# Psalms for Healing

# Psalms for Healing

## Praying with Those in Need

GRETCHEN PERSON

MINNEAPOLIS

*This book is dedicated to my parents, Eldon and Elaine, with love and appreciation for their sustaining and nurturing prayers across the years and to my husband, Mark, for his love, help, and encouragement.*

PSALMS FOR HEALING
Praying with Those in Need

Scripture quotations are from the New Revised Standard Version Bible, copyright © 1989 by the Division of Christian Education of the National Council of the Churches of Christ in the U.S.A. and used by permission.

Cover design by Michelle L. Norstad
Book design by Timothy W. Larson

ISBN 0-8066-4161-4

The paper used in this publication meets the minimum requirements of American National Standard for Information Sciences—Permanence of Paper for Printed Library Materials, ANSI Z329.48-1984.

Manufactured in the U.S.A.                                        AF 9-4161

11   10   09   08   07   06              5   6   7   8   9   10

# Contents

# Introduction

THIS BOOK DEVELOPED from my work as a resident chaplain at Rochester Methodist Hospital. During my work there, I met many patients who were facing illness or crisis situations. Many of these patients and their families asked me to pray with or for them.

The psalms are one of the richest sources of support and strength that clergy, lay ministers, and caregivers can offer in hospital settings. Not every verse of every psalm, however, is helpful in a given situation. In this book I have compiled psalms (or particular verses of them) that may be most appropriate in the situations named. Although I wrote the prayers that follow the psalms to be prayed with patients, the prayers may be easily adapted by patients for personal or family use.

Use these psalms and prayers for those not only in the hospital but for those in hospices and nursing homes. The psalms and prayers are also useful for times of personal worship and meditation. Regardless of setting or situation, God is attentive to our prayers and comes with healing.

Please note that throughout this book, I have used the New Revised Standard Version Bible translation of the psalms. Clergy and family may choose to use the King James Bible version of Psalm 23, as many people are familiar with it. Patients and family may derive greater comfort from this familiarity.

Also note that the psalms and prayers contain parenthetical material. Most of the words, phrases, and verses in parentheses are options to be included or excluded based on their helpfulness or appropriateness. The *(P)* in the prayers, which stands for *patient,* is an indication that the reader may personalize the prayers by inserting the patient's name. Gender specific pronouns also appear in parentheses.

# Diagnosis

HEARING A DIAGNOSIS can be a life-changing event in an individual's and a family's life. It can be a frightening, lonely time, yet it may also be a time when vulnerability opens one to new relationships with God, family, and friends.

**Ps. 6:2-7, 8-9:** Be gracious to me, O Lord, for I am languishing; O LORD heal me, for my bones are shaking with terror. My soul also is struck with terror, while you, O Lord—how long? Turn, O Lord, save my life; deliver me for the sake of your steadfast love. For in death there is no remembrance of you; in Sheol who can give you praise? I am weary with my moaning; every night I flood my bed with tears; I drench my couch with my weeping. My eyes waste away because of grief. . . . The Lord has heard the sound of my weeping. The Lord has heard my supplication; the Lord accepts my prayer.

*Prayer: Lord, be gracious to (P) for (he/she) is in pain and is scared by this diagnosis—physically and spiritually. Restore (his/her) health for the sake of your steadfast love—for who can praise you in death? You know (P's) grief, tears, and fears. Thank you for hearing us.*

**Ps. 9:9-10, 12, 13-14, 18:** The Lord is a stronghold for the oppressed, a stronghold in times of trouble. And those who know your name put their trust in you, for you, O Lord, have not forsaken those who seek you. The Lord does not forget the cry of the afflicted; you are the one who lifts me up from the gates of death so that I may recount all your praises and rejoice in your deliverance. For the needy shall not always be forgotten, nor the hope of the poor perish forever.

*Prayer: Lord God, you are (P's) stronghold in times of trouble. Help (P) to trust you in the face of this diagnosis. Help (him/her) to know that you do not forget the cry of the afflicted but lift them up from the gates of death. You are (P's) undying hope.*

**Ps. 25:1-2, 4-6, (11), 15-(18):** To you, O Lord, I lift up my soul. O my God, in you I trust. Make me to know your ways, O Lord; teach me your paths. Lead me in your truth, and teach me, for you are the God of my salvation; for you I wait all day long. Be mindful of your mercy, O Lord, and of your steadfast love, for they have been from of old. (For your name's sake, O Lord, pardon my guilt, for it is great.) My eyes are ever toward the Lord, for he will pluck my feet out of the net. Turn to me and be gracious to me, for I am lonely and afflicted. Relieve the troubles of my heart and bring me out of my distress. (Consider my affliction and my trouble, and forgive all my sins.)

*Prayer:* Lord God, we lift up (P's) needs to you because we trust in you. (P) looks to you for help; be gracious to (him/her), Lord. Relieve the troubles of (his/her) heart, especially (his/her) concerns about this diagnosis, and bring (him/her) out of distress. Consider (P's) affliction and trouble and bring relief to (him/her).

**Ps. 50:15:** Call on me in the day of trouble; I will deliver you, and you shall glorify me.

*Prayer:* Lord, you have promised to deliver us in the day of trouble. And so we turn to you and ask you to hear our cries as (P) faces this diagnosis. Come to (P) and deliver (him/her) from pain and suffering.

**Ps. 55:1-2, 4-8, 16-17, 22:** Give ear to my prayer, O God; do not hide yourself from my supplication. Attend to me, and answer me; I am troubled in my complaint. My heart is in anguish within me, the terrors of death have fallen upon me. Fear and trembling come upon me, and horror overwhelms me. And I say, "O that I had wings like a dove! I would fly away and be at rest; truly, I would flee far away; I would lodge in the wilderness; I would hurry to find a shelter for myself from the raging wind and tempest." But I call upon God, and the Lord will save me. Evening and morning and at noon I utter my complaint and moan, and he will hear my voice. Cast your burden

on the Lord, and he will sustain you; he will never permit the righteous to be moved.

*Prayer: Listen to our prayer, O God. Death and all its terrors have come to (P) with this diagnosis. (He/She) comes to you with a troubled heart. It is very frightening for (P) to face death; the thought of death brings fear, trembling, and even horror. Attend to (P) and answer (him/her). Help (him/her) to trust that (he/she) can give (his/her) burdens to you and that you will sustain (him/her).*

**Ps. 69:1-3, 13, 15-17, 29, 33:** Save me, O God, for the waters have come up to my neck. I sink in deep mire where there is no foothold; I have come into deep waters, and the flood sweeps over me. I am weary with my crying; my throat is parched. My eyes grow dim with waiting for my God. But as for me, my prayer is to you, O Lord. At an acceptable time, O God, in the abundance of your steadfast love, answer me. With your faithful help rescue me from sinking in the mire. Do not let the flood sweep over me, or the deep swallow me up, or the Pit close its mouth over me. Answer me, O Lord, for your steadfast love is good; according to your abundant mercy, turn to me. Do not hide your face from your servant, for I am in distress—make haste to answer me. I am lowly and in

pain; let your salvation, O God, protect me. For the Lord hears the needy, and does not despise his own that are in bonds.

*Prayer: Lord God, this diagnosis feels to (P) like dangerous floodwaters that are sweeping over (him/her). Listen to our prayers and answer (P) according to your steadfast love and mercy. Give (him/her) a sense of your presence. We trust that you hear us.*

**Ps. 77:1-12:** I cry aloud to God, that he may hear me. In the day of trouble I seek the Lord; in the night my hand is stretched out without wearying; my soul refuses to be comforted. I think of God, and I moan; I meditate, and my spirit faints. You keep my eyelids from closing; I am so troubled that I cannot speak. I consider the days of old, and remember the years of long ago. I commune with my heart in the night; I meditate and search my spirit: "Will the Lord spurn forever, and never again be favorable? Has his steadfast love ceased forever? Are his promises at an end for all time? Has God forgotten to be gracious? Has he in anger shut up his compassion?" And I say, "It is my grief that the right hand of the Most High has changed." I will call to mind the deeds of the Lord; I will remember your wonders of old. I will meditate on all your work, and muse on your mighty deeds.

*Prayer: Lord, having heard this diagnosis, we cry to you for help. In the day and in the middle of the night, (P) reaches out to you; yet it is difficult to sense your presence and (he/she) is not comforted. Where is your love, Lord? Are you angry? Will you not show (P) your compassion? It seems that you have forgotten to be gracious to (him/her). In these times of difficulty too great for words, help (P) to remember how you cared for (him/her) in the past. Let those memories comfort and strengthen (him/her) now. Help (P) to trust in you.*

**Ps. 86:1-7, 13, 15-16:** Incline your ear, O Lord, and answer me, for I am poor and needy. Preserve my life, for I am devoted to you; save your servant who trusts in you. You are my God; be gracious to me, O Lord, for to you do I cry all day long. Gladden the soul of your servant, for to you, O Lord, I lift up my soul. For you, O Lord, are good and forgiving, abounding in steadfast love to all who call on you. Give ear, O Lord, to my prayer; listen to my cry of supplication. In the day of my trouble I call on you, for you will answer me. Great is your steadfast love toward me; you have delivered my soul from the depths of Sheol. You, O Lord, are a God merciful and gracious, slow to anger and abounding in steadfast love and faithfulness. Turn to me and be gracious to me; give your strength to your servant.

*Prayer: Lord, (P) cries to you all day long. This diagnosis has brought sadness and hardship; please listen to (P's) calls for help and answer. Be gracious to (him/her) and give (him/her) strength. Help (him/her) to see your graciousness and make (him/her) glad again.*

**Ps. 105:4-5:** Seek the Lord and his strength; seek his presence continually. Remember the wonderful works he has done and his miracles.

*Prayer: Lord, (P) seeks your presence and your strength. As (he/she) faces this diagnosis, it would be easy for (him/her) to let fear and despair overtake (him/her). But keep (P) from despair! Comfort (him/her) with the memory of your wonderful works and miracles.*

**Ps. 109:21-22, 26, 31:** But you, O Lord my Lord, act on my behalf for your name's sake; because your steadfast love is good, deliver me. For I am poor and needy, and my heart is pierced within me. Help me, O Lord my God! Save me according to your steadfast love . . . and stand at the right hand of the needy.

*Prayer: Lord, (P) is in need of your help. (He/She) is fearful and anxious for what lies ahead. Stand with (P) whose heart is broken by this diagnosis and assure (him/her) of your steadfast love and your help.*

**Ps. 142:1-3, 5-6:** With my voice I cry to the Lord; with my voice I make supplication to the Lord. I pour out my complaint before him; I tell my trouble before him. When my spirit is faint, you know my way. I cry to you, O Lord; I say, "You are my refuge, my portion in the land of the living." Give heed to my cry, for I am brought very low.

*Prayer: Lord, this diagnosis brings (P) very low. Hear (his/her) cries and complaints. Renew (his/her) spirit; watch over (his/her) way.*

**Ps. 143:1-4, 6-8:** Hear my prayer, O Lord; give ear to my supplications in your faithfulness; answer me in your righteousness. Do not enter into judgment with your servant, for no one living is righteous before you. For the enemy has pursued me, crushing my life to the ground, making me sit in darkness like those long dead. Therefore my spirit faints within me; my heart within me is appalled. I stretch out my hands to you; my soul thirsts for you like a parched land. Answer me quickly, O Lord; my spirit fails. Do not hide your face from me, or I shall be like those who go down to the Pit. Let me hear of your steadfast love in the morning, for in you I put my trust. Teach me the way I should go, for to you I lift up my soul.

***Prayer:*** *Lord, when (P) is crushed by this diagnosis, when (his/her) world seems dark, when (his/her) spirit is weak, when you seem absent from (P), then help (him/her), Lord, to trust in you. Renew (his/her) spirit; surround (P) with your steadfast love, and show (him/her) your guidance.*

# Life-Threatening Illnesses

PATIENTS WITH life-threatening illnesses, along with their families, may experience a wide spectrum of emotions, including feelings of being out of control and yearning for stability. Prayers can bring a powerful sense of calm and peace.

**Ps. 6:2-7, 8-9:** Be gracious to me, O Lord, for I am languishing; O Lord, heal me, for my bones are shaking with terror. My soul also is struck with terror, while you, O Lord—how long? Turn, O Lord, save my life; deliver me for the sake of your steadfast love. For in death there is no remembrance of you; in Sheol who can give you praise? I am weary with my moaning; every night I flood my bed with tears; I drench my couch with my weeping. My eyes waste away because of grief. . . . The Lord has heard the sound of my weeping. The Lord has heard my supplication; the Lord accepts my prayer.

*Prayer: Lord, be gracious to (P), for (he/she) is in pain and is physically and spiritually scared. Restore (his/her) health for the sake of your steadfast love—for who can praise you in death? You know (P's) grief, tears, and fears. Thank you for hearing us.*

**Ps. 9:9-10, 12, 13-14, 18:** The Lord is a stronghold for the oppressed, a stronghold in times of trouble. And those who know your name put their trust in you, for you, O Lord, have not forsaken those who seek you. The Lord does not forget the cry of the afflicted; you are the one who lifts me up from the gates of death so that I may recount all your praises and rejoice in your deliverance. For the needy shall not always be forgotten, nor the hope of the poor perish forever.

*Prayer: Lord God, you are (P's) stronghold in times of trouble, such as this sickness. Help (him/her) to know that you do not forget the cry of the afflicted but lift them up from the gates of death. And you are (P's) undying hope.*

**Ps. 22:1-2, (4-5), (6-7), 9-11, 14-15, 16-17, 19, 24:** My God, my God, why have you forsaken me? Why are you so far from helping me, from the words of my groaning? O my God, I cry by day, but thou dost not answer; and by night, but find no rest. (In you our ancestors trusted; they trusted, and you delivered them. To you they cried, and were saved; in you they trusted, and were not put to shame.) (But I am a worm, and not human; scorned by others, and despised by the people. All who see me mock at me; they make mouths at me, they shake their heads. . . .) Yet it was you who took me from the womb; you

20

kept me safe on my mother's breast. On you I was cast from my birth, and since my mother bore me you have been my God. Do not be far from me, for trouble is near and there is no one to help. I am poured out like water, and all my bones are out of joint; my heart is like wax; it is melted within my breast; my mouth is dried up like a potsherd, and my tongue sticks to my jaws; you lay me in the dust of death. My hands and feet have shriveled; I can count all my bones. . . . But you, O Lord, do not be far away! O my help, come quickly to my aid! For the Lord did not despise or abhor the affliction of the afflicted; he did not hide his face from me, but heard when I cried to him.

*Prayer: God, why have you forsaken (P)? Why are you far from (his/her) suffering? We cry day and night to you, but find no rest. Yet it was you who gave (P) life and sustained (him/her) from childhood. This knowledge gives us the courage to come to you with our requests and pleas, for we know that you do not abhor (his/her) sickness. In your tender mercy, hear us, Lord.*

**Ps. 31:1-5, 7-12, 14-15, 16, 19, 21-22, 23, 24:** In you, O Lord, I seek refuge; do not let me ever be put to shame; in your righteousness deliver me. Incline your ear to me; rescue me speedily. Be a rock of refuge for me, a strong fortress to save me. You are indeed my

rock and my fortress; for your name's sake lead me and guide me, take me out of the net that is hidden for me, for you are my refuge. Into your hand I commit my spirit; you have redeemed me, O Lord, faithful God. I will exult and rejoice in your steadfast love, because you have seen my affliction; you have taken heed of my adversities, and have not delivered me into the hand of the enemy; you have set my feet in a broad place. Be gracious to me, O Lord, for I am in distress; my eye wastes away from grief, my soul and body also. For my life is spent with sorrow, and my years with sighing; my strength fails because of my misery, and my bones waste away. I am the scorn of all my adversaries, a horror to my neighbors, an object of dread to my acquaintances; those who see me in the street flee from me. I have passed out of mind like one who is dead; I have become like a broken vessel. But I trust in you, O Lord; I say, "You are my God." My times are in your hand. Let your face shine upon your servant; save me in your steadfast love. O how abundant is your goodness that you have laid up for those who fear you, and accomplished for those who take refuge in you, in the sight of everyone! Blessed be the Lord, for he has wondrously shown his steadfast love to me when I was beset as a city under siege. I had said in my alarm, "I am driven far from your sight." But you heard my supplications when I cried out to you for help. Love the Lord, all you his saints. The Lord preserves the faithful. Be strong, and let your heart take courage, all you who wait for the Lord.

***Prayer:*** *Lord, you are (P's) refuge and fortress. You know (his/her) grief and sickness; you see (his/her) distress. Sometimes in the past it seemed to (P) that you were not listening to (his/her) cries for help, but (he/she) has come to trust that you do listen. And because (he/she) trusts you, we ask that during this difficult time, you give (him/her) the calm and confidence that only you can give.*

**Ps. 38:6, 7, 8-11, 15, 17-18, 21-22:** I am utterly bowed down and prostrate; all day long I go around mourning. There is no soundness in my flesh. I am utterly spent and crushed; I groan because of the tumult of my heart. O Lord, all my longing is known to you; my sighing is not hidden from you. My heart throbs, my strength fails me; as for the light of my eyes—it also has gone from me. My friends and companions stand aloof from my affliction, and my neighbors stand far off. But it is for you, O Lord, that I wait; it is you, O Lord my God, who will answer. My pain is ever with me. I confess my iniquity; I am sorry for my sin. Do not forsake me, O Lord; O my God, do not be far from me; make haste to help me, O Lord, my salvation.

*Prayer:* Lord God, (P) is exhausted and crushed by this sickness. (His/Her) heart and mind are in chaos. Lord, you know (his/her) longings and you see even (his/her) tired sighs. . . . The news from the doctors is not good, Lord. Hearing it and thinking about what it means makes (P) feel weak and sometimes numb. The light is gone from (his/her) eyes; friends stay away because they are afraid of what is happening and feel awkward. So Lord God, (P) needs you. Do not forsake (him/her); hurry to help and stay near to (him/her).

**Ps. 41:3:** The Lord sustains those on their sickbed; in their illness you, Lord, heal all their infirmities.

*Prayer:* Lord, sustain (P) in (his/her) illness. It is hard for (P) to lie here all day—it makes (him/her) feel useless. Sustain (P) through frustration, pain, anger, and loneliness. Heal (his/her) sickness and other weaknesses and make (him/her) strong.

**Ps. 50:15:** Call on me in the day of trouble; I will deliver you, and you shall glorify me.

*Prayer:* Lord, you have promised to deliver us in the day of trouble. And so we turn to you and ask you to hear our cries for (P) in these difficult days of sickness. Come to (P) and deliver (him/her) from pain and suffering.

**Ps. 55:1-2, 4-8, 16-17, 22:** Give ear to my prayer, O God; do not hide yourself from my supplication. Attend to me, and answer me; I am troubled in my complaint. My heart is in anguish within me, the terrors of death have fallen upon me. Fear and trembling come upon me, and horror overwhelms me. And I say, "O that I had wings like a dove! I would fly away and be at rest; truly, I would flee far away; I would lodge in the wilderness; I would hurry to find a shelter for myself from the raging wind and tempest." But I call upon God, and the Lord will save me. Evening and morning and at noon I utter my complaint and moan, and he will hear my voice. Cast your burden on the Lord, and he will sustain you; he will never permit the righteous to be moved.

*Prayer: Listen to our prayer, O God. Death and all its terrors have come to (P), wrapped in this sickness. (He/She) comes to you with a troubled heart. It is very frightening for (P) to face death; the thought of death brings fear, trembling, and even horror. Attend to (P) and answer (him/her). Help (him/her) to trust that (he/she) can give (his/her) burdens to you and that you will sustain (him/her).*

**Ps. 63:1, 3, 4-8:** O God, you are my God, I seek you, my soul thirsts for you; my flesh faints for you, as in a dry and weary land where there is no water. Because your steadfast love is better than life, my lips will praise

you. I will lift up my hands and call on your name. My soul is satisfied as with a rich feast, and my mouth praises you with joyful lips when I think of you on my bed, and meditate on you in the watches of the night; for you have been my help, and in the shadow of your wings I sing for joy. My soul clings to you; your right hand upholds me.

*Prayer: Lord God, we need you as one needs water in the desert. Your love is better than life itself and so we lift up our prayers to you. You have been (P's) help in the past; (he/she) has found joy in the shadow of your wings. Therefore, uphold (P) even now during this illness and let (his/her) soul find satisfaction in you.*

**Ps. 69:1-3, 13, 15-17, 29, 33:** Save me, O God, for the waters have come up to my neck. I sink in deep mire where there is no foothold; I have come into deep waters, and the flood sweeps over me. I am weary with my crying; my throat is parched. My eyes grow dim with waiting for my God. But as for me, my prayer is to you, O Lord. At an acceptable time, O God, in the abundance of your steadfast love, answer me. With your faithful help rescue me from sinking in the mire. Do not let the flood sweep over me, or the deep swallow me up, or the Pit close its mouth over me. Answer me, O Lord, for your steadfast love is good; according to your abundant mercy, turn to me.

Do not hide your face from your servant, for I am in distress—make haste to answer me. I am lowly and in pain; let your salvation, O God, protect me. For the Lord hears the needy, and does not despise his own that are in bonds.

*Prayer: Lord God, sometimes, in the throes of this sickness, it feels to (P) like dangerous floodwaters are sweeping over (him/her). (He/She) wears (himself/herself) out with crying. (He/She) waits for you to help, but it seems that you do not listen. In your time, O God, answer (P). Listen to our prayers and answer (P) according to your steadfast love and mercy. Give (him/her) a sense of your presence.*

**Ps. 77:1-12:** I cry aloud to God, that he may hear me. In the day of trouble I seek the Lord; in the night my hand is stretched out without wearying; my soul refuses to be comforted. I think of God, and I moan; I meditate, and my spirit faints. You keep my eyelids from closing; I am so troubled that I cannot speak. I consider the days of old, and remember the years of long ago. I commune with my heart in the night; I meditate and search my spirit: "Will the Lord spurn forever, and never again be favorable? Has his steadfast love ceased forever? Are his promises at an end for all time? Has God forgotten to be gracious? Has he in anger shut up his compassion?" And I say, "It is my

grief that the right hand of the Most High has changed." I will call to mind the deeds of the Lord; I will remember your wonders of old. I will meditate on all your work, and muse on your mighty deeds.

*Prayer: Lord, in the midst of this troubling sickness we cry to you for help. In the middle of the night (P) reaches out to you; yet it is difficult to sense your presence and (he/she) is not comforted. Where is your love, Lord? Are you angry? Will you not show (P) your compassion? It seems that you have forgotten to be gracious to (him/ her). In these times of difficulty too great for words, help (P) to remember how you cared for (him/her) in the past. Let those memories comfort and strengthen (him/ her) now. Help (P) to trust in you.*

**Ps. 86:1-7, 13, 15-16:** Incline your ear, O Lord, and answer me, for I am poor and needy. Preserve my life, for I am devoted to you; save your servant who trusts in you. You are my God; be gracious to me, O Lord, for to you do I cry all day long. Gladden the soul of your servant, for to you, O Lord, I lift up my soul. For you, O Lord, are good and forgiving, abounding in steadfast love to all who call on you. Give ear, O Lord, to my prayer; listen to my cry of supplication. In the day of my trouble I call on you, for you will answer me. Great is your steadfast love toward me; you have delivered my soul from the depths of Sheol. You,

O Lord, are a God merciful and gracious, slow to anger and abounding in steadfast love and faithfulness. Turn to me and be gracious to me; give your strength to your servant.

*Prayer: Lord, (P) cries to you all day long because of (his/her) sickness. Listen to (his/her) calls for help and answer. Be gracious to (P) and give (him/her) strength. Help (him/her) to see your graciousness and make (him/her) glad again.*

**Ps. 102:1-7, 9, 11-12, 17-20, 23-28:** Hear my prayer, O Lord; let my cry come to you. Do not hide your face from me in the day of my distress. Incline your ear to me; answer me speedily in the day when I call. For my days pass away like smoke, and my bones burn like a furnace. My heart is stricken and withered like grass; I am too wasted to eat my bread. Because of my loud groaning my bones cling to my skin. I am like an owl of the wilderness, like a little owl of the waste places. I lie awake; I am like a lonely bird on the housetop. For I eat . . . bread, and mingle tears with my drink. My days are like an evening shadow; I wither away like grass. But you, O Lord, are enthroned forever; your name endures to all generations. The Lord will regard the prayer of the destitute, and will not despise their prayer. Let this be recorded for a generation to come, so that a people yet unborn may praise the Lord: that

he looked down from his holy height, from heaven the Lord looked at the earth, to hear the groans of the prisoners, to set free those who were doomed to die .... He has broken my strength in midcourse; he has shortened my days. "O my God," I say, "do not take me away at the midpoint of my life, you whose years endure throughout all generations." Long ago you laid the foundation of the earth, and the heavens are the work of your hands. They will perish, but you endure; they will all wear out like a garment. You change them like clothing, and they pass away; but you are the same, and your years have no end. (The children of your servants shall live secure; their offspring shall be established in your presence.)

*Prayer: Lord, listen to our cries. (P) is in terrible pain and it is difficult for (him/her) to eat—so difficult that it seems that tears often become (his/her) food. (P's) body is wasting away; this sickness makes (him/her) lonely and frightened. Look on (P's) fragile life, Lord, and be tender with (him/her).*

**Ps. 105:4-5:** Seek the Lord and his strength; seek his presence continually. Remember the wonderful works he has done and his miracles.

*Prayer: Lord, (P) seeks your presence and your strength. As (he/she) faces sickness, it would be easy for (him/her) to let fear and despair overtake (him/her). But keep (P) from despair. Comfort (him/her) with the memory of your wonderful works and miracles.*

**Ps. 109:21-24, 26, 31:** But you, O Lord my Lord, act on my behalf for your name's sake; because your steadfast love is good, deliver me. For I am poor and needy, and my heart is pierced within me. I am gone like a shadow at evening; I am shaken off like a locust. My knees are weak through fasting; my body has become gaunt. Help me, O Lord my God! Save me according to your steadfast love . . . and stand at the right hand of the needy.

*Prayer: Lord, (P) seeks your presence. As (he/she) faces sickness or other difficulties, comfort (him/her) with memories of your wonderful works and miracles. Help us to trust that through doctors and nurses your miracles of healing still occur.*

# Transplants

INTENSE WAITING. Wondering. Ups and downs. Patients requiring transplants travel a rough road. These psalms help transplant patients know that they are not alone on their difficult journey.

**Ps. 5:1-3, 7, 11-12:** Give ear to my words, O Lord; give heed to my sighing. Listen to the sound of my cry, my King and my God, for to you I pray. O Lord, in the morning you hear my voice; in the morning I plead my case to you and watch. I, through the abundance of your steadfast love will enter your house . . . in awe of you. Let all who take refuge in you rejoice; let them ever sing for joy. Spread your protection over them, so that those who love your name may exult in you. For you bless the righteous, O Lord, you cover them with favor as with a shield.

*Prayer: Listen to our cries, O Lord, for we plead (P's) case for a transplant. We ask you to help and restore (P's) health. As (he/she) waits moment by moment and hour by hour in this hospital, help (him/her) to know the presence and abundance of your steadfast*

*love. Spread your protection over (him/her) and give
(him/her) confidence that those who love your name
and take refuge in you will know your joy.*

**Ps. 6:2-7, 8-9:** Be gracious to me, O Lord, for I am languishing; O Lord, heal me, for my bones are shaking with terror. My soul also is struck with terror, while you, O Lord—how long? Turn, O Lord, save my life; deliver me for the sake of your steadfast love. For in death there is no remembrance of you; in Sheol who can give you praise? I am weary with my moaning; every night I flood my bed with tears; I drench my couch with my weeping. My eyes waste away because of grief. . . . The Lord has heard the sound of my weeping. The Lord has heard my supplication; the Lord accepts my prayer.

*Prayer: Lord, be gracious to (P), for (he/she) is in pain
physically and emotionally. The waiting and wondering
if a life-saving organ will become available are overwhelming. We ask that you bring life and health to (P)
for the sake of your steadfast love—for who can praise
you in death? Thank you for hearing us.*

**Ps. 9:9-10, 12, 13-14, 18:** The Lord is a stronghold for the oppressed, a stronghold in times of trouble. And those who know your name put their trust in you, for you, O Lord, have not forsaken those who seek

you. The Lord does not forget the cry of the afflicted; you are the one who lifts me up from the gates of death so that I may recount all your praises and rejoice in your deliverance. For the needy shall not always be forgotten, nor the hope of the poor perish forever.

*Prayer: Lord God, you are a stronghold in times of trouble. Be with (P), who waits for a suitable donor organ and has many concerns. Help (him/her) to know that you do not forsake those who seek you or forget the cry of the afflicted. You lift us up from the gates of death; you are our hope that will never perish. Give to (P) the calm and confidence that only you can give.*

Ps. 20:1-2, 4-5: The Lord answer you in the day of trouble! The name of the God of Jacob protect you! May he send you help from the sanctuary, and give you support from Zion. May he grant you your heart's desire, and fulfill all your plans. May we shout for joy over your victory, and in the name of our God set up our banners. May the Lord fulfill all your petitions.

*Prayer: Lord, hear the cries of our hearts in this difficult time; protect, support, and help (P). There is so much in life (he/she) still wants to do; (he/she) has many plans and dreams yet to fulfill. Be present with (him/her) during this transplant. Be present also with all the medical staff who will attend to (him/her) in the coming hours and days. Grant a successful surgery and let (P) know joy again.*

**Ps. 33:18-22:** Truly the eye of the Lord is on those who fear him, on those who hope in his steadfast love, to deliver their soul from death, and to keep them alive in famine. Our soul waits for the Lord; he is our help and shield. Our heart is glad in him, because we trust in his holy name. Let your steadfast love, O Lord, be upon us, even as we hope in you.

*Prayer: Lord, watch over (P) with your love. You promise to deliver your children from death and nourish our hungry spirits and bodies. (P) has waited patiently for a donor organ and has endured the ups and downs of hopes and disappointments. Be mindful of your promise and of (P). (He/She) waits for you in these difficult times; (his/her) hope is in you.*

**Ps. 38:6, 7, 8-11, 15, 17-18, 21-22:** I am utterly bowed down and prostrate; all day long I go around mourning. There is no soundness in my flesh. I am utterly spent and crushed; I groan because of the tumult of my heart. O Lord, all my longing is known to you; my sighing is not hidden from you. My heart throbs, my strength fails me; as for the light of my eyes—it also

has gone from me. My friends and companions stand aloof from my affliction, and my neighbors stand far off. But it is for you, O Lord, that I wait; it is you, O Lord my God, who will answer. My pain is ever with me. I confess my iniquity; I am sorry for my sin. Do not forsake me, O Lord; O my God, do not be far from me; make haste to help me, O Lord, my salvation.

*Prayer: Lord God, (P) is exhausted and crushed by (his/her) sickness and the waiting for a transplant. (His/her) heart and mind are in chaos; (he/she) feels weak, even numb. So much work at home has gone neglected and (he/she) wonders about how the medical bills will be paid. The light is gone from (his/her) eyes because of all the concerns. Lord God, (P) needs you. Do not forsake (him/her), hurry to help (him/her) in these difficult times and stay near to (him/her).*

**Ps. 41:3:** The Lord sustains those on their sickbed; in their illness you, Lord, heal all their infirmities.

*Prayer: Lord, sustain (P) in (his/her) illness and in (his/her) waiting for a transplant. Come quickly with healing in your wings.*

**Ps. 50:15:** Call on me in the day of trouble; I will deliver you, and you shall glorify me.

*Prayer: Lord, you have promised to deliver us in the day of trouble and so we turn to you. We ask that you would hear (P's) cries in these hours before (his/her) transplant. Bring (him/her) successfully through this surgery.*

৵

**Ps. 55:1-2, 4-8, 16-17, 22:** Give ear to my prayer, O God; do not hide yourself from my supplication. Attend to me, and answer me; I am troubled in my complaint. My heart is in anguish within me, the terrors of death have fallen upon me. Fear and trembling come upon me, and horror overwhelms me. And I say, "O that I had wings like a dove! I would fly away and be at rest; truly, I would flee far away; I would lodge in the wilderness; I would hurry to find a shelter for myself from the raging wind and tempest. But I call upon God, and the Lord will save me. Evening and morning and at noon I utter my complaint and moan, and he will hear my voice. Cast your burden on the Lord, and he will sustain you; he will never permit the righteous to be moved.

*Prayer: Listen to our prayer, O God. Death and all its terrors have come to (P). (He/She) comes to you with an anguished heart. It is very frightening for (him/her) to face death; the thought of it brings fear, trembling, and even horror. Be present with (him/her) while (he/she) waits for a transplant and attend to (him/her) during the surgery. Help (him/her) to trust that (he/she) can give (his/her) burdens to you and that you will sustain (him/her). We call upon you, O God, and trust that you will save us.*

∾

**Ps. 69:1-3, 13, 15-17, 29, 33:** Save me, O God, for the waters have come up to my neck. I sink in deep mire, where there is no foothold; I have come into deep waters, and the flood sweeps over me. I am weary with my crying; my throat is parched. My eyes grow dim with waiting for my God. But as for me, my prayer is to you, O Lord. At an acceptable time, O God, in the abundance of your steadfast love, answer me. With your faithful help rescue me from sinking in the mire. Do not let the flood sweep over me, or the deep swallow me up, or the Pit close its mouth over me. Answer me, O Lord, for your steadfast love is good; according to your abundant mercy, turn to me. Do not hide your face from your servant, for I am in distress—make haste to answer me. I am lowly and in pain; let your salvation, O God, protect me. For the Lord hears the needy, and does not despise his own that are in bonds.

*Prayer: Lord God, sometimes it feels to (P) like (he/ she) is sinking and can get no foothold; sometimes it seems that dangerous floodwaters are sweeping over (him/her). (P) is in pain and weary with crying and waiting for a transplant. Do not hide from (P) but give (him/her) a sense of your presence and let your face shine upon (him/her) through the faces of the staff who attend to (him/her). In these difficult times, O Lord, sustain (his/her) life. Listen to our prayers and answer (P) according to your steadfast love and mercy.*

❧

**Ps. 86:1-7, 13, 15-16:** Incline your ear, O Lord, and answer me, for I am poor and needy. Preserve my life, for I am devoted to you; save your servant who trusts in you. You are my God; be gracious to me, O Lord, for to you do I cry all day long. Gladden the soul of your servant, for to you, O Lord, I lift up my soul. For you, O Lord, are good and forgiving, abounding in steadfast love to all who call on you. Give ear, O Lord, to my prayer; listen to my cry of supplication. In the day of my trouble I call on you, for you will answer me. Great is your steadfast love toward me; you have delivered my soul from the depths of Sheol. You, O Lord, are a God merciful and gracious, slow to anger and abounding in steadfast love and faithfulness. Turn to me and be gracious to me; give your strength to your servant.

*Prayer: Lord, (P) has many needs, and the hospital expenses threaten to make (him/her) financially poor. (He/She) is tired of negotiating with insurance companies and is exhausted by the transplant experience. Lord, be gracious to (P) and make (him/her) glad again. Listen to our calls to you in this day of anxiety; make your strength, steadfast love, and faithfulness known to (P).*

**Ps. 102:1-7, 9, 11-12, 17-20, 23-27, (28):** Hear my prayer, O Lord; let my cry come to you. Do not hide your face from me in the day of my distress. Incline your ear to me; answer me speedily in the day when I call. For my days pass away like smoke, and my bones burn like a furnace. My heart is stricken and withered like grass; I am too wasted to eat my bread. Because of my loud groaning my bones cling to my skin. I am like an owl of the wilderness, like a little owl of the waste places. I lie awake; I am like a lonely bird on the housetop. For I eat . . . bread, and mingle tears with my drink. My days are like an evening shadow; I wither away like grass. But you, O Lord, are enthroned forever; your name endures to all generations. The Lord will regard the prayer of the destitute, and will not despise their prayer. Let this be recorded for a generation to come, so that a people yet unborn may praise the Lord: that he looked down from his holy height, from heaven the Lord looked at the earth, to hear the groans of the prisoners, to set free those who were doomed to die . . . . He has broken my strength in midcourse; he has shortened my days. "O my God," I say, "do not take me away at the midpoint of my life, you whose years endure throughout all generations." Long ago you laid the foundation of the earth, and the heavens are the work of your hands. They will perish, but you endure; they will all wear out like a garment. You change them like clothing, and they pass away; but you are the same, and your years have no end. (The children of your servants shall live secure; their off-spring shall be established in your presence.)

*Prayer: Lord, do not hide from (P). Hours and days of (his/her) life vanish like smoke. Because of this illness and the concerns it brings, (P) sometimes cannot eat or sleep. Waiting in the hospital or transplant residence with others whose needs are similar is helpful to (him/her), Lord, for there is support in community. Yet the separation from family and friends is lonely. God, you are strong and endure forever; you promise to hear our groans and set free those doomed to die. Therefore, look on (P's) fragile life and needs and be tender with (him/her).*

**Ps. 105:4-5:** Seek the Lord and his strength; seek his presence continually. Remember the wonderful works he has done and his miracles.

*Prayer: Lord, we seek your presence. As (P) faces a transplant, comfort (him/her) with memories of your wonderful works and miracles. Help (him/her) to trust that through doctors and nurses your miracles of healing most certainly occur.*

# Sick Children
and Their Families

WHAT CAN be more agonizing than watching your child struggle with sickness? During a child's illness, surrounding the child and family with prayers can bring comfort, confidence, and healing.

**Ps. 4:1, 3, 5, 8:** Answer me when I call, O God of my right! You gave me room when I was in distress. Be gracious to me, and hear my prayer. Know that the Lord has set apart the faithful for himself; the Lord hears when I call to him. Put your trust in the Lord. I will both lie down and sleep in peace; for you alone, O Lord, make me lie down in safety.

*Prayer: Lord God, hear and help (P) and (his/her) family. They need you so desperately. Give this family the confidence to believe that you do set apart the faithful for yourself; let this truth be comforting to them. Calm (P's) fears and anxieties as (he/she) waits in this hospital. Strengthen this family. As the night (now) enfolds us, bring us peaceful sleep and safety.*

**Ps. 5:1-3, 7, 11-12:** Give ear to my words, O Lord; give heed to my sighing. Listen to the sound of my cry, my King and my God, for to you I pray. O Lord, in the morning you hear my voice; in the morning I plead my case to you and watch. I, through the abundance of your steadfast love will enter your house . . . in awe of you. Let all who take refuge in you rejoice; let them ever sing for joy. Spread your protection over them, so that those who love your name may exult in you. For you bless the righteous, O Lord, you cover them with favor as with a shield.

*Prayer: O God, our Great Physician, hear our cries and the little sighs of our child. You are mighty, we are broken and in need of your care and healing. We plead our case before you and watch. Please bring us joy again.*

**Ps. 17:1, 6, 8:** Hear a just cause, O Lord; attend to my cry. I call upon you, for you will answer me, O God; incline your ear to me, hear my words. Guard me as the apple of the eye; hide me in the shadow of your wings.

*Prayer: Gentle God, guard our child (P) as the apple of your eye —for (he/she) is surely the apple of our eye. We ask for healing for this little child—our plea is for a just cause. Listen to us; look deeply into our hearts and see how much we treasure this child and (his/her) health.*

**Ps. 20:1-2, 4-5:** The Lord answer you in the day of trouble! The name of the God of Jacob protect you! May he send you help from the sanctuary, and give you support from Zion. May he grant you your heart's desire, and fulfill all your plans. May we shout for joy over your victory, and in the name of our God set up our banners. May the Lord fulfill all your petitions.

*Prayer: Our Heavenly Parent, hear our prayers for our child (P) and answer us. Send us your help and support quickly. We have plans, hopes, and dreams as a family, and (P) is an integral part of those dreams. Send your healing to this child and sustain us in our waiting.*

**Ps. 44:23-26:** Lord, rouse yourself! Why do you sleep? Awake, do not cast us off forever! Why do you hide your face? Why do you forget our affliction and oppression? For we sink down to the dust; our bodies cling to the ground. Rise up, come to our help. Redeem us for the sake of your steadfast love.

*Prayer: God, are you sleeping? How can you let this little child suffer? Why do you hide from (P) and from us? Why do you forget (his/her) affliction? We are weighed down by this illness. Remember that all your children are fragile dust and in need of your help. For the sake of your steadfast love, save our child (P).*

**Ps. 46:1-2, 7:** God is our refuge and strength, a very present help in trouble. Therefore we will not fear, though the earth should change. The Lord of hosts is with us; the God of Jacob is our refuge.

*Prayer: Lord God, be our child (P's) refuge and strength. Be very present to (him/her) in (his/her) sickness. Hold (his/her) little body in your strong arms. Though everything in (his/her) life is changing, help (him/her) not to be afraid, but rather to find refuge in you, through us, (his/her) parents.*

**Ps. 56:3-4, 8, 9, 10-11, 12-13:** O Most High, when I am afraid, I put my trust in you. In God, whose word I praise, in God I trust; I am not afraid; what can flesh do to me? You have kept count of my tossings; put my tears in your bottle. Are they not in your record? This I know, that God is for me. In God, whose word I praise, in the Lord, whose word I praise, in God I trust; I am not afraid. My vows to you I must perform, O God; I will render thank offerings to you. For you have delivered my soul from death, and my feet from falling, so that I may walk before God in the light of life.

*Prayer: Lord God, you know our child (P) so well. You know (his/her) fears and ours and even the very number of tossings and turnings those fears cause. You record our tears. You know that we are afraid and heart-sick right now. Help us to trust you; ease our anxiety. Restore our child's health, that we may give you thanks.*

**Ps. 61:1-3, 4-5:** Hear my cry, O God; listen to my prayer. From the end of the earth I call to you, when my heart is faint. Lead me to the rock that is higher than I; for you are my refuge. Let me abide in your tent forever, find refuge under the shelter of your wings. For you, O God, have heard my vows; you have given me the heritage of those who fear your name.

*Prayer: Listen to our prayer, Lord God. (P) is weak. Give our child the knowledge that wherever (he/she) is—at home or in the hospital—you are still (his/her) strong refuge. We thank you, Lord, for our loving and supportive family and friends through whom (he/she) experiences the shelter of your wings.*

**Ps. 103:13:** As a father has compassion for his children, so the Lord has compassion for those who fear him.

*Prayer: Lord, you know what it is to be a parent; you know the pain of seeing one's own child suffer. Because you are compassionate, we have the courage to ask for your help and healing for (P). We ask also that you give us and (P) your strength and endurance and an awareness of your love.*

**Ps. 130:1-2, (3-4), 5-6, 7:** Out of the depths I cry to you, O Lord. Lord, hear my voice! Let your ears be attentive to the voice of my supplications! (If you, O Lord, should mark iniquities, Lord, who could stand? But there is forgiveness with you. . . .) I wait for the Lord, my soul waits, and in his word I hope; my soul waits for the Lord more than those who watch for the morning. For with the Lord there is steadfast love, and with him is great power to redeem.

*Prayer: God, our Heavenly Parent, we cry from the depths—from a place so deep we could never have imagined it. You know what it is to lose a child. Spare us that experience, O God!*

**Ps. 147:2, 3, 6:** The Lord . . . heals the brokenhearted, and binds up their wounds. The Lord lifts up the downtrodden.

*Prayer: Lord, bind up the wounds of our child (P) and heal us who are brokenhearted over (his/her) (injuries/ sickness). Lift us up and keep us strong.*

# Before and After Surgery

Waiting for surgery, its results, and recovery can make days seem long and nights seem endless. Sensitivity to a patient's needs is crucial to healing. Pray before you enter a hospital room that God will give you words to ease the patient's mind and body.

## Before Surgery

**Ps. 17:1, 6, 8:** Hear a just cause, O Lord; attend to my cry. I call upon you, for you will answer me, O God; incline your ear to me, hear my words. Guard me as the apple of the eye; hide me in the shadow of your wings.

*Prayer: We call upon you, O God, for you promise to hear and answer us. Show your love to (P), who seeks refuge in you in these tense hours before surgery. Guard (him/her) as the apple of your eye and hide (him/her) in the protective shadow of your wings. Guide the doctors and nurses in the operating room and grant (P) a good recovery.*

**Ps. 20:1-2, 4-5:** The Lord answer you in the day of trouble! The name of the God of Jacob protect you! May he send you help from the sanctuary, and give you support from Zion. May he grant you your heart's desire, and fulfill all your plans. May we shout for joy over your victory, and in the name of our God set up our banners. May the Lord fulfill all your petitions.

*Prayer: Lord, hear us in this time of anxiety; protect, support, and help (P) in these hours before surgery. Hear the cries of (his/her) heart. There is so much in life (P) would like to accomplish; (he/she) has plans and dreams yet to fulfill. Grant (P) a successful surgery, send your healing, and let (P) know joy again.*

**Ps. 41:3:** The Lord sustains those on their sickbed; in their illness you, Lord, heal all their infirmities.

*Prayer: Lord, sustain (P) in these days and hours before surgery. Heal (his/her) sickness and other weaknesses and make (him/her) strong.*

**Ps. 59:9-10, 16-17:** O my strength, I will watch for you; for you, O God, are my fortress. My God in his steadfast love will meet me; my God will let me look in triumph on my enemies. But I will sing of your might; I will sing aloud of you steadfast love in the morning. For you have been a fortress for me and a refuge in the

day of my distress. O my strength, I will sing praises to you, for you, O God, are my fortress, the God who shows me steadfast love.

*Prayer: Lord God, in this time before surgery, we watch for you. You are (P's) fortress—a refuge in times of need. Show your steadfast love to (P) now and bring (him/her) safely through surgery.*

**Ps. 91:9-12, 14-16:** Because you have made the Lord your refuge, and the Most High your dwelling place, no evil shall befall you, no scourge come near your tent. For he will command his angels concerning you to guard you in all your ways. On their hands they will bear you up, so that you will not dash your foot against a stone. Those who love me, I will deliver; I will protect those who know my name. When they call to me, I will answer them; I will be with them in trouble, I will rescue them and honor them. With long life I will satisfy them and show them my salvation.

*Prayer: Lord, we ask your presence with (P) in these troubling times, for you are our refuge. Bear (him/her) up in this time before surgery and guard (him/her) during surgery. Answer when we call, O God, and satisfy (P) with long life.*

**Ps. 97:10:** The Lord guards the lives of his faithful.

*Prayer: Lord, guard and keep (P) through this surgery, for (he/she) knows your name and is faithful.*

**Ps. 138:1, 3, 7-8:** I give you thanks, O Lord, with my whole heart. On the day I called, you answered me, you increased my strength of soul. Though I walk in the midst of trouble, . . . you stretch out your hand, and your right hand delivers me. The Lord will fulfill his purpose for me; your steadfast love, O Lord, endures forever. Do not forsake the work of your hands.

*Prayer: Lord, the psalmist offers the assurance that you answer us on the day we call to you. The psalmist tells us that you walk with us and take us by the hand in times of trouble. So do not forsake (P) now in these hours of waiting before surgery but take (him/her) by the hand, grant (P) a peaceful confidence, and help (him/her) to realize your purpose for (him/her).*

**Ps. 142:1-3, 5-6:** With my voice I cry to the Lord; with my voice I make supplication to the Lord. I pour out my complaint before him; I tell my trouble before him. When my spirit is faint, you know my way. I cry to you, O Lord; I say, "You are my refuge, my portion in the land of the living." Give heed to my cry, for I am brought very low.

*Prayer: Lord God, in this time before surgery, we call on you for help. Listen to the complaints and troubles of (P); strengthen (his/her) faint spirit. When sickness, surgery, or other events in (P's) life bring (him/her) low, Lord, hear (his/her) cries. Renew (his/her) spirit; watch over (his/her) way.*

## AFTER SURGERY

**Ps. 18:1-2, 4-6, 16, 30:** I love you, O Lord, my strength. The Lord is my rock, my fortress, and my deliverer, my God, my rock in whom I take refuge, my shield, and the horn of my salvation, my stronghold. The cords of death encompassed me; the torrents of perdition assailed me; the cords of Sheol entangled me; the snares of death confronted me. In my distress I called upon the Lord; to my God I cried for help. From his temple he heard my voice, and my cry to him reached his ears. He reached down from on high, he took me; he drew me out of mighty waters. This God—his way is perfect; the promise of the Lord proves true; he is a shield for all who take refuge in him.

*Prayer: Lord God, as (P) recovers from surgery, we thank you for being (his/her) strength and refuge. In the face of death (he/she) called upon you and you heard (his/her) cry. And now with relief and joy we give you thanks.*

**Ps. 30:2-4, 5-12:** O Lord my God, I cried to you for help, and you have healed me. O Lord, you brought up my soul from Sheol, restored me to life from among those gone down to the Pit. Sing praises to the Lord, O you his faithful ones, and give thanks to his holy name. Weeping may linger for the night, but joy comes with the morning. As for me, I said in my prosperity, "I shall never be moved." By your favor, O Lord, you had established me as a strong mountain; you hid your face; I was dismayed. To you, O Lord, I cried, and to the Lord I made supplication: "What profit is there in my death, if I go down to the Pit? Will the dust praise you? Will it tell of your faithfulness? Hear, O Lord, and be gracious to me! O Lord, be my helper!" You have turned my mourning into dancing; you have taken off my sackcloth and clothed me with joy, so that my soul may praise you and not be silent. O Lord my God, I will give thanks to you forever.

*Prayer: We give you thanks, Lord God, for you heard (P's) cry for help and healed (him/her). You saw (his/her) tears in the nights preceding surgery—tears of fatigue and concern. And now you have restored (his/her) joy. In (P's) distress, it seemed that you were not listening. But (he/she) cried to you and asked, "What good will it do if I die? For if I die, who can take my place in telling of your faithfulness?" Lord God, we give you thanks for joy—for turning (P's) mourning into dancing.*

**Ps. 34:4-8, 15, 17-19, 22:** I sought the Lord and he answered me, and delivered me from all my fears. Look to him and be radiant; so your faces shall never be ashamed. This poor soul cried, and was heard by the Lord, and was saved from every trouble. The angel of the Lord encamps around those who fear him, and delivers them. O taste and see that the Lord is good; happy are those who take refuge in him. The eyes of the Lord are on the righteous, and his ears are open to their cry. When the righteous cry for help, the Lord hears, and rescues them from all their troubles. The Lord is near to the brokenhearted, and saves the crushed in spirit. Many are the afflictions of the righteous, but the Lord rescues them from them all. The Lord redeems the life of his servants; none of those who take refuge in him will be condemned.

*Prayer: Lord, poor as we are toward you, you still hear our cries and watch over us. You came near to (P), who was brokenhearted in the face of the surgery that awaited (him/her). You saved (him/her) when (he/she) was crushed in spirit. We give you thanks for rescuing (P) from (his/her) troubles. You are good and we delight to take refuge in you.*

**Ps. 66:8-9, 20:** Bless our God, O peoples, let the sound of his praise be heard, who has kept us among the living. Blessed be God because he has not rejected my prayer or removed his steadfast love from me.

*Prayer: Lord, thank you for sustaining (P's) life during surgery. Thank you for accepting our prayers concerning (P) and for protecting (him/her).*

**Ps. 89:1-2:** I will sing of your steadfast love, O Lord, forever; with my mouth I will proclaim your faithfulness to all generations. I will declare that your steadfast love is established forever, your faithfulness is as firm as the heavens.

*Prayer: We are grateful for the steadfast love you have shown to (P), Lord. We thank you for your faithfulness and for bringing (him/her) safely through surgery.*

**Ps. 92:1-2, 4:** It is good to give thanks to the Lord, to sing praises to your name, O Most High; to declare your steadfast love in the morning, and your faithfulness by night. For you, O Lord, have made me glad by your work; at the works of your hands I sing for joy.

*Prayer: Through the doctors and nurses (P) has experienced the healing work of your hands, Lord. We thank you, for you have made (him/her) glad.*

**Ps. 94:17-19, 22:** If the Lord had not been my help, my soul would soon have lived in the land of silence. When I thought, "My foot is slipping," your steadfast

love, O Lord, held me up. When the cares of my heart are many, your consolations cheer my soul. The Lord has become my stronghold, and my God the rock of my refuge.

*Prayer: Lord, we thank you for being (P's) help during surgery. (He/She) still has concerns; yet we are grateful for your steadfast love that holds (P) up and cheers (his/her) soul. Be (P's) refuge this day.*

Ps. 98:1, 3, 4, 7-9: O sing to the Lord a new song, for he has done marvelous things. He has remembered his steadfast love and faithfulness. . . . Make a joyful noise to the Lord, all the earth; break forth into joyous song and sing praises. Let the sea roar, and all that fills it; the world and those who live in it. Let the floods clap their hands; let the hills sing together for joy at the presence of the Lord.

*Prayer: Lord, we give you thanks for the gifts of life and healing. You do marvelous things through the skills of your people; today we give special thanks for those who did the intricate work of surgery that has brought healing to (P). We offer you our joy.*

Ps. 103:1-5, 13-18: Bless the Lord, O my soul, and all that is within me, bless his holy name. Bless the Lord, O my soul, and do not forget all his benefits—who

forgives all your iniquity, who heals all your diseases, who redeems your life from the Pit, who crowns you with steadfast love and mercy, who satisfies you with good as long as you live so that your youth is renewed like the eagle's. As a father has compassion for his children, so the Lord has compassion for those who fear him. For he knows how we were made; he remembers that we are dust. As for mortals, their days are like grass; they flourish like a flower of the field; for the wind passes over it, and it is gone, and its place knows it no more. But the steadfast love of the Lord is from everlasting to everlasting on those who fear him, and his righteousness to children's children, to those who keep his covenant and remember to do his commandments.

*Prayer: In this time of recovery after surgery, Lord, we thank you for all your gifts—especially your healing, love, and mercy. Still we ask for your compassion for (P), because (he/she) is in pain, Lord. You know how we are made. Be tender with (him/her) and renew (his/-her) strength.*

**Ps. 126:6:** Those who go out weeping . . . shall come home with shouts of joy.

**Prayer:** *Lord, (P) is in pain after surgery; in these difficult days, remind (him/her) of the joyful homecoming that will be (his/hers)—both when (he/she) leaves this hospital and at the last when you welcome all your children into your heavenly home.*

# Fear and Doubt

SICKNESS CAN BRING fears and doubts of all kinds. These psalms and prayers acknowledge these realities and bring them to God.

## FEAR

**Ps. 10:1, (4), (6), 14:** Why, O Lord, do you stand far off? Why do you hide yourself in times of trouble? (In the pride of their countenance . . . the thoughts [of the wicked] are, "There is no God.") (They think in their heart, "We shall not be moved; throughout all generations we shall not meet adversity.") But you do see! Indeed you note trouble and grief, that you may take it into your hands; the helpless commit themselves to you.

*Prayer: Lord God, it feels like you are far away from (P)—even hiding from (him/her). (Sometimes there is the temptation to think that there is no God or that we will never meet adversity. But now, O Lord, (P) has met suffering and adversity.) Be present with (him/her) now. Give (him/her) the confidence to know that you see (his/her) trouble and grief. Help (P) to commit (himself/herself) and (his/her) troubles into your hands.*

**Ps. 22:1-2, (4-5), (6-7), 9-11, 14-15, 16-17, 19, 24:** My God, my God, why have you forsaken me? Why are you so far from helping me, from the words of my groaning? (In you our ancestors trusted; they trusted, and you delivered them. To you they cried, and were saved; in you they trusted, and were not put to shame.) (But I am a worm, and not human; scorned by others, and despised by the people. All who see me mock at me; they make mouths at me, they shake their heads. . . .) It was you who took me from the womb; you kept me safe on my mother's breast. On you I was cast from my birth, and since my mother bore me you have been my God. Do not be far from me, for trouble is near and there is no one to help. I am poured out like water, and all my bones are out of joint; my heart is like wax; it is melted within my breast; my mouth is dried up like a potsherd, and my tongue sticks to my jaws; you lay me in the dust of death. My hands and feet have shriveled; I can count all my bones. . . . But you, O Lord, do not be far away! O my help, come quickly to my aid! For the Lord did not despise or abhor the affliction of the afflicted; he did not hide his face from me, but heard when I cried to him.

*Prayer: God, why have you forsaken (P)? Why are you far from (his/her) suffering? (P) cries day and night to you, but finds no rest. (He/She) fears the physical changes in (his/her) body; (he/she) sees and experiences things in this illness that are frightening and that make it so hard to believe that you are a caring God. Yet it was you who gave (P) life and sustained (him/her) from childhood. Come to (P's) aid. Although (he/she) is fearful, (he/she) still trusts the words of the psalmist that say that you do not abhor the affliction of the afflicted. Hear our cry to you.*

**Ps. 27:1-5, 7-10, 13-14:** The Lord is my light and my salvation; whom shall I fear? The Lord is the stronghold of my life; of whom shall I be afraid? When evildoers assail me to devour my flesh—my adversaries and foes—they shall stumble and fall. Though an army encamp against me, my heart shall not fear; though war rise up against me, yet I will be confident. One thing I have asked of the Lord, that will I seek after; to live in the house of the Lord all the days of my life, to behold the beauty of the Lord, and to inquire in his temple. For he will hide me in his shelter in the day of trouble; he will conceal me under the cover of his tent; he will set me high on a rock. Hear, O Lord, when I cry aloud, be gracious to me and answer me! "Come," my heart says, "seek his face!" Your face, Lord, do I seek. Do not hide your face from me. Do not turn your servant away in anger, you who have been my help. Do not cast me off, do not forsake me, O God of my salvation! If my father and mother forsake me, the Lord will take me up. I believe that I shall

see the goodness of the Lord in the land of the living. Wait for the Lord; be strong, and let your heart take courage; wait for the Lord!

*Prayer: Lord, calm (P's) fears and anxieties; assure (him/her) that you are the stronghold of life. Shelter (him/her) in these difficult days. Be gracious to (him/her) and hear (him/her); do not forsake (P), but give (him/her) courage and strength to wait for you.*

**Ps. 31:1-5, (7-8), 9-12, 14-15, 16, 19, (21-22), 23, 24:** In you, O Lord, I seek refuge; do not let me ever be put to shame; in your righteousness deliver me. Incline your ear to me; rescue me speedily. Be a rock of refuge for me, a strong fortress to save me. You are indeed my rock and my fortress; for your name's sake lead me and guide me, take me out of the net that is hidden for me, for you are my refuge. Into your hand I commit my spirit; you have redeemed me, O Lord, faithful God. (I will exult and rejoice in your steadfast love, because you have seen my affliction; you have taken heed of my adversities, and have not delivered me into the hand of the enemy; you have set my feet in a broad place.) Be gracious to me, O Lord, for I am in distress; my eye wastes away from grief, my soul and body also. For my life is spent with sorrow, and my years with sighing; my strength fails because of my misery, and my bones waste away. I am the scorn

of all my adversaries, a horror to my neighbors, an object of dread to my acquaintances; those who see me in the street flee from me. I have passed out of mind like one who is dead; I have become like a broken vessel. But I trust in you, O Lord; I say, "You are my God." My times are in your hand. Let your face shine upon your servant; save me in your steadfast love. O how abundant is your goodness that you have laid up for those who fear you, and accomplished for those who take refuge in you, in the sight of everyone! (Blessed be the Lord, for he has wondrously shown his steadfast love to me when I was beset as a city under siege. I had said in my alarm, "I am driven far from your sight.") But you heard my supplications when I cried out to you for help. Love the Lord, all you his saints. The Lord preserves the faithful. Be strong, and let your heart take courage, all you who wait for the Lord.

*Prayer: Lord, you know (P's) sickness, fears, and grief. You know that (his/her) life is spent in sorrow. And now, Lord, (his/her) strength is failing and it is even difficult for (him/her) to feel the stares of those who meet (him/her) in the halls. Lord, be gracious to (P); let your face shine on (him/her) through those who care for (him/her) so that (he/she) may know gladness again.*

**Ps. 46:1-2, 7:** God is our refuge and strength, a very present help in trouble. Therefore we will not fear, though the earth should change. The Lord of hosts is with us; the God of Jacob is our refuge.

*Prayer: Lord God, be (P's) refuge and strength. Be very present to (him/her) in (his/her) affliction. Though everything in (his/her) life is changing, help (him/her) not to be afraid, but rather to find refuge in you.*

**Ps. 56:3-4, 8, 9, 10-11, 12-13:** O Most High, when I am afraid, I put my trust in you. In God, whose word I praise, in God I trust; I am not afraid; what can flesh do to me? You have kept count of my tossings; put my tears in your bottle. Are they not in your record? This I know, that God is for me. In God, whose word I praise, in the Lord, whose word I praise, in God I trust; I am not afraid. My vows to you I must perform, O God; I will render thank offerings to you. For you have delivered my soul from death, and my feet from falling, so that I may walk before God in the light of life.

*Prayer: Lord God, you know (P) so well. You know (his/her) fears and even the very number of tossings and turnings those fears cause. You record (his/her) tears. When (P) is numb with fear over sickness or the results of biopsies or other medical tests, help (him/her) to trust that you always hold (his/her) life in your hands.*

**Ps. 91:9-12, 14-16:** Because you have made the Lord your refuge, and the Most High your dwelling place, no evil shall befall you, no scourge come near your tent. For he will command his angels concerning you to guard you in all your ways. On their hands they will bear you up, so that you will not dash your foot against a stone. Those who love me, I will deliver; I will protect those who know my name. When they call to me, I will answer them; I will be with them in trouble, I will rescue them and honor them. With long life I will satisfy them and show them my salvation.

*Prayer: Protect (P), Lord, for (he/she) knows your name. Bear (him/her) up in these difficult days, for (he/she) loves you. Be with (P) in this day of trouble; rescue (him/her) and show (him/her) your salvation.*

**Ps. 118:5-6, 7, 13-14, 17:** Out of my distress I called on the Lord; the Lord answered me and set me in a broad place. With the Lord on my side I do not fear; . . . the Lord is on my side to help me. I was pushed hard, so that I was falling, but the Lord helped me. The Lord is my strength and my might; he has become my salvation. I shall not die, but I shall live, and recount the deeds of the Lord.

*Prayer: Lord, when (P) is afraid; when (he/she) is pushed so hard that it seems (he/she) is falling, help (him/her). (P) has many fears; (he/she) fears what this sickness means and what may be ahead. Be (his/her) strength; listen to (his/her) cries of distress and answer (him/her).*

**Ps. 139:1-18:** O Lord, you have searched me and known me. You know when I sit down and when I rise up; you discern my thoughts from far away. You search out my path and my lying down, and are acquainted with all my ways. Even before a word is on my tongue, O Lord, you know it completely. You hem me in, behind and before, and lay your hand upon me. Such knowledge is too wonderful for me; it is so high that I cannot attain it. Where can I go from your spirit? Or where can I flee from your presence? If I ascend to heaven, you are there; if I make my bed in Sheol, you are there. For it was you who formed by inward parts; you knit me together in my mother's womb. I praise you, for I am fearfully and wonderfully made. Wonderful are your works; that I know very well. My frame was not hidden from you, when I was being made in secret, intricately woven in the depths of the earth. Your eyes beheld my unformed substance. In your book were written all the days that were formed for me, when none of them as yet existed. How weighty to me are your thoughts, O God! How vast is the sum of them! I try to count them—they are more than the sand; I come to the end—I am still with you.

*Prayer: Almighty and yet vulnerable God, you know the fears (P) has. Yet the psalmist reminds us that there is no place, not even in this hospital, where we are separated from your presence. You know us better than we know ourselves. You care for us and are with us always. Let that assurance calm our fears and settle our doubts.*

## DOUBT

**Ps. 8:4-6:** What are human beings that you are mindful of them, mortals that you care for them? Yet you have made them a little lower than God, and crowned them with glory and honor. You have given them dominion over the works of your hands; you have put all things under their feet.

*Prayer: Lord God, sometimes (P) wonders if you care for (him/her). (He/She) wonders where you are in (his/her) pain. In these times give (him/her) faith, Lord, to realize that you do care for (him/her). In fact, you have made (P) only a little lower than yourself and crowned (him/her) with glory and honor. You have entrusted to (him/her) the care of all that your own hands created. Therefore, remind (P) of how very much you do care for (him/her) and how invaluable (he/she) is to you.*

**Ps. 13:1-2, 3:** How long, O Lord? Will you forget me forever? How long will you hide your face from me? How long must I bear pain in my soul and have

sorrow in my heart all day long? Consider and answer me, O Lord my God! Give light to my eyes, or I will sleep the sleep of death. . . .

*Prayer: Lord, it seems that you have forgotten (P) or are hiding from (him/her). How long must (P) endure pain and sorrow? Please answer us, O Lord.*

**Ps. 39:1-8, 12:** I said, "I will guard my ways that I may not sin with my tongue; I will keep a muzzle on my mouth as long as the wicked are in my presence." I was silent and still; I held my peace to no avail; my distress grew worse, my heart became hot within me. While I mused, the fire burned; then I spoke with my tongue: "Lord, let me know my end, and what is the measure of my days; let me know how fleeting my life is. You have made my days a few handbreadths, and my lifetime is as nothing in your sight. Surely everyone stands as a mere breath. Surely everyone goes about like a shadow. Surely for nothing they are in turmoil; they heap up, and do not know who will gather. And now, O Lord, what do I wait for? My hope is in you. Deliver me from all my transgressions. Do not make me the scorn of the fool. Hear my prayer, O Lord, and give ear to my cry; do not hold your peace at my tears. For I am your passing guest, an alien, like all my forebears."

*Prayer: Lord, why is life what it is? You have made the lives of humans short—like passing shadows. All our work and worry do not seem to amount to anything in the face of death. Lord, do not ignore (P's) tears. Teach us that our hope is in you. Help us to see the purpose in our vocations and the significance of our lives.*

**Ps. 42:1-6, 7-9, 10-11:** As a deer longs for flowing streams, so my soul longs for you, O God. My soul thirsts for God, for the living God. When shall I come and behold the face of God? My tears have been my food day and night, while people say to me continually, "Where is your God?" These things I remember as I pour out my soul: how I went with the throng, and led them in procession to the house of God, with glad shouts and songs of thanksgiving, a multitude keeping festival. Why are you cast down, O my soul, and why are you disquieted within me? Hope in God; for I shall again praise him, my help and my God. My soul is cast down within me; therefore I remember you. . . . Deep calls to deep at the thunder of your cataracts; all your waves and your billows have gone over me. By day the Lord commands his steadfast love, and at night his song is with me, a prayer to the God of my life. I say to God, my rock, "Why have you forgotten me? Why must I walk about mournfully. . . ?" As with a deadly

wound in my body, my adversaries taunt me, while they say to me continually, "Where is your God?" Why are you cast down, O my soul, and why are you disquieted within me? Hope in God; for I shall again praise him, my help and my God.

*Prayer: Lord, why must (P) be sad and restless? Tears have been (his/her) food day and night. Why is (his/her) soul in turmoil? Have you forgotten (him/her)? Send your love to (P) by day; surround (him/her) with your song by night. Help (P) to hope in you and praise you again.*

Ps. 44:23-26: Lord, rouse yourself! Why do you sleep, O Lord? Awake, do not cast us off forever! Why do you hide your face? Why do you forget our affliction and oppression? For we sink down to the dust; our bodies cling to the ground. Rise up, come to our help. Redeem us for the sake of your steadfast love.

*Prayer: God, are you sleeping? Why do you hide from (P)? Why does it seem that you have forgotten (his/her) affliction? Remember that humans are dust and come to our help. For the sake of your steadfast love, save (P).*

Ps. 73:13-17, 21-26, 28: All in vain I have kept my heart clean and washed my hands in innocence. For all day long I have been plagued, and am punished every

morning. If I had said, "I will talk on in this way," I would have been untrue to the circle of your children. But when I thought how to understand this, it seemed to me a wearisome task, until I went into the sanctuary of God. When my soul was embittered, when I was pricked in heart, I was stupid and ignorant; I was like a brute beast toward you. Nevertheless, I am continually with you; you hold my right hand. You guide me with your counsel, and afterward you will receive me with honor. Whom have I in heaven but you? And there is nothing on earth that I desire other than you. My flesh and my heart may fail, but God is the strength of my heart and my portion forever. For me it is good to be near God; I have made the Lord God my refuge, to tell of all your works.

*Prayer: Lord God, it is impossible to understand why (P) must suffer. It is tiring to try to think about it. Yet coming into your presence in prayer offers relief. Hold (P) by the hand even when (he/she) fights and argues against you. For whom does (he/she) finally have but you? You, O Lord, are (his/her) greatest treasure. When our bodies fail us and when our friends and families disappoint us, you are still with us. It is good to be near you; you are our refuge.*

# Trust
# and Confidence

WE LONG TO TRUST that all will be well no matter what a sickness brings. These prayers express yearning, hope, and trust in God, even in bewildering times.

**Ps. 3:3-5:** But you, O Lord, are a shield around me, my glory, and the one who lifts up my head. I cry aloud to the Lord, and he answers me from his holy hill. I lie down and sleep; I wake again, for the Lord sustains me.

*Prayer: Lord God, set your love and care like a shield around (P). Give to all who hurt or suffer the confidence to know that you lift our heads from sadness and weakness and you do hear our prayers. (Lord, we now commit this evening to your care for you sustain us even in our sleep.)*

**Ps. 4:1, 3, 5, (8):** Answer me when I call, O God of my right! You gave me room when I was in distress. Be gracious to me, and hear my prayer. Know that the Lord has set apart the faithful for himself; the Lord hears when I call to him. Put your trust in the Lord.

(I will both lie down and sleep in peace; for you alone, O Lord, make me lie down in safety.)

*Prayer: Lord God, hear (P) now when (he/she) needs you so desperately—for you do promise to hear your children in need. Give (him/her) the confidence to believe that you do set apart the faithful for yourself. Calm (P's) fears and anxieties, help (him/her) to trust in you.*

❧

**Ps. 14:1, 5, 6:** Fools say in their hearts, "There is no God." God is with the company of the righteous. . . . The Lord is their refuge.

*Prayer: O Lord, in difficult times it is easy to feel that there is no God. But when (P) feels that way, help (him/her) somehow to know that you are present with those who love you and that you are (his/her) refuge always.*

❧

**Ps. 16:1-2, 5, 8-11:** Protect me, O God, for in you I take refuge. I say to the Lord, "You are my Lord; I have no good apart from you." The Lord is my chosen portion and my cup; you hold my lot. I keep the Lord always before me; because he is at my right hand, I shall not be moved. Therefore my heart is glad, and my soul rejoices; my body also rests secure. For you do not give me up to Sheol, or let the faithful one see the Pit.

You show me the path of life. In your presence there is fullness of joy; in your right hand are pleasures forevermore.

*Prayer: Protect (P), O God, for you are (his/her) refuge. Lord, stay before (him/her) and help (him/her) to rest securely in body and soul. Give (P) the confidence to trust that in you are life and joy.*

**Ps. 18:1-2, 4-6, 16, 30:** I love you, O Lord, my strength. The Lord is my rock, my fortress, and my deliverer, my God, my rock in whom I take refuge, my shield, and the horn of my salvation, my stronghold. The cords of death encompassed me; the torrents of perdition assailed me; the cords of Sheol entangled me; the snares of death confronted me. In my distress I called upon the Lord; to my God I cried for help. From his temple he heard my voice, and my cry to him reached his ears. He reached down from on high, he took me; he drew me out of mighty waters. This God—his way is perfect; the promise of the Lord proves true; he is a shield for all who take refuge in him.

*Prayer: Lord God, we confidently name you as our rock, fortress, shield, and refuge. We trust that when we cry to (from this hospital room), you will hear and answer. Sustain our confidence in you, O Lord. Show us your goodness and healing.*

**Ps. 23:1-6:** The Lord is my shepherd, I shall not want. He makes me lie down in green pastures; he leads me beside still waters; he restores my soul. He leads me in right paths for his name's sake. Even though I walk through the darkest valley, I fear no evil; for you are with me; your rod and your staff—they comfort me. You prepare a table before me in the presence of my enemies; you anoint my head with oil; my cup overflows. Surely goodness and mercy shall follow me all the days of my life, and I shall dwell in the house of the Lord my whole life long.

*Prayer: Dearest Shepherd, walk with (P) now through these dark times. Comfort, restore, and pursue (P) with your goodness. Give (P) the confidence and comfort of knowing that (he/she) will dwell in your house forever.*

**Ps. 27:1-5, 7-10, 13-14:** The Lord is my light and my salvation; whom shall I fear? The Lord is the stronghold of my life; of whom shall I be afraid? When evildoers assail me to devour my flesh—my adversaries and foes—they shall stumble and fall. Though an army encamp against me, my heart shall not fear; though war rise up against me, yet I will be confident. One thing I have asked of the Lord, that will I seek after; to live in the house of the Lord all the days of my life, to behold the beauty of the Lord, and to inquire in his temple. For he will hide me in his shelter in the day of

trouble; he will conceal me under the cover of his tent; he will set me high on a rock. Hear, O Lord, when I cry aloud, be gracious to me and answer me! "Come," my heart says, "seek his face!" Your face, Lord, do I seek. Do not hide your face from me. Do not turn your servant away in anger, you who have been my help. Do not cast me off, do not forsake me, O God of my salvation! If my father and mother forsake me, the Lord will take me up. I believe that I shall see the goodness of the Lord in the land of the living. Wait for the Lord; be strong, and let your heart take courage; wait for the Lord!

*Prayer: Lord, when sickness, like an enemy army, seems to eat at (P's) strength and body, help (him/her) to be confident in the truth that you are the stronghold of life. Shelter (P) in these difficult days. Be gracious to (him/her) and hear (his/her) prayers; do not forsake (him/her). Give (him/her) courage and strength to wait for you.*

**Ps. 28:1-2, 6-9:** To you, O Lord, I call; my rock, do not refuse to hear me, for if you are silent to me, I shall be like those who go down to the Pit. Hear the voice of my supplication, as I cry to you for help, as I lift up my hands toward your most holy sanctuary. Blessed be the Lord, for he has heard the sound of my pleadings. The Lord is my strength and my shield; in him my heart trusts; so I am helped, and my heart exults,

and with my song I give thanks to him. The Lord is the strength of his people; he is the saving refuge of his anointed. O save your people, and bless your heritage; be their shepherd, and carry them forever.

*Prayer: Lord, trusting in you is a help to us. We know that you hear our pleading for (P's) life and health. Carry (him/her) in your arms in these difficult days, even as a tender shepherd carries sheep.*

**Ps. 31:1-5, 7-12, 14-15, 16, 19, 21-22, 23, 24:** In you, O Lord, I seek refuge; do not let me ever be put to shame; in your righteousness deliver me. Incline your ear to me; rescue me speedily. Be a rock of refuge for me, a strong fortress to save me. You are indeed my rock and my fortress; for your name's sake lead me and guide me, take me out of the net that is hidden for me, for you are my refuge. Into your hand I commit my spirit; you have redeemed me, O Lord, faithful God. I will exult and rejoice in your steadfast love, because you have seen my affliction; you have taken heed of my adversities, and have not delivered me into the hand of the enemy; you have set my feet in a broad place. Be gracious to me, O Lord, for I am in distress; my eye wastes away from grief, my soul and body also. For my life is spent with sorrow, and my years with sighing; my strength fails because of my misery, and my bones waste away. I am the scorn of all my adversaries, a horror to my neighbors, an object of dread to

my acquaintances; those who see me in the street flee from me. I have passed out of mind like one who is dead; I have become like a broken vessel. But I trust in you, O Lord; I say, "You are my God." My times are in your hand. Let your face shine upon your servant; save me in your steadfast love. O how abundant is your goodness that you have laid up for those who fear you, and accomplished for those who take refuge in you, in the sight of everyone! Blessed be the Lord, for he has wondrously shown his steadfast love to me when I was beset as a city under siege. I had said in my alarm, "I am driven far from your sight." But you heard my supplications when I cried out to you for help. Love the Lord, all you his saints. The Lord preserves the faithful. Be strong, and let your heart take courage, all you who wait for the Lord.

*Prayer: Lord, (P) commits (his/her) spirit into your hand, for you are (his/her) refuge and fortress. Some friends of (P) seem to have forgotten (him/her). Perhaps they do not know what to say, but it hurts (P) to be treated as if (he/she) does not exist. We trust that you hear (his/her) cries for help and that you preserve the lives of those faithful to you. You know the sickness of (P); be gracious to (him/her), for (he/she) is in distress.*

**Ps. 33:18-22:** Truly the eye of the Lord is on those who fear him, on those who hope in his steadfast love, to deliver their soul from death, and to keep them alive

in famine. Our soul waits for the Lord; he is our help and shield. Our heart is glad in him, because we trust in his holy name. Let your steadfast love, O Lord, be upon us, even as we hope in you.

*Prayer: Tender God, we trust that you are (P's) help. We depend on your strong name and ask that your love surround us as a shield against pain, infection, and sickness. Come to (P) with healing and hope.*

**Ps. 34:4-8, 15, 17-19, 22:** I sought the Lord and he answered me, and delivered me from all my fears. Look to him and be radiant; so your faces shall never be ashamed. This poor soul cried, and was heard by the Lord, and was saved from every trouble. The angel of the Lord encamps around those who fear him, and delivers them. O taste and see that the Lord is good; happy are those who take refuge in him. The eyes of the Lord are on the righteous, and his ears are open to their cry. When the righteous cry for help, the Lord hears, and rescues them from all their troubles. The Lord is near to the brokenhearted, and saves the crushed in spirit. Many are the afflictions of the righteous, but the Lord rescues them from them all. The Lord redeems the life of his servants; none of those who take refuge in him will be condemned.

*Prayer: Lord, poor as we are toward you, you still hear our cries and watch over us. You came near to (P), who was brokenhearted and crushed in spirit. And because you rescued (him/her) from (his/her) fears, we look to you with confidence and joyful faces and offer you our thanks.*

**Ps. 62:1-2, 5-8:** For God alone my soul waits in silence, from him comes my salvation. He alone is my rock and my salvation, my fortress, I shall never be shaken. For God alone my soul waits in silence, for my hope is from him. He alone is my rock and my salvation, my fortress; I shall not be shaken. On God rests my deliverance and my honor; my mighty rock, my refuge is in God. Trust in him at all times, O people; pour out your heart before him; God is refuge for us.

*Prayer: Lord God, you are the source of (P's) hope, honor, and salvation. We pour out our hearts to you in this difficult time and ask that you keep (P) firm in the knowledge that you are (his/her) refuge.*

**Ps. 71:1-3, 5-9, 12, 18:** In you, O Lord, I take refuge; let me never be put to shame. In your righteousness deliver and rescue me; incline your ear to me and save me. Be to me a rock of refuge, a strong fortress to save me, for you are my rock and my fortress. For you, O Lord, are my hope, my trust, O Lord, from my youth. Upon you I have leaned from my birth; it was you who took me from my mother's womb, my praise is

continually of you. I have been like a portent to many, but you are my strong refuge. My mouth is filled with your praise, and with your glory all day long. Do not cast me off in the time of old age; do not forsake me when my strength is spent. O God, do not be far from me; O my God, make haste to help me! So even to old age and gray hairs, O God, do not forsake me, until I proclaim your might to all the generations to come.

*Prayer: Lord God, (P) trusts in you; be (his/her) rock and refuge. (He/She) has leaned on you since birth; so now, when (he/she) is older, O Lord, do not forsake (him/her); but make haste to help. Give (P) strength to tell generations still to come of your might.*

**Ps. 84:1-5, 8, 11-12:** How lovely is your dwelling place, O Lord of hosts! My soul longs, indeed it faints for the courts of the Lord; my heart and my flesh sing for joy to the living God. Even the sparrow finds a home, and the swallow a nest for herself, where she may lay her young, at your altars, O Lord of hosts, my King and my God. Happy are those who live in your house, ever singing your praise. Happy are those whose strength is in you. O Lord God of hosts, hear my prayer; give ear, O God of Jacob! For the Lord God is a sun and shield; he bestows favor and honor. No good thing does the Lord withhold from those who walk uprightly. O Lord of hosts, happy is everyone who trusts in you.

*Prayer: Lord, help us to trust that your dwelling place is a good place where we will know and be safe in your great love.*

**Ps. 145:8-9, 13-20:** The Lord is gracious and merciful, slow to anger and abounding in steadfast love. The Lord is good to all, and his compassion is over all that he has made. The Lord is faithful in all his words, and gracious in all his deeds. The Lord upholds all who are falling, and raises up all who are bowed down. The eyes of all look to you, and you give them their food in due season. You open your hand, satisfying the desire of every living thing. The Lord is just in all his ways, and kind in all his doings. The Lord is near to all who call on him, to all who call on him in truth. He fulfills the desire of all who fear him; he also hears their cry, and saves them. The Lord watches over all who love him.

*Prayer: We trust that you are gracious and merciful, Lord God. We trust that you uphold those who are falling and that you raise up those who are bowed down in grief. Therefore, we commend (P's) sorrows to you, trusting that you will be tender and kind with (him/her).*

# Abandonment
and Loneliness

SICKNESS CAN bring feelings of devastating abandonment and loneliness. It may even seem as though one's voice has been taken away. Jesus, too, knew these feelings when he cried, "My God, my God, why have you forsaken me?" Praying these psalms, making one's home in them for a while, can help one find a voice again and recognize that God never abandons us.

Ps. 22:1-2, (4-5), 6-7, 9-11, 14-15, 16-17, 19, 24: My God, my God, why have you forsaken me? Why are you so far from helping me, from the words of my groaning? O my God, I cry by day, but thou dost not answer; and by night, but find no rest. (In you our ancestors trusted; they trusted, and you delivered them. To you they cried, and were saved; in you they trusted, and were not put to shame.) But I am a worm, and not human; scorned by others, and despised by the people. All who see me mock at me; they make mouths at me, they shake their heads. . . . Yet it was you who took me from the womb; you kept me safe on my mother's breast. On you I was cast from my birth, and since my mother bore me you have been

99

my God. Do not be far from me, for trouble is near and there is no one to help. I am poured out like water, and all my bones are out of joint; my heart is like wax; it is melted within my breast; my mouth is dried up like a potsherd, and my tongue sticks to my jaws; you lay me in the dust of death. My hands and feet have shriveled; I can count all my bones. . . . But you, O Lord, do not be far away! O my help, come quickly to my aid! For the Lord did not despise or abhor the affliction of the afflicted; he did not hide his face from me, but heard when I cried to him.

*Prayer: God, why have you forsaken (P)? Why are you far from (his/her) suffering? (He/She) cries day and night to you but finds no rest. Yet it was you who gave (P) life and sustained (him/her) from childhood. For this reason, we plead with you not to be far from (him/her) in this time of trouble. Hear our cry!*

**Ps. 25:15-18:** My eyes are ever toward the Lord, for he will pluck my feet out of the net. Turn to me and be gracious to me, for I am lonely and afflicted. Relieve the troubles of my heart and bring me out of my distress. Consider my affliction and my trouble, and forgive all my sins.

*Prayer: Lord God, (P) is lonely and sick. It seems that you have forsaken (him/her); in fact, it is difficult to maintain hope that you care. But still, somehow, (P) looks to you for help. Be gracious to (him/her), Lord, for this hospital can be frightening as well as lonely. Relieve the troubles of (his/her) heart and bring (him/her) out of (his/her) distress. Think about (P's) affliction and answer (him/her).*

❧

**Ps. 27:7-10, 13-14:** Hear, O Lord, when I cry aloud, be gracious to me and answer me! "Come," my heart says, "seek his face!" Your face, Lord, do I seek. Do not hide your face from me. Do not turn your servant away in anger, you who have been my help. Do not cast me off, do not forsake me, O God of my salvation! If my father and mother forsake me, the Lord will take me up. I believe that I shall see the goodness of the Lord in the land of the living. Wait for the Lord; be strong, and let your heart take courage; wait for the Lord!

*Prayer: Lord, when sickness diminishes (P's) strength and body, do not forsake (him/her). When it seems that you are hiding from (him/her), help (him/her) somehow to be confident in the truth that you are the stronghold of life and that you do care for (him/her). Shelter (P) in these difficult days. Give (him/her) courage and strength to wait for you.*

**Ps. 44:23-26:** Lord, rouse yourself! Why do you sleep? Awake, do not cast us off forever! Why do you hide your face? Why do you forget our affliction and oppression? For we sink down to the dust; our bodies cling to the ground. Rise up, come to our help. Redeem us for the sake of your steadfast love.

*Prayer: God, are you sleeping? Why do you hide from (P)? Why do you forget (his/her) affliction? (He/She) feels crushed by this illness. Remember that all your children are fragile dust and in need of your help. For the sake of your steadfast love, save (P).*

**Ps. 61:1-3, 4-5:** Hear my cry, O God; listen to my prayer. From the end of the earth I call to you, when my heart is faint. Lead me to the rock that is higher than I; for you are my refuge. Let me abide in your tent forever, find refuge under the shelter of your wings. For you, O God, have heard my vows; you have given me the heritage of those who fear your name.

*Prayer: Listen to our prayer, Lord God. (P) has come to this medical center from far away, and this place seems very foreign to (him/her). Give (P) the knowledge that wherever (he/she) is, you are still (his/her) refuge. Under the shelter of your wings (he/she) may live in safety. We thank you for being our shelter, Lord, and for placing us in families and with other people who confess your name.*

**Ps. 73:13-17, 21-26, 28:** All in vain I have kept my heart clean and washed my hands in innocence. For all day long I have been plagued, and am punished every morning. If I had said, "I will talk on in this way," I would have been untrue to the circle of your children. But when I thought how to understand this, it seemed to me a wearisome task, until I went into the sanctuary of God. . . . When my soul was embittered, when I was pricked in heart, I was stupid and ignorant; I was like a brute beast toward you. Nevertheless, I am continually with you; you hold my right hand. You guide me with your counsel, and afterward you will receive me with honor. Whom have I in heaven but you? And there is nothing on earth that I desire other than you. My flesh and my heart may fail, but God is the strength of my heart and my portion forever. For me it is good to be near God; I have made the Lord God my refuge, to tell of all your works.

*Prayer: Lord God, even when our hearts fail physically, you are still the strength of our hearts spiritually. In this very difficult time, help (P) to find strength and comfort in this truth. (He/She) is wearied by trying to understand why this is happening. (He/She) needs to know that you are with (him/her) even in the midst of things (he/she) cannot understand; give (P) eyes to see your presence. Hold (him/her) by the hand even when (he/she) feels forsaken or fights and argues against you. For whom do we finally have but you? You, O Lord, are our greatest treasure.*

**Ps. 102:1-7, 9, 11-12, 17-20, 23-27, (28):** Hear my prayer, O Lord; let my cry come to you. Do not hide your face from me in the day of my distress. Incline your ear to me; answer me speedily in the day when I call. For my days pass away like smoke, and my bones burn like a furnace. My heart is stricken and withered like grass; I am too wasted to eat my bread. Because of my loud groaning my bones cling to my skin. I am like an owl of the wilderness, like a little owl of the waste places. I lie awake; I am like a lonely bird on the housetop. For I eat . . . bread, and mingle tears with my drink. My days are like an evening shadow; I wither away like grass. But you, O Lord, are enthroned forever; your name endures to all generations. The Lord will regard the prayer of the destitute, and will not despise their prayer. Let this be recorded for a generation to come, so that a people yet unborn may praise the Lord: that he looked down from his holy height, from heaven the Lord looked at the earth, to hear the groans of the prisoners, to set free those who were doomed to die . . . . He has broken my strength in midcourse; he has shortened my days. "O my God," I say, "do not take me away at the midpoint of my life, you whose years endure throughout all generations." Long ago you laid the foundation of the earth, and the heavens are the work of your hands. They will perish, but you endure; they will all wear out like a garment. You change them like clothing, and they pass away; but you are the same, and your years have no end. (The children of your servants shall live secure; their offspring shall be established in your presence.)

*Prayer: Lord, it seems that you are hiding from (P) and (his/her) troubles. (He/She) feels lonely and forsaken by you. The psalmist assures us that you do regard the prayers of those who cry to you. Sometimes though, in the depths of feeling forsaken, that is difficult to believe. (P) comes before you now with (his/her) doubts, anger, fears, pain. We beg you to listen to (his/her) cries. (He/She) is in terrible pain. God, you endure throughout all generations; look on us and be tender with (P) and all of us.*

**Ps. 142:1-3, 5-6:** With my voice I cry to the Lord; with my voice I make supplication to the Lord. I pour out my complaint before him; I tell my trouble before him. When my spirit is faint, you know my way. I cry to you, O Lord; I say, "You are my refuge, my portion in the land of the living." Give heed to my cry, for I am brought very low.

*Prayer: Lord, (P) has told you (his/her) troubles and complaints. When feelings of abandonment and loneliness make (his/her) spirit faint, Lord, hear (his/her) cries. Renew (his/her) heart; watch over (his/her) way and lead (him/her).*

**Ps. 143:1-4, 6-8:** Hear my prayer, O Lord; give ear to my supplications in your faithfulness; answer me in your righteousness. Do not enter into judgment with your servant, for no one living is righteous before you. For the enemy has pursued me, crushing my life to the ground, making me sit in darkness like those long dead. Therefore my spirit faints within me; my heart within me is appalled. I stretch out my hands to you; my soul thirsts for you like a parched land. Answer me quickly, O Lord; my spirit fails. Do not hide your face from me, or I shall be like those who go down to the Pit. Let me hear of your steadfast love in the morning, for in you I put my trust. Teach me the way I should go, for to you I lift up my soul.

*Prayer: Lord, when (P) feels crushed, abandoned, and lonely, when (his/her) world seems dark, when (his/her) spirit faints and (his/her) heart is frightened, when you seem absent, help (P), Lord, to trust in you. Renew (his/her) spirit; surround (him/her) with your steadfast love and lead (him/her).*

# Struggle,
# Acceptance,
# and Peace

Sickness involves wrestling with difficult questions as well as physical ailments. Do not avoid the struggle! Let your prayers reflect your multifaceted struggles and eventually you may also sense acceptance and even peace.

**Ps. 5:1-3, 7, 11-12:** Give ear to my words, O Lord; give heed to my sighing. Listen to the sound of my cry, my King and my God, for to you I pray. O Lord, in the morning you hear my voice; in the morning I plead my case to you and watch. I, through the abundance of your steadfast love will enter your house . . . in awe of you. Let all who take refuge in you rejoice; let them ever sing for joy. Spread your protection over them, so that those who love your name may exult in you. For you bless the righteous, O Lord, you cover them with favor as with a shield.

*Prayer: Lord, we come before you pleading (P's) case—asking you to restore (his/her) health. (He/She) is tired and desperate. Help (him/her) to know the presence and abundance of your steadfast love. Spread*

*your protection over (P) and give (him/her) confidence*
*that those who love your name and take refuge in you*
*will know your joy.*

❧

**Ps. 7:1, 3, 5, 6 ,8, 10-11, 17:** O Lord my God, in you I take
refuge; save me from all my pursuers, and deliver me.
O Lord my God, if I have done this, if there is wrong
in my hands, . . . then let the enemy pursue and and
overtake me, trample my life to the ground, and lay
my soul in the dust. The Lord judges the peoples;
judge me, O Lord, according to my righteousness and
according to the integrity that is in me. God is my
shield, who saves the upright in heart. God is a righteous judge, and a God who has indignation every day.
I will give to the Lord the thanks due to his righteousness, and sing praise to the name of the Lord, the Most
High.

*Prayer: Lord, (P) takes refuge in you. Save (him/her)*
*from this sickness that pursues (him/her) like an enemy.*
*Rise up, O Lord! Show your anger at (P's) illness! Test*
*(his/her) heart and see (his/her) integrity. Be gracious to*
*(P), O Lord, that (he/she) may again sing your praises.*

❧

**Ps. 13:1-3, 5-6:** How long, O Lord? Will you forget me
forever? How long will you hide your face from me?
How long must I bear pain in my soul, and have sorrow in my heart all day long? How long shall my

enemy be exalted over me? Consider and answer me, O Lord my God! Give light to my eyes, or I will sleep the sleep of death. . . . But I trusted in your steadfast love; my heart shall rejoice in your salvation. I will sing to the Lord, because he has dealt bountifully with me.

*Prayer: Lord, (P) is struggling with many difficult feelings and questions. Have you forgotten (him/her)? Where are you? Why must there be pain? How long shall this evening of sickness last? Lord, hear and answer (P's) prayers and deal bountifully with (him/her). Bring your peace into this room and calm our hearts.*

**Ps. 27:1-5, 7-10, 13-14:** The Lord is my light and my salvation; whom shall I fear? The Lord is the stronghold of my life; of whom shall I be afraid? When evildoers assail me to devour my flesh—my adversaries and foes—they shall stumble and fall. Though an army encamp against me, my heart shall not fear; though war rise up against me, yet I will be confident. One thing I have asked of the Lord, that will I seek after; to live in the house of the Lord all the days of my life, to behold the beauty of the Lord, and to inquire in his temple. For he will hide me in his shelter in the day of trouble; he will conceal me under the cover of his tent; he will set me high on a rock. Hear, O Lord, when I cry aloud, be gracious to me and answer me!

"Come," my heart says, "seek his face!" Your face, Lord, do I seek. Do not hide your face from me. Do not turn your servant away in anger, you who have been my help. Do not cast me off, do not forsake me, O God of my salvation! If my father and mother forsake me, the Lord will take me up. I believe that I shall see the goodness of the Lord in the land of the living. Wait for the Lord; be strong, and let your heart take courage; wait for the Lord!

*Prayer: (P) is not well physically and there are procedures and times of waiting that make (him/her) fearful. Let the words of the psalmist that say, "My heart shall not fear" and "Let your heart take courage" be true for (him/her) both physically and spiritually, Lord. Take away the struggles and fears of (his/her) heart and replace those fears with health, acceptance, and peace. You are the stronghold of life. Help (P) to be confident in that truth. Shelter (him/her) in these difficult days.*

**Ps. 57:1-3:** Be merciful to me, O God, be merciful to me, for in you my soul takes refuge; in the shadow of your wings I will take refuge, until the destroying storms pass by. I cry to God Most High, to God who fulfills his purpose for me. He will send from heaven and save me. . . . God will send forth his steadfast love and his faithfulness.

*Prayer: Lord, why must there be sickness or other storms in life that seem to destroy the people who are most important to us? Surround (P) with your steadfast love and faithfulness. Give us the confidence to believe that in the shadow of your wings there is refuge from the storms of life. Keep (P) in your care, O God.*

**Ps. 73:13-17, 21-26, 28:** All in vain I have kept my heart clean and washed my hands in innocence. For all day long I have been plagued, and am punished every morning. If I had said, "I will talk on in this way," I would have been untrue to the circle of your children. But when I thought how to understand this, it seemed to me a wearisome task, until I went into the sanctuary of God. When my soul was embittered, when I was pricked in heart, I was stupid and ignorant; I was like a brute beast toward you. Nevertheless, I am continually with you; you hold my right hand. You guide me with your counsel, and afterward you will receive me with honor. Whom have I in heaven but you? And there is nothing on earth that I desire other than you. My flesh and my heart may fail, but God is the strength of my heart and my portion forever. For me it is good to be near God; I have made the Lord God my refuge, to tell of all your works.

*Prayer: Lord God, it is impossible to understand why (P) must suffer. We struggle with this overwhelming question but it only makes us frustrated and tired. Hold (P) by the hand even when (he/she) fights and argues against you. For whom does (he/she) finally have but you? You, O Lord, are our heart's desire. It is good to be near you and take refuge in you. Guide (P) in these wearisome days.*

**Ps. 77:1-12:** I cry aloud to God, that he may hear me. In the day of my trouble I seek the Lord; in the night my hand is stretched out without wearying; my soul refuses to be comforted. I think of God, and I moan; I meditate, and my spirit faints. You keep my eyelids from closing; I am so troubled that I cannot speak. I consider the days of old, and remember the years of long ago. I commune with my heart in the night; I meditate and search my spirit: "Will the Lord spurn forever, and never again be favorable? Has his steadfast love ceased forever? Are his promises at an end for all time? Has God forgotten to be gracious? Has he in anger shut up his compassion?" And I say, "It is my grief that the right hand of the Most High has changed." I will call to mind the deeds of the Lord; I will remember your wonders of old. I will meditate on all your work, and muse on your mighty deeds.

*Prayer: Lord, we cry to you for help and yet it is difficult to sense your presence. (P) struggles with many questions. Have you forgotten (him/her), God? Will you ever again be gracious to (him/her)? In these times of difficulty too great for words, help (P) to remember how you have cared for (him/her) in the past and to find strength and comfort in those memories. Help (him/her) to trust that you still care for (him/her).*

**Ps. 85:7-8:** Show us your steadfast love, O Lord, and grant us your salvation. Let me hear what God the Lord will speak, for he will speak peace to his people, to his faithful, to those who turn to him in their hearts.

*Prayer: Lord, it is very difficult for (P) to know or feel peace during this illness. But you do speak words of shalom to us, and we ask that through the doctors, nurses, and chaplains (P) may hear those words. Help (him/her) to see and hear the ways in which your love comes to (him/her), O Lord, and let (him/her) find peace in its steadfast nature.*

**Ps. 94:17-19, 22:** If the Lord had not been my help, my soul would soon have lived in the land of silence. When I thought, "My foot is slipping," your steadfast love, O Lord, held me up. When the cares of my heart

are many, your consolations cheer my soul. The Lord has become my stronghold, and my God the rock of my refuge.

**Prayer:** *Lord God, the cares of (P's) heart are heavy and many. When it seemed that (he/she) was slipping, you held (him/her) up with your steadfast love. Cheer and lighten (him/her) with your consolations and be (his/her) refuge this day.*

**Ps. 119:17, 25, 28, 41, 49-50, 76-77, 81-82, 84, 88, 107, 114, 143, 147, 149, 153, 154, 156, 159, 169-170:** Deal bountifully with your servant, so that I may live and observe your word. My soul clings to the dust; revive me according to your word. My soul melts away for sorrow; strengthen me according to your word. Let your steadfast love come to me, O Lord, your salvation according to your promise. Remember your word to your servant, in which you have made me hope. This is my comfort in my distress, that your promise gives me life. Let your steadfast love become my comfort according to your promise to your servant. Let your mercy come to me, that I may live. My soul languishes for your salvation; I hope in your word. My eyes fail with watching for your promise; I ask, "When will you comfort me?" How long must your servant endure? In your steadfast love spare my life. I am severely afflicted; give me life, O Lord,

according to your word. You are my hiding place and my shield; I hope in your word. Trouble and anguish have come upon me. . . . I rise before dawn and cry for help; I put my hope in your words. In your steadfast love hear my voice; O Lord, in your justice preserve my life. Look upon my misery and rescue me, . . . plead my cause and redeem me, give me life according to your promise. Great is your mercy, O Lord; give me life according to your justice. Preserve my life according to your steadfast love. Let my cry come before you, O Lord; give me understanding according to your word. Let my supplication come before you.

*Prayer: Lord, (P's) soul has been brought very low. (He/She) has known sorrow that (he/she) never imagined (he/she) could endure. (He/She) cries for help at all hours of the day and night. Let your mercy be with (P), Lord, for in distress (he/she) realizes that it is your word—your promise—that gives life. In (P's) affliction and anguish, hear (his/her) cries. Comfort (him/her) with your love and mercy.*

∽

Ps. 146:5-6, 7, 8-9: Happy are those whose help is the God of Jacob, whose hope is in the Lord their God, who made heaven and earth, the sea, and all that is in them; who keeps faith forever. The Lord sets the prisoners free; the Lord opens the eyes of the blind. The

Lord lifts up those who are bowed down. The Lord watches over the strangers; he upholds the orphan and the widow.

*Prayer: Lord, (P's) help and hope is in you. (He/She) is bowed down under the weight of suffering and many other concerns. Set (him/her) free from a prison of mental anguish and unanswerable questions. Bear (him/her) up. Watch over and uphold (him/her).*

# Grief

GRIEF CAN BE OVERWHELMING. Loss and potential loss can be so frightening and painful that it feels like the world is simply caving in; sometimes it seems that there is no end to the pain. In times of grief, prayers become a lifeline that upholds and guides us when we do not know the way. Minute by minute and hour by hour, God sustains us.

**Ps. 10:14:** Indeed you, Lord, note trouble and grief, that you may take it into your hands; the helpless commit themselves to you.

*Prayer: Lord, you know (P's) trouble and grief; we ask you to take (his/her) concerns into your gentle hands. In helplessness and sorrow, (he/she) commits (himself/herself) to you.*

**Ps. 12:1, 5:** Help, O Lord. . . . "Because the needy groan, I will now rise up," says the Lord; "I will place them in the safety for which they long."

*Prayer: Help, O Lord, because in this time of death there is great need and suffering. Be with this family in their anguish and loss. Help them to trust that both (P) and they themselves are in your safekeeping.*

**Ps. 23:1-6:** The Lord is my Shepherd, I shall not want. He makes me lie down in green pastures; he leads me beside still waters; he restores my soul. He leads me in right paths for his name's sake. Even though I walk through the darkest valley, I fear no evil; for you are with me; your rod and your staff—they comfort me. You prepare a table before me in the presence of my enemies; you anoint my head with oil; my cup overflows. Surely goodness and mercy shall follow me all the days of my life, and I shall dwell in the house of the Lord my whole life long.

*Prayer: Dearest Shepherd, walk with (P) now through these darkest times of life, and comfort (him/her) with your love.*

**Ps. 25:15-18:** Turn to me and be gracious to me, for I am lonely and afflicted. Relieve the troubles of my heart and bring me out of my distress. Consider my affliction and my trouble, and forgive all my sins.

*Prayer:* *Lord, be gracious to (P). Relieve (his/her) grief and affliction. Ease the weight of distress and uncertainty about the future. Grant (P) calm and peace.*

❧

**Ps. 31:9-10, (11-12), 14-15, 16, 22, 23, 24:** Be gracious to me, O Lord, for I am in distress; my eye wastes away from grief, my soul and body also. For my life is spent with sorrow, and my years with sighing; my strength fails because of my misery, and my bones waste away. (I am the scorn of all my adversaries, a horror to my neighbors, an object of dread to my acquaintances; those who see me in the street flee from me. I have passed out of mind like one who is dead; I have become like a broken vessel.) But I trust in you, O Lord; I say, "You are my God." My times are in your hand. Let your face shine upon your servant; save me in your steadfast love. You heard my supplications when I cried out to you for help. The Lord preserves the faithful. Be strong, and let your heart take courage, all you who wait for the Lord.

*Prayer:* *Lord, you know (P's) sickness and grief. You know how physically tiring grief itself is—how the tears (he/she) cries make (his/her) eyes sore and (his/her) body exhausted. Be gracious to (P), for (he/she) is in distress. (His/Her) strength is failing and that in itself is difficult to experience; but along with that, people stare at (him/her) in shock and dread. Give (him/her) strength for this battle with sickness and for the grief that accompanies it, Lord.*

**Ps. 34:(4, 6-7), 15, 17-19, 22:** (I sought the Lord and he answered me, and delivered me from all my fears. This poor soul cried, and was heard by the Lord, and was saved from every trouble. The angel of the Lord encamps around those who fear him, and delivers them.) The eyes of the Lord are on the righteous, and his ears are open to their cry. When the righteous cry for help, the Lord hears, and rescues them from all their troubles. The Lord is near to the brokenhearted, and saves the crushed in spirit. Many are the afflictions of the righteous, but the Lord rescues them from them all. The Lord redeems the life of his servants; none of those who take refuge in him will be condemned.

*Prayer: Lord, you know that (P) is brokenhearted and crushed in spirit. It is difficult to find words to express (his/her) deep grief. We need you to pray in us and for us, Lord; stay near to (P) now and be tender with (him/her).*

**Ps. 38:6, 7, 8(-11), 15, 17 (-18), 21-22:** I am utterly bowed down and prostrate; all day long I go around mourning. There is no soundness in my flesh. I am utterly

spent and crushed; I groan because of the tumult of my heart. O Lord, all my longing is known to you; my sighing is not hidden from you. My heart throbs, my strength fails me; as for the light of my eyes—it also has gone from me. (My friends and companions stand aloof from my affliction and my neighbors stand far off.) But it is for you, O Lord, that I wait; it is you, O Lord my God, who will answer. My pain is ever with me. (I confess my iniquity; I am sorry for my sin.) Do not forsake me, O Lord; O my God, do not be far from me; make haste to help me, O Lord, my salvation.

*Prayer: Lord God, (P) is exhausted and crushed by this sickness. (His/Her) heart and mind are in chaos and buffeted with grief. Lord, you know (his/her) longings and you even see (his/her) tired sighs. The news from the doctors is not good; hearing it and thinking about what it means makes (his/her) heart throb and strength fail. (P) feels weak, even numb. The light is gone from (his/her) eyes; (his/her) friends stay away because they are afraid of what is happening and feel awkward. Lord God, (P) needs you. Do not forsake (him/her), hurry to help (him/her) and stay near to (him/her).*

**Ps. 43:2, 3, 5:** Why must I walk about mournfully. . . ? O send out your light and your truth; let them lead me; let them bring me to your holy hill and to your

dwelling. Why are you cast down, O my soul, and why are you disquieted within me? Hope in God, for I shall again praise him, my help and my God.

*Prayer: Lord, in the midst of the grief (P) is now experiencing, give (him/her) hope. Take (him/her) by the hand and lead (him/her).*

**Ps. 56:3-4, 8, 9:** O Most High, when I am afraid, I put my trust in you. In God, whose word I praise, in God I trust. . . . You have kept count of my tossings; put my tears in your bottle. Are they not in your record? This I know, that God is for me.

*Prayer: Lord God, you know (P) so well. You know how many times (he/she) tosses and turns at night because of grief; you even record (his/her) tears. In the midst of (his/her) anguish, help (him/her) to trust you.*

**Ps. 68:5, 10, 19, 35:** Father of orphans and protector of widows is God in his holy habitation. In your goodness, O God, you provide for the needy. Blessed be the Lord, who daily bears us up; God is our salvation. He gives power and strength to his people.

*Prayer: Lord God, be with the family of (P), whom we now commend to your care. Remind us that you will always be our Father and the protector of (spouse and children). In the midst of death, give this family strength. Bear them up in the days to come.*

**Ps. 88:1-6, 8-9, 13-14:** O Lord, God of my salvation, when at night, I cry out in your presence, let my prayer come before you; incline your ear to my cry. For my soul is full of troubles and my life draws near to Sheol. I am counted among those who go down to the Pit; I am like those who have no help, like those forsaken among the dead, like the slain that lie in the grave, like those whom you remember no more, for they are cut off from your hand. You have put me in the depths of the Pit, in the regions dark and deep. You have caused my companions to shun me; you have made me a thing of horror to them. I am shut in so that I cannot escape.; my eye grows dim with sorrow. Every day I call to you, O Lord; I spread out my hands to you. But I, O Lord, cry out to you; in the morning my prayer comes before you. O Lord, why do you cast me off? Why do you hide your face from me?

*Prayer: Lord, these nights of grief seem unbearable. It seems that you have abandoned (P) in darkness and hidden your face from (him/her). Hear our cries, O Lord, and answer.*

**Ps. 106:4-5:** Remember me, O Lord, when you show favor to your people; help me when you deliver them; that I may see the prosperity of your chosen ones, that I may rejoice in the gladness of your nation, that I may glory in your heritage.

*Prayer: Lord, remember (P) so that (he/she) may be with you always and know your abundance and joy.*

**Ps. 116:15:** Precious in the sight of the Lord is the death of his faithful ones.

*Prayer: Lord, help this family to entrust their loved one to your care. Help them to know that (P) is precious to you and is in your care and keeping always.*

**Ps. 130:1-2, (3-4), 5-6, 7:** Out of the depths I cry to you, O Lord. Lord, hear my voice! Let your ears be attentive to the voice of my supplications! (If you, O Lord, should mark iniquities, Lord, who could stand? But there is forgiveness with you. . . .) I wait for the Lord, my soul waits, and in his word I hope; my soul waits

for the Lord more than those who watch for the morning. For with the Lord there is steadfast love, and with him is great power to redeem.

*Prayer: Lord, (P) cries to you from (his/her) deepest pain; (his/her) grief is overwhelming. Listen, Lord! Give attention to our cries. Give (P) hope even in unspeakable grief.*

**Ps. 137:1-4:** By the rivers of Babylon—there we sat down and there we wept when we remembered Zion. On the willows there we hung up our harps. For there our captors asked us for songs, and our tormentors asked for mirth, saying, "Sing us one of the songs of Zion!" How could we sing the Lord's song in a foreign land?

*Prayer: Lord God, just as those who were carried into exile wept at the memories of their past, so (P) and (his/her) family also weep at memories of their past. They are grateful for the good memories; they treasure the wonderful times they have shared; because of this they now weep both with thanks for the past and with sadness at the uncertainty of the future. Lord, grant them more opportunities to create good memories together! Right now, it feels as though (P's) illness is holding (him/her) captive and tormenting not only (P) but (his/her) entire family as well. And it seems impossible to sing your song, O Lord; for how can we sing praise to you when life hurts so much? How can we sing in gladness to you in what feels like a very foreign land physically and emotionally—a foreign land of hospitals and sickness and grief? Lord, stay near us in this difficult time, lead us out of this foreign place and restore us to gladness once more.*

**Ps. 143:1-4, 6-8:** Hear my prayer, O Lord; give ear to my supplications in your faithfulness; answer me in your righteousness. Do not enter into judgment with your servant, for no one living is righteous before you. For the enemy has pursued me, crushing my life to the ground, making me sit in darkness like those long dead. Therefore my spirit faints within me; my heart within me is appalled. I stretch out my hands to you; my soul thirsts for you like a parched land. Answer me quickly, O Lord; my spirit fails. Do not hide your face from me, or I shall be like those who go down to the Pit. Let me hear of your steadfast love in the morning, for in you I put my trust. Teach me the way I should go, for to you I lift up my soul.

*Prayer: Lord, now when (P) feels crushed . . . when (his/her) world seems dark with grief . . . when (he/she) feels physically faint . . . when you seem absent from (him/her) . . . help (him/her), Lord. Do not hide from (him/her). (P) needs you to show (him/her) the way, for right now it is not clear. Lord, even in the midst of grief, help (P) to hear of your steadfast love when (he/she) rises in the morning; (he/she) needs to hear of that love to make it through the day. To you we lift up our souls. Renew (P's) spirit; surround (him/her) with your steadfast love.*

**Ps. 146:8-9:** The Lord lifts up those who are bowed down. The Lord watches over the strangers; he upholds the orphan and the widow.

*Prayer: Lord, bear up the members of this family, who are bowed down in grief over the loss of their loved one. Give them the knowledge that you uphold your children and watch over them in their grief.*

**Ps. 147:2, 3, 6:** The Lord gathers the outcasts, . . . heals the brokenhearted, and binds up their wounds. The Lord lifts up the downtrodden.

*Prayer: (It is grief that brings this family together now, O Lord. Yet some family members feel excluded, like outcasts, because of past disagreements or feuds. Gather them together so that they may bear each other up in their grief.) Lord, the hearts of this family are broken— heal them. They are wounded in body and soul—bind them up. They are downtrodden, on the verge of despair. Bear them in your hands.*

# Help and Healing

We come to hospitals for help and healing. Deep inside, we long to be made whole. Sometimes, marvelously, sickness can lead to greater wholeness. Wherever the sickness takes us, we pray for God's "shalom."

**Ps. 3:3-5:** But you, O Lord, are a shield around me, my glory, and the one who lifts up my head. I cry aloud to the Lord, and he answers me from his holy hill. I lie down and sleep; I wake again, for the Lord sustains me.

*Prayer: Lord God, set your love and care like a shield around (P). Give to all who hurt or suffer the confidence to know that you lift our heads from sadness and weakness; you do hear our prayers and help us.*

**Ps. 12:1, 5:** Help, O Lord. . . . "Because the needy groan, I will now rise up," says the Lord; "I will place them in the safety for which they long."

*Prayer: Help, O Lord, because your child, (P), is crying in anguish. Rise up to help (him/her). Lord, bring (P) the safety (he/she) longs for in body and soul.*

**Ps. 17:1, 6, 8:** Hear a just cause, O Lord; attend to my cry. I call upon you, for you will answer me, O God; incline your ear to me, hear my words. Guard me as the apple of the eye; hide me in the shadow of your wings.

*Prayer: We call upon you for help, O God, and plead (P's) case before you because you promise to hear and answer us. Show your love to (P), who seeks refuge in you. Guard (him/her) as your treasure and hide (him/her) in the shadow of your wings.*

**Ps. 23:1-6:** The Lord is my Shepherd, I shall not want. He makes me lie down in green pastures; he leads me beside still waters; he restores my soul. He leads me in right paths for his name's sake. Even though I walk through the darkest valley, I fear no evil; for you are with me; your rod and staff—they comfort me. You prepare a table before me in the presence of my enemies; you anoint my head with oil; my cup overflows. Surely goodness and mercy shall follow me all the days of my life, and I shall dwell in the house of the Lord my whole life long.

*Prayer: Dearest Shepherd, help (P); walk with (him/her) now through the darkest times of life. Comfort, restore, and pursue (him/her) with your goodness.*

**Ps. 28:1-2, 6-9:** To you, O Lord, I call; my rock, do not refuse to hear me, for if you are silent to me, I shall be like those who go down to the Pit. Hear the voice of my supplication, as I cry to you for help, as I lift up my hands toward your most holy sanctuary. Blessed be the Lord, for he has heard the sound of my pleadings. The Lord is my strength and my shield; in him my heart trusts; so I am helped, and my heart exults, and with my song I give thanks to him. The Lord is the strength of his people; he is the saving refuge of his anointed. O save your people, and bless your heritage; be their shepherd, and carry them forever.

*Prayer: Lord, we lift our hands and hearts to you; we know that you hear our pleading for (P's) life and health. Carry (him/her) in your arms in these difficult days, as a shepherd carries his sheep.*

**Ps. 30:8-10:** To you, O Lord, I cried. and to the Lord I made my supplication: "What profit is there in my death, if I go down to the Pit? Will the dust praise you? Will it tell of your faithfulness? Hear, O Lord, and be gracious to me! O Lord, be my helper!"

*Prayer: Gracious God, we cry to you for help and healing. Please hear our case. What good would there be in (P's) death? The dust cannot tell others of your love! Save (P's) life, O Lord, that (he/she) may praise you.*

**Ps. 46:1-2, 7:** God is our refuge and strength, a very present help in trouble. Therefore we will not fear, though the earth should change. The Lord of hosts is with us; the God of Jacob is our refuge.

*Prayer: Lord God, be a very present help to (P) in times of trouble. Though everything in (his/her) life is changing, help (him/her) not to be afraid, but rather to find refuge and strength in your love.*

**Ps. 54:1-2, 4, 7:** Save me, O God, by your name, and vindicate me by your might. Hear my prayer, O God; give ear to the words of my mouth. God is my helper; the Lord is the upholder of my life. For he has delivered me from every trouble.

*Prayer: Lord God, you are (P's) helper—the one who upholds (his/her) life. Listen to (his/her) words of pleading, longing, anger, and complaint and come to (his/her) aid.*

**Ps. 57:1-3, 7-10:** Be merciful to me, O God, be merciful to me, for in you my soul takes refuge; in the shadow of your wings I will take refuge, until the destroying storms pass by. I cry to God Most High, to God who fulfills his purpose for me. He will send from heaven and save me. . . . God will send forth his steadfast love and his faithfulness. My heart is steadfast, O God, my heart is steadfast. I will sing and make melody. Awake,

my soul! Awake, O harp and lyre! I will awake the dawn. I will give thanks to you, O Lord, among the peoples; I will sing praises to you among the nations. For your steadfast love is as high as the heavens; your faithfulness extends to the clouds.

*Prayer: Lord, surround (P) with your steadfast love and faithfulness; help (him/her) in the midst of life's storms. Give (him/her) the confidence to know that in the shadow of your wings there is refuge. O God, restore (P's) health so that (he/she) may awake the dawn with songs of praise and thanksgiving to you.*

**Ps. 59:9-10, 16:** O my strength, I will watch for you; for you, O God, are my fortress. My God in his steadfast love will meet me. For you have been a fortress for me and a refuge in the day of my distress.

*Prayer: Lord, (P) watches and waits for you because (he/she) needs to know of your steadfast love in the midst of (his/her) sickness, fear, and uncertainty. The psalmist assures us that you are a refuge and fortress in the day of distress; so come to (P) now and help (him/her).*

**Ps. 70:5:** But I am poor and needy; hasten to me, O God! You are my help and my deliverer; O Lord, do not delay!

*Prayer: Lord, we come to you in great need of your help. We beg you to come quickly to (P), who is in need, for you are (his/her) helper and deliverer. Do not delay, O Lord!*

**Ps. 80:14-15, 18:** Turn again, O God of hosts; look down from heaven, and see; have regard for this vine, the stock that your right hand planted. Then we will never turn back from you; give us life and we will call on your name.

*Prayer: Look in mercy, O God, up (P). You created (him/her) and established (him/her) as cherished vine. Now do not reject the work of your hands. Come quickly with your help and healing.*

**Ps. 91:9-12, 14-16:** Because you have made the Lord your refuge, and the Most High your dwelling place, no evil shall befall you, no scourge come near your tent. For he will command his angels concerning you to guard you in all your ways. On their hands they will bear you up, so that you will not dash your foot against a stone. Those who love me, I will deliver; I will protect those who know my name. When they call to me, I will answer them; I will be with them in trouble, I will rescue them and honor them. With long life I will satisfy them and show them my salvation.

*Prayer: Lord, be with (P) now in this time of trouble. Help (him/her), guard (his/her) life, and protect (him/her), for (he/she) knows your name. Bear (P) up, Lord, in these difficult days, and send your healing to ease the long hours.*

**Ps. 113:7:** He raises the poor from the dust, and lifts up the needy from the ash heap.

*Prayer: Lift (P) from the depths of despair, Lord. Help and bear (him/her) up with your love and strength.*

**Ps. 121:1-3, 4, 5, 7-8:** I lift up my eyes to the hills—from where will my help come? My help comes from the Lord, who made heaven and earth. He will not let your foot be moved; he who keeps you will not slumber; . . . he will neither slumber nor sleep. The Lord is your keeper; . . . he will keep you from all evil; he will keep your life. The Lord will keep your going out and your coming in from this time on and forever.

*Prayer: You are (P's) helper, Lord, and you neither slumber nor sleep. Let (P) who is weary—but too worried to sleep—find comfort and rest in the promise that you will watch over (him/her) always. Keep (his/her) life in your creative hands.*

**Ps. 130:1-2, (3-4), 5-6, 7:** Out of the depths I cry to you, O Lord. Lord, hear my voice! Let your ears be attentive to the voice of my supplications! (If you, O Lord, should mark iniquities, Lord, who could stand? But there is forgiveness with you. . . .) I wait for the Lord, my soul waits, and in his word I hope; my soul waits for the Lord more than those who watch for the morning. For with the Lord there is steadfast love, and with him is great power to redeem.

*Prayer: Lord, (P) cries to you. Be attentive to (his/her) voice! (He/She) did not know how desperate (he/she) could be for help or how low (he/she) could be brought. Give (him/her) hope, health, and healing, Lord.*

**Ps. 142:1-2:** With my voice I cry to the Lord; with my voice I make supplication to the Lord. I pour out my complaint before him; I tell my trouble before him.

*Prayer: Come to (P) quickly, O Lord, when (he/she) calls on you. (He/She) lifts up (his/her) hands and heart to you. Hear (P's) voice, have regard for (his/her) situation, and make your presence known in gentle ways.*

**Ps. 143:7-8, 11:** Answer me quickly, O Lord; my spirit fails. Do not hide your face from me, or I shall be like those who go down in the Pit. Let me hear of your steadfast love in the morning, for in you I put my

trust. Teach me the way I should go, for to you I lift up my soul. For your name's sake, O Lord, preserve my life. in your righteousness, bring me out of trouble.

*Prayer: Gracious healer, do not hide your face from (P). Bear up (his/her) failing spirit, preserve (his/her) life, and restore (his/her) health.*

# Confession
# and Forgiveness

SICKNESS OFTEN LEADS US to examine life. We think about things we wish we would not have done. We ponder things we wish we would have done. In Christ there is mercy and forgiveness. This absolution often opens the door to healing. In him we may begin anew.

Ps. 25:1-2, 4-6, (11), 15-(18): To you, O Lord, I lift up my soul. O my God, in you I trust. Make me to know your ways, O Lord; teach me your paths. Lead me in your truth, and teach me, for you are the God of my salvation; for you I wait all day long. Be mindful of your mercy, O Lord, and of your steadfast love, for they have been from of old. (For your name's sake, O Lord, pardon my guilt, for it is great.) My eyes are ever toward the Lord, for he will pluck my feet out of the net. Turn to me and be gracious to me, for I am lonely and afflicted. Relieve the troubles of my heart and bring me out of my distress. (Consider my affliction and my trouble, and forgive all my sins.)

*Prayer: Lord God, we lift up (P's) needs to you, for we trust in you. (P) looks to you for help; be gracious to (him/her), Lord. Relieve the troubles of (his/her) heart and bring (him/her) out of distress. Consider (P's) affliction and trouble and bring comfort to (him/her) as quickly as possible.*

**Ps. 32:1-7:** Happy are those whose transgression is forgiven, whose sin is covered. Happy are those to whom the Lord imputes no iniquity, and in whose spirit there is no deceit. While I kept silence, my body wasted away through my groaning all day long. For day and night your hand was heavy upon me; my strength was dried up as by the heat of summer. Then I acknowledged my sin to you, and I did not hide my iniquity; I said, "I will confess my transgressions to the Lord," and you forgave the guilt of my sin. Therefore let all who are faithful offer prayer to you; at a time of distress, the rush of mighty waters shall not reach them. You are a hiding place for me; you preserve me from trouble; you surround me with glad cries of deliverance.

*Prayer: Lord, thank you for removing the heaviness of (P's) guilt. Thank you for forgiveness that frees (him/her) to live life.*

**Ps. 51:1-12, 17:** Have mercy on me, O God, according to your steadfast love; according to your abundant mercy blot out my transgressions. Wash me thoroughly from my iniquity, and cleanse me from my sin. For I know my transgressions, and my sin is ever

before me. Against you, you alone, have I sinned, and done what is evil in your sight, so that you are justified in your sentence and blameless when you pass judgment. Indeed, I was born guilty, a sinner when my mother conceived me. You desire truth in the inward being; therefore teach me wisdom in my secret heart. Purge me with hyssop, and I shall be clean; wash me, and I shall be whiter than snow. Let me hear joy and gladness; let the bones that you have crushed rejoice. Hide your face from my sins, and blot out all my iniquities. Create in me a clean heart, O God, and put a new and right spirit within me. Do not cast me away from your presence, and do not take your holy spirit from me. Restore to me the joy of your salvation, and sustain in me a willing spirit. The sacrifice acceptable to God is a broken spirit; a broken and contrite heart, O God, you will not despise.

*Prayer: Lord God, thank you that there is forgiveness with you. In your mercy, wash away (P's) sins and teach (him/her) wisdom, that (he/she) may sin no more. Create in (P) a clean heart, O God, and put a new and right spirit within (him/her). Keep (P) in your presence, sustain (him/her) with a willing spirit, and restore to (him/her) the joy of your salvation.*

**Ps. 57:1-3:** Be merciful to me, O God, be merciful to me, for in you my soul takes refuge; in the shadow of your wings I will take refuge, until the destroying

storms pass by. I cry to God Most High, to God who fulfills his purpose for me. He will send from heaven and save me. . . . God will send forth his steadfast love and his faithfulness.

*Prayer: Lord, be merciful to (P) and let (him/her) take refuge from the storms of life in the shadow of your wings. (He/She) looks to you for purpose in life and trusts that you will send your steadfast love and faithfulness to (him/her).*

**Ps. 67:1:** May God be gracious to us and bless us and make his face to shine upon us.

*Prayer: Lord, be gracious and merciful to (P) in this hospital. Look upon (him/her) in (his/her) distress and let the light of your face shine on (him/her) through those who care for (him/her).*

**Ps. 78:39:** God remembered that they were but flesh, a wind that passes and does not come again.

*Prayer: Lord, remember that humans are fragile beings, mere flesh and blood. We are easily broken in body and spirit; therefore, be mercifully tender with all who suffer.*

**Ps. 79:8:** Let your compassion come speedily to meet us, for we are brought very low.

*Prayer: Lord God, hurry to (P) with your compassion and mercy. (He/She) has been brought low by this experience, Lord, and needs your tenderness.*

**Ps. 80:3:** Restore us, O God; let your face shine, that we may be saved.

*Prayer: Look on (P), O God, see (his/her) needs, and in your mercy restore (him/her).*

**Ps. 113:7:** The Lord raises the poor from the dust, and lifts up the needy from the ash heap.

*Prayer: In your mercy, lift (P) up, O God. (He/She) is weighed down with sickness and needs; bear (him/her) up with your love and strength.*

**Ps. 115:12, 13, 15:** The Lord has been mindful of us; he will bless us; . . . he will bless those who fear the Lord, both small and great. May you be blessed by the Lord, who made heaven and earth.

**Prayer:** *Lord, as you have been mindful of your people in the past, so be mindful of (P) now. Show your mercy to (him/her). Bless and sustain all the members of (P's) family in this time of (his/her) illness, for they are all (small and great, young and old) the work of your hands and in need of your care.*

# Thanksgiving (for Restored and Continued Health)

How GOOD IT IS to give thanks for help and healing in whatever form it may come during an illness.

**Ps. 18:1-3, 4, 5-6, 16, 30:** I love you, O Lord, my strength. The Lord is my rock, my fortress, and my deliverer, my God, my rock in whom I take refuge, my shield, and the horn of my salvation, my stronghold. I call upon the Lord, who is worthy to be praised. The cords of death encompassed me; the snares of death confronted me. In my distress I called upon the Lord; to my God I cried for help. From his temple he heard my voice, and my cry to him reached his ears. He reached down from on high, he took me; he drew me out of mighty waters. This God—his way is perfect; the promise of the Lord proves true; he is a shield for all who take refuge in him.

*Prayer: Lord God, we thank you for being our strength and refuge. In the face of death (P) called upon you; you heard (his/her) cry, and now we give you thanks.*

**Ps. 30:2-4, 5-12:** O Lord my God, I cried to you for help, and you have healed me. O Lord, you brought up my soul from Sheol, restored me to life from among those gone down to the Pit. Sing praises to the Lord, O you his faithful ones, and give thanks to his holy name. Weeping may linger for the night, but joy comes with the morning. As for me, I said in my prosperity, "I shall never be moved." By your favor, O Lord, you had established me as a strong mountain; you hid your face; I was dismayed. To you, O Lord, I cried, and to the Lord I made supplication: "What profit is there in my death, if I go down to the Pit? Will the dust praise you? Will it tell of your faithfulness? Hear, O Lord, and be gracious to me! O Lord, be my helper!" You have turned my mourning into dancing; you have taken off my sackcloth and clothed me with joy, so that my soul may praise you and not be silent. O Lord my God, I will give thanks to you forever.

*Prayer: We give you thanks, Lord God, for you heard (P's) cry for help and healed (him/her). You saw (his/her) tears in the night and restored (his/her) joy. Lord, we are grateful that you turned (P's) mourning into dancing.*

**Ps. 34:4-8, 15, 17-19, 22:** I sought the Lord and he answered me, and delivered me from all my fears. Look to him and be radiant; so your faces shall never be ashamed. This poor soul cried, and was heard by

the Lord, and was saved from every trouble. The angel of the Lord encamps around those who fear him, and delivers them. O taste and see that the Lord is good; happy are those who take refuge in him. The eyes of the Lord are on the righteous, and his ears are open to their cry. When the righteous cry for help, the Lord hears, and rescues them from all their troubles. The Lord is near to the brokenhearted, and saves the crushed in spirit. Many are the afflictions of the righteous, but the Lord rescues them from them all. The Lord redeems the life of his servants; none of those who take refuge in him will be condemned.

*Prayer: Lord, (P) came to you with (his/her) fears, and you were with (him/her) during (his/her) medical procedures and tests. You came near to (P) when (he/she) was brokenhearted and crushed in spirit. We now give you thanks.*

**Ps. 40:1-3, 5-6, 8-11, 16:** I waited patiently for the Lord; he inclined to me and heard my cry. He drew me up from the desolate pit, out of the miry bog, and set my feet upon a rock, making my steps secure. He put a new song in my mouth, a song of praise to our God. Many will see and fear, and put their trust in the Lord. You have multiplied, O Lord my God, your wondrous deeds and your thoughts toward us; none can compare with you. Were I to proclaim and tell of them, they would be more than can be counted. Sacrifice

and offering you do not desire, but you have given me an open ear. I delight to do your will, O my God; your law is within my heart. I have told the glad news of deliverance in the great congregation; see, I have not restrained my lips, as you know, O Lord. I have not hidden your saving help within my heart, I have spoken of your faithfulness and your salvation; I have not concealed your steadfast love and your faithfulness from the great congregation. Do not, O Lord, withhold your mercy from me; let your steadfast love and your faithfulness keep me safe forever. May all who seek you rejoice and be glad in you; may those who love your salvation say continually, "Great is the Lord!"

*Prayer: Lord, you have heard (P's) cries. You drew (him/her) out of a desolate sickness and put a new song in (his/her) mouth. (He/She) is eager to tell others of your deliverance and steadfast love. Thank you for your wonderful deeds that (P) has experienced in healing.*

**Ps. 63:1, 3, 4-8:** O God, you are my God, I seek you, my soul thirsts for you; my flesh faints for you, as in a dry and weary land where there is no water. Because your steadfast love is better than life, my lips will praise you. I will lift up my hands and call on your name. My soul is satisfied as with a rich feast, and my mouth praises you with joyful lips when I think of you on my bed, and meditate on you in the watches of the night;

for you have been my help, and in the shadow of your wings I sing for joy. My soul clings to you; your right hand upholds me.

*Prayer: Lord God, we thank you for helping (P) during (his/her) sickness and for being a refuge to (him/her) when (he/she) was weary. When we think about you we realize how your hand has upheld (him/her) and how dependent we all are on you.*

**Ps. 66:8-9, 20:** Bless our God, O peoples, let the sound of his praise be heard, who has kept us among the living. Blessed be God because he has not rejected my prayer or removed his steadfast love from me.

*Prayer: Lord, thank you for sustaining (P's) life. We cried to you day and night for help, and now we thank you for accepting our prayers and surrounding (P) with your steadfast love and healing.*

**Ps. 92:1-2, 4:** It is good to give thanks to the Lord, to sing praises to your name, O Most High; to declare your steadfast love in the morning, and your faithfulness by night. For you, O Lord, have made me glad by your work; at the works of your hands I sing for joy.

*Prayer: Through the doctors and nurses, (P) has experienced the healing work of your hands, Lord. We thank you, for you have made (him/her) glad.*

**Ps. 94:17-19, 22:** If the Lord had not been my help, my soul would soon have lived in the land of silence. When I thought, "My foot is slipping," your steadfast love, O Lord, held me up. When the cares of my heart are many, your consolations cheer my soul. The Lord has become my stronghold, and my God the rock of my refuge.

**Prayer:** *We thank you, gracious God, for being (P's) help and for sustaining (him/her) in sickness. (P) has had many cares and concerns during this illness, and through it all you have been (his/her) stronghold and refuge. We are grateful for your steadfast love that bears up your children.*

**Ps. 96:1-4, 5-6:** O sing to the Lord a new song; sing to the Lord, all the earth. Sing to the Lord, bless his name; tell of his salvation from day to day. Declare his glory among the nations, his marvelous works among all the peoples. For great is the Lord, and greatly to be praised. The Lord made the heavens. Honor and majesty are before him; strength and beauty are in his sanctuary.

**Prayer:** *Lord, (P) has experienced your goodness through the skills you have given to those who work in this hospital, and we are grateful. Restoration of health is a marvelous work of yours; experiencing it has given (P) a new song. As (he/she) leaves this hospital, give* *(him/her) the courage and desire to tell others of the strength you have been to (him/her) and all the healing you have brought to (him/her).*

**Ps. 98:1, 3, 4, 7-9:** O sing to the Lord a new song, for he has done marvelous things. He has remembered his steadfast love and faithfulness. . . . Make a joyful noise to the Lord, all the earth; break forth into joyous song and sing praises. Let the sea roar, and all that fills it; the world and those who live in it. Let the floods clap their hands; let the hills sing together for joy at the presence of the Lord.

*Prayer: Lord, we give you thanks for the marvelous gift of life and for the skills you give to doctors and nurses to sustain life and health. You have made (P) glad by restoring (his/her) health; we offer you our joy.*

**Ps. 103:1-5, 8-18:** Bless the Lord, O my soul, and all that is within me, bless his holy name. Bless the Lord, O my soul, and do not forget all his benefits—who forgives all your iniquity, who heals all your diseases, who redeems your life from the Pit, who crowns you with steadfast love and mercy, who satisfies you with good as long as you live so that your youth is renewed like the eagle's. The Lord is merciful and gracious, slow to anger and abounding in steadfast love. He will not always accuse, nor will he keep his anger forever.

He does not deal with us according to our sins, nor repay us according to our iniquities. For as the heavens are high above the earth, so great is his steadfast love toward those who fear him; as far as the east is from the west, so far he removes our transgressions from us. As a father has compassion for his children, so the Lord has compassion for those who fear him. For he knows how we were made; he remembers that we are dust. As for mortals, their days are like grass; they flourish like a flower of the field; for the wind passes over it, and it is gone, and its place knows it no more. But the steadfast love of the Lord is from everlasting to everlasting on those who fear him, and his righteousness to children's children, to those who keep his covenant and remember to do his commandments.

*Prayer: Lord, we thank you for healing (P's) sickness and for the many gifts you have given to (him/her). Thank you for rest that has renewed (him/her) and for your love and mercy. In your compassion you remember that your children are dust. Thank you for dealing with (P)—and all of us—tenderly.*

**Ps. 107:1-2, 6, 8-9, 13-15, 19-22, 25-31, 41, 43:** O give thanks to the Lord, for he is good; for his steadfast love endures forever. Let the redeemed of the Lord say so, those he redeemed from trouble. . . . They cried to the Lord in their trouble, and he delivered them from

their distress. . . . Let them thank the Lord for his steadfast love, for his wonderful works to humankind. For he satisfies the thirsty, and the hungry he fills with good things. They cried to the Lord in their trouble, and he saved them from their distress; he brought them out of darkness and gloom, and broke their bonds asunder. Let them thank the Lord for his steadfast love, for his wonderful works to humankind. They cried to the Lord in their trouble, and he saved them from their distress; he sent out his word and healed them, and delivered them from destruction. Let them thank the Lord for his steadfast love, for his wonderful works to humankind. And let them offer thanksgiving sacrifices, and tell of his deeds with songs of joy. For he commanded and raised the stormy wind, which lifted up the waves of the sea. They mounted up to heaven, they went down to the depths; their courage melted away in their calamity; they reeled and staggered like drunkards, and were at their wits' end. Then they cried to the Lord in their trouble, and he brought them out from their distress; he made the storm be still, and the waves of the sea were hushed. Then they were glad because they had quiet, and he brought them to their desired haven. Let them thank the Lord for his steadfast love, for his wonderful works to humankind. He raises up the needy out of distress, and makes their families like flocks. Let those who are wise give heed to these things, and consider the steadfast love of the Lord.

*Prayer: Lord, thank you for your steadfast love and healing that have been made known to (P) through the medical staff. Like a tender shepherd, you listened to our cries for (P) and brought (him/her) out of distress, calming this storm in (his/her) life.*

**Ps. 116:1-10:** I love the Lord, because he has heard my voice and my supplications. Because he inclined his ear to me, therefore I will call on him as long as I live. The snares of death encompassed me; I suffered distress and anguish. Then I called on the name of the Lord: "O Lord, I pray, save my life!" Gracious is the Lord and righteous; our God is merciful. The Lord protects. . . . When I was brought low, he saved me. Return, O my soul to your rest, for the Lord has dealt bountifully with you. For you have delivered my soul from death, my eyes from tears, my feet from stumbling. I walk before the Lord in the land of the living. I kept my faith, even when I said, "I am greatly afflicted."

*Prayer: Lord, thank you for hearing (P's) cries to you; thank you for rescuing (him/her) from death. This has been a difficult time for (P); (he/she) has known tremendous anxiety and tension. (He/She) has waited for test results—some of which were very discouraging—and cried many tears. But now (P) is recovering, and we thank you for your mercy and for keeping faith strong in the face of death.*

**Ps. 126:6:** Those who go out weeping . . . shall come home with shouts of joy.

*Prayer: Lord, (P) came to this hospital with many worries and tears. But now (his/her) heart is brimming with thanks and joy for health restored. Bless (his/her) homecoming.*

**Ps. 138:1, 3, 7-8:** I give you thanks, O Lord, with my whole heart. On the day I called, you answered me, you increased my strength of soul. Though I walk in the midst of trouble, . . . you stretch out your hand, and your right hand delivers me. The Lord will fulfill his purpose for me; your steadfast love, O Lord, endures forever. Do not forsake the work of your hands.

*Prayer: Thank you, Lord, for offering strength to (P) in body and soul; thank you for taking (him/her) by the hand in the midst of trouble and helping (him/her) through it. You give us life, Lord; help us all to realize your purpose for our years.*

**Ps. 145:8-9, 13-20:** The Lord is gracious and merciful, slow to anger and abounding in steadfast love. The Lord is good to all, and his compassion is over all that he has made. The Lord is faithful in all his words, and gracious in all his deeds. The Lord upholds all who are falling, and raises up all who are bowed down.

The eyes of all look to you, and you give them their food in due season. You open your hand, satisfying the desire of every living thing. The Lord is just in all his ways, and kind in all his doings. The Lord is near to all who call on him, to all who call on him in truth. He fulfills the desire of all who fear him; he also hears their cry, and saves them. The Lord watches over all who love him.

*Prayer: Lord, (P) has known your goodness and compassion. You upheld (him/her) when (he/she) was falling in worry and grief; you raised (him/her) up when (he/she) was crushed by disturbing results of medical tests. Thank you for being near when we call to you; show (P) your kindness always.*

# Index

# About the Author

Yusef Komunyakaa, originally from Bogalusa, Louisiana, served in Vietnam as a correspondent and managing editor of the *Southern Cross*. Within the five year period between 1975 and 1980, he received a B.A. in English and sociology, a M.A. in creative writing for poetry at Colorado State University, and a M.F.A. in creative writing for poetry at the University of California in Irvine. During the last twenty years, Komunyakaa has published nine books of poems, including *Neon Vernacular: New and Selected Poems 1977–1989* (Wesleyan/New England), as well as won the 1994 Pulitzer Prize for poetry and the Kingsley-Tufts Poetry Award from the Claremont Graduate School in California. This volume selects from previously published titles—*Lost in the Bonewheel Factory, Copacetic, I Apologize for the Eyes in My Head,* and *Dien Cai Dau.* For *Thieves of Paradise* (1998), his most recent volume of poems, Komunyakaa was named finalist for the 1999 National Book Critics Circle Award. On the recording *Love Notes from the Madhouse* (1998), performed live with jazz musician John Tchicai and ensemble, Komunyakaa reads poems from *Neon Vernacular* and *Thieves of Paradise.* Komunyakaa is professor in the Council of Humanities and Creative Writing Program at Princeton University.

# Editor's Introduction

Although the poetry of Yusef Komunyakaa has its basis firmly rooted in the stylistic innovations of early-twentieth-century American modernists, much of what he writes reflects his inextricable link to a sentiment seldom acknowledged in African American poetics—the idea that a "black" experience should not particularlize the presentation of art. Like his predecessors Robert Hayden and Melvin Tolson, Komunyakaa transcends Cullen's conundrum and establishes a voice outside of the parochial schema constructed by nationalisms and other institutional imperatives. His use of social portraiture is reminiscent of *Angle of Ascent* while his arcane sensibility and vernacular juxtapositioning recalls *Harlem Gallery*. Of course, there is an apparent danger in constructing Komunyakaa's work within this strict matrix, but few poets have taken such an approach to the democratization of aesthetics prior to his arrival. As early as *Copacetic* (1984), Komunyakaa's interpretations of popular mythology and legend have given readers alternative access to cultural lore. Epic human imperfections, ancient psychological profiles, and the haunting resonance of the South are now explained by those who slow drag to Little Willie John and rendezvous at MOMA.

This volume of essays, interviews, and commentaries is an attempt to understand Komunyakaa's critical eclecticism within the context of his own words. That he has chosen *Blue Notes* as his central thematic element says a great deal about how he imagines the temporal landscape of his poetic craft. The appellation not only leaves us on the steps of his childhood memories, as suggested by the introductory prose poem "Blue," but takes us through a number of associative expressions and images that fragment and coalesce as if governed by the improvisational idiom of jazz itself.

*Blue Notes* consists of four sections. The first is compiled of essays and statements that examine the artistic craft of several poets and jazz musicians who have been influential to Komunyakaa's work. Note the interchangeable critique that he uses for musicians and poets. The second section, a collection of poems that include the poet's own commentary, illuminates content and structure. All but one of the poems ("Trueblood's Blues") originally appeared in the *Best American Poetry Series* and are interesting because of how Komunyakaa chooses to construct their social historical contexts. His comments may suggest that each of these poems are "uniquely" concerned, but the poems themselves elicit a far more complex response. The third section, interviews, were all conducted within this decade but reveal the development of Komunyakaa's aesthetic sensibility. Significantly, the poet also shares his insight into experiential moments and the notion of a Great American poetry. The final section consists of six artistic explorations, two of which have already been performed ("Tenebrae" and "Buddy's Monologue"). They represent Komunyakaa's present interests and along with the most current interview, "Notations in Blue," suggest future areas of concern.

Radiclani Clytus

# Contents

# I.

# Essays

# Blue

I have always loved blue. One of my first memories is my teen-aged mother standing in the bedroom doorway in a silk slip pale as the shine inside an abalone. From grub worm to midday sky on the plains, blue is the insides of something mysterious and lonely. I'd look at fish and birds, thinking the sky and water colored them. The first abyss is blue. An artist must go beyond the mercy of satin or water—from a gutty hue to that which is close to royal purple. All the seasons and blossoms inbetween. Lavender. Theatrical and outrageous electric. Almost gray. True and false blue. Water and oil. The gas jet breathing in oblivion. The unstruck match. The blue of absence. The blue of deep presence. The insides of something perfect. Primary: we can only subtract what it is from what it is, and what's left is almost what it is. A feather on a bed of pine needles. My father's work clothes at the end of two seasons of blood, sweat, and tears. The blackened iron wash pot filled with white things and Red Devil Lye—the glow of pine knots under a winter sky in Bogalusa. The 1950s. Bluing in a #3 galvanized tub of whites, and the sheets and pillowcases and Sunday shirts pinned to the clothesline like a painter's daytime. The future. The red Kissing Camels against a Colorado sky in the Garden of the Gods. The South China Sea. Skin beneath the palest blue in Saigon. Mosaic tiles on walls and floors. I lingered for hours at a window in Urbino, gazing at poppies on low hills against the sky. A hue precious as lapis lazuli crushed into ultramarine, as Perugino washed his brushes one hundred times to steal the only color that brightened his nightmares.

# Shape and Tonal Equilibrium

Jazz discovers the emotional mystery behind things; it provides a spiritual connection to the land, reconnecting us to places where its forms originated. A poem doesn't have to have an overt jazz theme in order to have a relationship to jazz, but it should embrace the whole improvisational spirit of this music.

Historically, the African American has survived by sheer nerve and wit. Often it seems we have created our art out of very little. Music is serious business in the black community mainly because it is so intricately interwoven with our identity. Our music, propelled by the drum, was deemed an immediate threat because it articulated cultural unity and communication. Thus, there is little wonder that the drum was outlawed in locales under the control of slaveowners. To replace the loss of one instrument, our ancestors clapped their hands and stomped their feet to maintain that unity of expression so important to their cultural heritage.

It's easy to recognize contemporary American culture in the graceful shadows swaying with the night in Congo Square. They committed an act of sabotage merely by dancing to keep forbidden gods alive That they refused to become only an antithesis—lost and incomplete—is almost Hegelian. Our music allowed us to stay connected to our heritage, yet propels us into the future. Being in motion—improvisation, becoming— this is the mode of our creativity. The accent is on the positive even when the negative pervades. Our music became an argument with the odds, a nonverbal articulation of our pathos.

In this sense, even the blues dirge is an affirmation creating

Originally appeared as "Jazz and Poetry: A Conversation between Yusef Komunyakaa and William Matthews (moderated by Robert Kelly)" in *Georgia Review* 46, no. 4 (1992): 642–61.

possibilities out of theft or song out of the violation of flesh. This music has always been the bridge to what Houston Baker calls the journey back, a requisite voyage to the source. As an African American poet, however, I resist being conveniently stereotyped as a jazz poet. I write about whatever captures my imagination, anything that touches me with significance: philosophy, psychology, nature, culture, folklore, history, sex, science, concerns from the gut level to the arcane. And yes, jazz as a necessary balm, moves through all these aspects of our daily lives.

We often hear jazz referred to as America's classical music. Unfortunately, until recently, many middle-class African Americans derided jazz as the devil's music, repeating the condemnation that it came out of the whorehouses of Storyville, that it wasn't sacred. Second-class citizens can be terribly puritanical and this is especially true when they're striving for acceptance by the dominant culture. Even among the luminaries of the Harlem Renaissance, it was only Langston Hughes who wholeheartedly embraced jazz and blues as major influences on the movement. Except for Hughes, Helene Johnson, and Zora Neale Hurston, most of the poets, including Claude McKay, Anne Spencer, and Countee Cullen, gravitated toward British Romantics such as Keats and Wordsworth. They pursued an interest in New England transcendentalism more than the folk traditions that produced the blues and jazz. Or they connected to the flight motif of the spiritual that had informed early black poetry.

Two voices associated with the postrenaissance period of the 1950s, Sterling Brown and Frank Marshall Davis, wrote jazz and blues-influenced poems as did Gwendolyn Brooks on occasion. However, I would argue that the first real synthesis of jazz and poetry originated with jazz/blues philosophers Larry Neal and Amiri Baraka or even someone like Jayne Cortez, whose body of work is tied to jazz. In the early 1970s when I was listening to Miles, Monk, and Coltrane along with other progressive players, I didn't notice at first how they were influencing my poetry. I just loved the sound; jazz was part of my life as a continuous score to the fleeting images my mind envisioned. The music signaled a kind of freedom and that's what I internalized. Jazz allowed me to make vivid excursions into my creative universe. More than what Villon or Ginsberg taught me, I learned from jazz that I could write anything into a poem. The music played off irony and from this I grasped the dynamics of insinuation. Jazz projects tonal insinuations. Discovering this, I now had access to an expanded spectrum of emotions and a pallette of linguistic colors that only enhanced the awareness that my intellectual pursuits provided.

Of special importance, jazz has worked as a way of reestablishing a kind of trust, a trust I had known earlier as a child. It directed me to the necessity to articulate clearly what my imagination brought me. Perhaps what I mean is best said in the poem "Blue Light Lounge Sutra for the Performance Poets at Harold Park Hotel":

> the need gotta be
> so deep words can't
> answer simple questions
> all night long notes
> stumble off the tongue
> & color the air indigo
> so deep fragments of gut
> & flesh cling to the song.

An essential element to jazz is improvisation and that requires taking risks. McKay's protest sonnet "If We Must Die" took few steps to challenge structural norms, but it took risks in content. Why else was it read into the *Congressional Record* by Senator Henry Cabot Lodge?

African American poets of the 1920s faced nearly the same dilemma as Phyllis Wheatley when Thomas Jefferson judged her work to be beneath critical response. That is, well into this century, European Americans withheld recognition from writers of African descent. It was up to African American communities to acknowledge their finest writers. In the meantime, African American poets bided for the day they would receive merit based on their works. Only when the defense of this nation depended on African American participation did the economic and political climate change to allow for gradual acceptance.

Poetry has always been associated with the elite, the leisure class, or the "high" culture of Europe. Consequently, few black poets willingly admitted the influence of jazz since it was associated with "low" culture, having been created by the descendants of Africans. In Greenwich Village of the 1930s, it was a jazz club, the Village Vanguard, that first integrated uptown and downtown artists—musicians, actors, comedians, and poets. Jazz provided the setting for breaking taboos. Jazz, too, was the culminating activity that all these artists shared. Harlem dance and jazz clubs from the 1930s to the 1950s and rock 'n' roll did the same much to the chagrin of the politicians.

In the post-civil rights era during the 1960s, many African Americans and African American artists redefined their cultural ties. Young black poets looked to Langston Hughes and Frank Horne. Young white poets associated with modernism; they recognized the inclusive American voice. They heard it. Indeed, jazz shaped the Beat aesthetic, but that movement had come a privileged route too. To many, the Beat movement was nothing more than the latest minstrel show in town with the new Jim Crows and Zip Coons, another social club that admitted few women or African Americans. Charlie Parker was their Buddha.

Just as a jam session invites anyone who wants to enter the fray of spontaneous composition, jazz poetry demands trust in others and in its mode of freedom. As I listen to Dolphy or Dexter, their music works like a refrain in keeping me focused. It seems that all my muses love the music too, that they are hip enough to link me to Soyinka or Robbe-Grillet. Ultimately Miles belongs side-by-side with Sartre. Anything is possible, that is what jazz teaches me. I like the implied freedom jazz brings to my work; a soloist can go to hell or heaven and back, bending a tune into an extended possibility.

Jazz offers something else: it has been the one thing that gives symmetry—shape and tonal equilibrium—to my poetry. For some, jazz-influenced poetry might appear as a threat to the canon, but it survives exclusionary cultural critics. This isn't new. Anything related to jazz has always been somewhat of a threat, and not only in the United States or England. Look at the stir jazz created in 1938 at the "Entartete Musik" exhibition in Dusseldorf, Germany with Ernst Krenek's *Jonny spilt auf.*

I feel blessed that something pulled jazz and poetry together inside me.

Here is an example of what I mean, the first and last stanzas of "No Good Blues":

1

I try to hide in Proust,
Mallarme, & Camus,
but the no-good blues
come looking for me. Yeah,
come sliding in like good love
on a tongue of grease & sham,
built up from the ground.
I used to think a super-8 gearbox
did the job, that a five-hundred-dollar suit
would keep me out of Robert Johnson's
shoes. I rhyme Baudelaire
with Apollinaire, hurting
to get beyond crossroads & goofer
dust, outrunning a twelve-bar
pulse-beat. But I pick up
a hitchhiker outside Jackson.
Tasseled boots & skin-tight
jeans. You know the rest.

6

I'm cornered at Birdland
like a two-headed man hexing
himself. But the no-good blues
come looking for me. A prayer
holds me in place,
balancing this sequined
constellation. I've hopped boxcars
& thirteen state lines to where
she stands like Ma Rainey.
Gold tooth & satin. Rotgut
& God Almighty. Moonlight
wrestling a Texas-jack.
A meteor of desire burns
my last plea to ash. Blues
don't care how many tribulations
you lay at my feet, I'll go
with you if you promise
to bring me home to Mercy.

# Journey into "(American Journal)"

In 1975, after years of admiring such poems as "The Ballad of Sue Ellen Westerfield," "Night, Death, Mississippi," and "Homage to the Empress of the Blues," I was fortunate to meet the formidable Robert Hayden. After his Friday-night reading at Colorado College in Colorado Springs, we made plans to meet Saturday afternoon.

I had no idea what I'd say to him. A barrage of elusive questions plagued me throughout the night. The next day I phoned Alex Blackburn, the founding editor of *Writers Forum,* and asked him if he wished to meet Hayden. Alex was elated, and I got off the hook. That afternoon we visited the Garden of the Gods.

Of course, years later, when Michael S. Harper gave me a copy of Hayden's *American Journal* in early 1981, I was surprised by the title poem. I remember how it rekindled sensations and images of that Colorado afternoon; I read the poem repeatedly, each time feeling Hayden's presence intensifying. The man had a penetrating, indecorous eloquence—so does his poetry. I felt linked to this poem personally. "(American Journal)" taught me how language and imagination can transform a physical landscape into a spiritual one. We had talked about how the Garden of the Gods parallels a moonscape, something otherworldly. It was from there that Hayden began to orbit his imaginative tableau. Where many of us would have written a realistic narrative to recreate that day as we gazed out at the rocky formations called Kissing Camels and Balanced Rock, as myriads of birds flashed in the high reddish crevices, Hayden's poem took a leap into the fantastic—a risk.

---

"Journey into '(American Journal)' " by Yusef Komunyakaa originally appeared in *Field: Contemporary Poetry and Poetics* 47 (fall 1992).

It is a voyage from the known to an approximated unknown that resonates with an almost-observed realism. It seems as if the narrator is on a spiritual quest, that this voyage into the brutal frontier of the American experience is a confrontation with his own alienation. He is transported through the power of reflection (the mind as spacecraft) in order to arrive at the scary truth of his species.

The poem's syntax suggests that everything is fused by a stream of consciousness—people, situations, ideas. Its satire is enhanced because numerous contradictions coexist, a tabulation of positives and negatives that insinuate: "new comers lately sprung up in our galaxy . . . yet no other beings / in the universe make more extravagant claims / for their importance and identity." The crude, egotistical Americans are attractive and repulsive; they are redeemable only if they can name their crimes and insanities or if someone can speak on their behalf—a seer, a poet, or a Christlike sympathizer. The poem's fractured syntax also highlights the narrator's alienation, as if spoken by a foreigner striving to grasp the structure and nuances of a new language.

Indeed, the "humanoid" among us narrates as might an early Western anthropologist, descending into the wilds of his galaxy to do fieldwork. He uses outdated jargon—"charming savages" and "enlightened primitives"—to describe us. Of course, this is the same ethnocentric lingo used by early anthropologists to dehumanize various peoples throughout the world. The narrator, however, employs the oxymorons in a satirical, almost cynical way, to articulate the supreme contradiction of our culture, the American Dream.

After interviewing an "earth man" at a tavern, who maintains he still believes in the dream, "irregardless of the some / times night mare facts we always try to double / talk our way around," the narrator, after further investigation of our society, records the American Dream as a great lie—a cultural materialism based on illusions and paradoxes. The idea that "everybody in the good old usa / should have the chance to get ahead . . . three squares a day" pales under the narrator's witnessing of "the squalid ghettoes in their violent cities." Like a mortified anthropologist, the narrator renames our dream as "vaunted liberty" and typically compares America with the more evolved society from which he traveled: "we are an ancient race and have outgrown / illusions cherished here."

As an outsider himself, he is able to ridicule this illusion, orchestrated by our mythmakers, because he, a "humanoid," like others who are physically or culturally "different," are not welcomed into American society, let alone given access to the means of attaining the Dream. The narrator can only exist in the American context if he prostitutes his individuality through "mimicry" and assimilation: "though i have easily passed for an american . . . exert greater caution twice have aroused / suspicion returned to the ship." The speaker is raceless, without gender or genus, but knows this fearful sense of otherness that had driven most Americans into the psychological melting pot.

The narrator speaks as an insider/outsider, a freak in an elastic limbo, whose sensitivity is violated by "unbearable decibels." This investigator knows the impending tragedy programmed by America's love of technology—its machine-oriented existence: "more faithful to their machine-made gods / technologists their shamans." Similarly, he records the cultivated national ignorance that protects and facilitates America's collective ego: "earth men / in antique uniforms play at the carnage whereby / the americans achieved identity."

Is the poet an anthropologist also? Are we responsible for what we witness? Perhaps the speaker is also an artist, one who must not only record the patterns of the universe one finds oneself in but decode, translate, and critique them also. In any case, for me this poem gains more and more authority and significance as the last piece in Hayden's *Collected Poems*. It is a perfect summation and coda to his career as a poet. He always saw himself and his work as totally *American*. Yet, I believe he identifies with the displaced speaker in "(American Journal)"—the outsider.

# Forces That Move the Spirit

## *Duende and Blues*

When Federico García Lorca talks about duende, the influence of Andalusian Gypsies on his poetry, how they shaped the concept of *cante jondo,* I feel that he's talking about a similar, if not the same, emotional soil from which has sprung the blues. I think of Son House, Leadbelly, Charley Patton, Ma Rainey, Blind Lemon Jefferson, etc., with the Mississippi as a slow-motion backdrop. I think of the delta's rich bottomland, the sweat and blood that have gone into endless rituals of survival, the brute force and almost obscene beauty of its peasantry, and how the music and songs are closer to prayers than anything else—and earthy atticism. If one can squeeze love out of these songs, he can taste distilled mercy. Or terror. Here's a class of people refusing to lie down and be counted as victims.

Willie Dixon says that "The whole of life itself expresses the blues. That's why I always says the blues are the true facts of life expressed in words and song, inspiration, feeling and understanding." Indeed, the blues are existential. They are also black and basic. And it is this down-to-earthness that I hope informs the main tenor of my poetry—a language that deals with the atrabilious nature of our existence as well as the emotional weight of its beauty. This is what Lorca saw in the *cante jondo.* Apparently, the Gypsy singer Manuel Torre said in 1922, as Manuel de Falla played *Nights in the Gardens of Spain,* that "Whatever has black sounds has *duende.*" The

From *What Will Suffice: Contemporary American Poets on the Art of Poetry,* ed. Christopher Buckley and Christopher Merrill (Salt Lake City: Gibbs Smith Publisher, 1995), 79–80.

sounds of the soil, of the earth turning around in its monumental mystery—conception and birth sounds that stumble out of the night, the violent serenity that Jean Toomer attempted to capture in *Cane,* and the fact that for one to embrace such moments is antithetical to the European psyche and its classic fear of the unknown.

I love the raw lyricism of the blues. Its mystery and conciseness. I admire and cherish how the blues singer attempts to avoid abstraction; he makes me remember that balance and rhythm keep our lives almost whole. The essence of mood is also important here. Mood becomes directive; it becomes the bridge that connects us to who we are philosophically and poetically. Emotional texture is drawn from the aesthetics of insinuation and nuance. But to do this well the poet has to have a sense of history. Of course, this often means that one has to reeducate oneself. James Baldwin talks about having taken recordings of Bessie Smith to Switzerland to begin to recreate where he came from before he could write *Another Country*—the natural tongue of his beginnings. Perhaps he desired only a certain mood. I agree with this analysis of Jahheinz Jahn: "The blues do not arise from a mood, but produce one. Like every art in African culture, song too is an attitude which affects something. The spiritual produces God, the secularized blues produce a mood."

The mood I desire in my poetry is one in which the truth can survive. I love satire. How the Fool operates in *King Lear* is brilliant: he is the wise man in the midst of a cultivated system of evasions and self-deception. Likewise, often the blues singer can get us closer to truth than the philosopher. This is the function of my poetry.

# Control Is the Mainspring

In spring of 1984 I found myself writing about my experiences and observations in Vietnam during 1969–70. The first three poems were "Somewhere near Phu Bai," "Starlight Scope Myopia," and "Missing in Action"; these poems seemed to have merely gushed out of me, and they surfaced with imagery that dredged up so much unpleasant psychic debris. All the guilt and anger coalesced into a confused stockpile of unresolved conflict. These poems were prompted by a need; they had fought to get out. I hadn't forgotten a single thread of evidence against myself.

However, I needed to slow down the pace of these volatile images since they were coming forth at such a panic-ridden haste. Something was happening to me, and I was afraid. I had purposefully evaded Vietnam-related literature and had seen only one "Vietnam War" movie, *Apocalypse Now,* about five years earlier in the pseudo-safety of southern California's Newport Beach. I remember leaving the movie house enraged—enraged at myself. But here I was in New Orleans, with the weight of the Old South pulsating underneath a thin facade, and I was readying myself to renovate an old house, 818 Piety Street, in the Bywater district. The ugly scars of history were all around me, and it became even more grotesque when moments of severe beauty showed through. Beneath the chipped and cracked horsehair plaster, the hundred-year-old oak slats looked new, untouched by mildew and ravages of poverty.

Those old houses have twelve- and fourteen-foot ceilings. The humid New Orleans summer had begun edging in, and I wanted to get the hard, high work finished first, where the

From *Hayden's Ferry Review* 10 (spring–summer 1992).

stifling heat collected. I put a pad of paper and pen on a table in the next room. This had a purpose. The images were coming so fast that, whenever I made a trek down the ladder, each line had to be worth its weight in sweat. That spring and summer I must've discarded thousands of images, ones that just a few months earlier I would've given up a thumb for. I learned that the body and the mind are indeed connected: good writing is physical and mental. I welcomed the knowledge of this because I am from a working-class people who believe that physical labor is sacred and spiritual.

My great-grandfather Melvin had been a carpenter; so was my father, and they both taught me the value of tools—saws, hammers, chisels, files, rulers, etc. It all dealt with conciseness and precision. It eliminated guesswork. One has to know his tools, so he doesn't work against himself. Tools make the job easier. More accuracy.

At this time I started rereading some of the Negritude poets such as Aimé Césaire, Nicolas Guillen, Réné Depestre, Leopold Sedar Senghor, and Jacques Rabenmananjara. I was also coming closer to the imagistic narrative: a poem moved by images and the inherent music in language. I wrote during the day and read at night.

Perched on the top rung of the ladder, each step down served as a kind of metrical device—made me plan each word and syllable. In the background, at the other end of the house, in the kitchen, jazz pulsed underneath the whole day. Sometimes I worked twelve to twenty hours. I realized that language is man's first music, and, consequently, I began to approach the poem with this in mind. Again, I was hungry for the essence and magic of language, of how it connects the poet to listener, elated that it all centers around communication. I believe that the apprenticeship I served with my father and great-grandfather years earlier guided my hand as I wrote poetry that spring and summer in the Crescent City. The rhythm of my breath and work was the metronome dividing the words I committed to paper, as I used rasps and sandpaper to scrape the wood back to its earlier symmetry and perfection.

# Tough Eloquence

*Poetry for the Free Peoples*

I began reading Etheridge Knight's poetry in the early 1970s, and what immediately caught my attention was his ability to balance an eloquence and toughness, exhibiting a complex man behind the words. His technique and content were one—the profane alongside the sacred—accomplished without disturbing the poem's tonal congruity and imagistic exactitude. Here was a streetwise poet who loved and revered language. Gwendolyn Brooks, Sterling Brown, and Langston Hughes seem to have been his mentors, but Knight appeared to have sprung into the literary world almost fully formed. He had so much control and authority; he was authentic from the onset. Irony pulsed beneath each phrase, urban and rural in the same breath. Maybe his duality evolved from the necessity of switching codes in his native Mississippi, having honed his ability to talk to whites and blacks simultaneously.

He was a poet who could play the dozens, who had been initiated into various jailhouse toasts, who had accomplished the grace of blues legend. Here was Robert Johnson back from the dead, a survivor speaking with biting lyricism automatically associated with spirituals and defined by the art of signifying. He had the tongue of a two-headed man—a Texas-jack that could cut two ways at once.

Etheridge Knight had been saved by poetry. As he says in *Colorado Review* (spring–summer 1987): "I first began to define myself as poet in prison. Guys in the joint was my first primary audience. I was sending poems to guys in the joint before I started sending them anyplace else. If you can play a guitar or paint or say poems, you have an audience. And you get affirmed. I got a lot of support. Guys thought I functioned

From *Trotter Review* (spring 1993).

like a village scribe. On weekends, they would come to me and bring their letters, I was supposed to be a 'poet' so they'd have me write letters to their wives and sweethearts. You got to do a lot of relating if you're going to do *that* right. You've got to listen. You've got to hear their story."

Knight was a chronicler of prison life and its immense pathos, and he conveyed each story with such clarity that the images would cut through almost anybody's armor. Poetry became his choice of weapons. The poem entitled "For Freckle-Faced Gerald" is a tragedy in motion, with all the nerves exposed: "Take Gerald. Sixteen years hadn't even done / a good job on his voice. He didn't even know / how to talk tough, or how to hide the glow / of life before he was thrown in a 'pigmeat' / for buzzards to eat." Of course, this young unseasoned convict was marked by his innocence, which makes one think of similar sideshows depicted by Genet. In Knight's poem it is Gerald's personality that makes him vulnerable. He is in a place where prisoners have to create their own cycle of victims out of situational greed: "Gerald could never quite win / with his precise speech and innocent grin / the trust and fists of the young black cats." Streetwise idioms work for Knight in a natural way; the "young black cats" become real, pacing the perimeter of their caged lives. They must claim their prey in order to nurture and qualify their psychological existence.

Experience is the caretaker of the imprisoned in Knight's poem "He Sees through Stone." This unnamed man becomes the prototypical survivor—a patriarch of the initiated: "he smiles / he knows / the hunt the enemy / he has the secret eyes / he sees through stone." The same "black cats," like shadows of the real men, who circled Gerald and brought him down like a young gazelle, also pace "this old black one," but they can't bring him down because of his experience. This prisoner is heroic, contrasting Gerald's almost antiheroic posture.

Knight knows that people in such a psychological clench need heroes of mythic proportions to fight their real and imaginary battles. Hard Rock is one they, and Knight, have claimed. He has a history of standing up to adversaries and symbols of authority, a figure of folkloric stature: "and he had the scars to prove it: / split purple lips, lumbed ears, welts above / His yellow eyes, and one long scar that cut / across his temple and plowed through a thick / canopy of kinky hair." This hero doesn't wear a white hat. He is crude, brute-looking, unsophisticated, but also noble. In order for him to belong to a group he must sacrifice himself; thus, he's misused by this fraternity of black victims. Also, one knows, like Hard Rock, what the collective "we" has been reduced to—that only savagery equals survival in such a hellhole. The situation has invented Hard Rock. This modern Frankenstein is unloved. When black manhood has been thwarted and misshapen, this is the reflection a black Narcissus sees.

Knight also knows that the threat of black manhood is what terrifies white America. This same fear drove lynch mobs out into the streets in recent history. When the poet gives us such poems as "On Seeing the Black Male as #1 Sex Object in America," he very consciously throws some inside jabs: "In bright jeans, tight jeans, bulging; / Shining their cars, / Hanging in the bars, Leaning on the corners . . ." He seems to be stacking the deck and playing with minds. But there is also a penetrating insight here; he knows the American psyche, and this is what makes him an expert signifier—playing the dozens with his reader—a speaker in control. Similar to the young men "wearing flashy red caps," Knight is also insinuating when he gives us a speaker who knows the score. This is a position of power. The masked persona has control not only because he can articulate the politics of the situation but also because he's the caretaker of a biting truth. He's a bona fide witness. He can speak for the victims, for the unaware, for the powerless who can only mock and shadowplay power with their audacious presence—as if their tongues have been cut out.

One of Knight's few war-related poems is "At a VA Hospital in the Middle of the United States of America: An Act in a Play." In it half-dead veterans of "five wars" are imprisoned in their doped-up dreamworlds. They are little more than phantoms: "words filled with ice and fear, / Nightflares and fogginess, and studied regularity." They can only daydream of their various exploits, real and imagined, contained in a blurred existence, but what is truly ironic is that their plausible histories and lies control them to the extent that they are imprisoned in numerous ways: "Midnight seeks the red-eyes, the tired /

Temper, the pains in the head." And: "For an end to sin, / For a surcease of sorrow. / He nods the days away, / And curses his Ranger Colonel in fluent Vietnamese." And: "Grant Trotter's war was the south side / Of Sand Diego. Storming the pastel sheets / of Mama Maria's, he got hit with a fifty / Dollar dose of syphilis. His feats / Are legends of masturbation, the constant coming / As he wanders the back streets of his mind." Importantly, the italicized refrain that ends each stanza comes from the spiritual "Down By the Riverside."

Such a construction reminds me of W. E. B. Du Bois's empathetic strategy in *The Souls of Black Folk* wherein he states: "They walked in darkness, sang songs in the olden days— Sorrow Songs—for they were weary at heart."[1] The refrain is Knight's antiwar statement. Knight had been an army medic in the Korean War and has written: "I died in Korea from a shrapnel wound, and narcotics resurrected me. I died in 1960 from a prison sentence and poetry brought me back to life." The only other mention of the Korean War is in his short poem for a Private First Class (PFC) in his first book, *Poems from Prison,* published in 1968 by Broadside Press. Perhaps there is an answer as to why Knight didn't write more war-related poems; I still wish he had. He could have filled a missing space in our literary canon.

Knight also knew how important it is to empower people with a sense of history, with an articulated presence in life: Hadn't poetry saved him? In early 1990 a young poet friend, Kenneth May, introduced me to the man who had been leading the Free Peoples Workshop at a bar called the Slippery Noodle in Indianapolis. It seemed as though I had known Knight for many years. He was kinfolk. There was something in his eyes that reminded me of the men in my family. He was another survivor, a hat-wearing shaman with a hint of Railroad Bill in his voice. He believed that a recitation or a reading was more academic, more removed, and more self-conscious. He was a poet who could talk the blues. The oral tradition was the basis of his personal aesthetics. Of course, this takes us straight back to the beginning of African American poetry, back to such voices as James M. Whitfield, Frances E. W. Harper, Paul Laurence Dunbar, and Langston Hughes.

What is most remarkable about Knight's poetry is that it avoids moralizing, and what I had learned earlier in the songs of Big Joe Turner, Johnny Ace, Bobby Blue Bland, T-Bone Walker, Muddy Waters, Ma Rainey, and a host of other blues legends, he brought back to me as I read "Cell Song," "The Warden Said to Me the Other Day," "A Poem for Black Relocation Centers," "The Stretching of the Belly," "No Moon Floods the Memory of that Night," "Feeling Fucked Up," "The Bones of My Father," "We Free Singers," and others.

As I tried to forget those old blues wrung from the flesh and soul, so had I attempted to cut out what troubled tenderness still clung to me, but Etheridge knew how to get close to his feminine side, so much so that you could almost hear a woman singing underneath his voice. Or, maybe there were the voices of many women there—mother, grandmother, sister, daughter—singing one collective acknowledgment. A passionate, naturalistic awareness informed many of his jaunty poems. Even when Etheridge gets caught up in signification, the humanness isn't undermined. Something genuine remains intact, untroubled. We find ourselves in the poem's center and must feel our way out. Thus, a poem like "As You Leave Me" stays with the reader. We might not want to know, but we do, at least in some measured way, what the narrator feels: "and I die as I watch you / disappear in the streets / to whistle and smile at the johns." This is hardcore, down-to-earth poetry. We feel the speaker's skin because we can hear some part of ourselves speaking. We know the woman in "The Violent Space" because she's like too many women (not just black women) who have been reduced by the hard facts of economics. We can also empathize with the poem's narrator, can taste his rage when he says, "I boil my tears in a twisted spoon / and dance like an angel on the point of a needle. / I sit counting syllables like Midas gold—I am not bold."

Although Etheridge was familiar with the rituals that made life painful, he was also aware of what could make us whole and vulnerable to simple beauty. And, sometimes, we realize that these are the most threatening moments, the affirmation of human existence. This is exemplified in "Circling the Daughter": "Now I sit, / Trembling in your presence.

Fourteen years / Have brought the moon-blood, the round-ness . . ." The poem continues: "Reach always within / For the Music and the Dance and the Circling." Of course, this circling is different from the "black cats" circling their prey in the poems discussed earlier. This circling is an affirmation; it says that sex is natural and beautiful. The poem has a poignant italicized couplet that appears twice, after the first stanza and at the poem's end, and it sounds like both a love call and a confession: "You break my eyes with your beauty: / OOOOuuoobaby-I-love-you." This is dedicated to his daughter, Tandi, celebrating womanhood with a quiet awe—as if whispered in a dark room.

Etheridge Knight died in March 1991. For more than a year before, at various readings, he'd *say* a poem by Melissa Orion, "Where Is the Poet?" He often used to say he wished he'd written it. Of course, he had memorized the poem, as if reciting his own elegy.

> So I went to Soweto and asked the wounded
> Have you seen my friend the poet?
>
> Oh no, answered the wounded, but we're longing to
> see him before we die
>
> Maybe you should go to the prisons, they said
> where there is loneliness, the poet should be

Knight had been there. He answered the calling like one of those old-timey Baptist preachers from Mississippi. Tough and eloquent, he was nothing if not a fall guy for beauty and truth, because he believed the poet was duty-bound to take chances. He was a man who had been roughed up by life, by bad luck, and he had the emotional and physical scars to prove it. This was the very quality about him that mystified so many of us, young and old, educated and unlettered, black and white, fulfilling our need to embrace him as our friend, the poet, who had been tried by water and baptized by fire.

NOTE

1. W. E. B. Du Bois, *The Souls of Black Folk* (Chicago: A. C. McClurg & Co., 1903), 250.

# It's Always Night

It's always night
or we wouldn't need light.
    —Thelonious Monk, qtd. in *Time*

Thelonious Monk was interested in how things struggle with opposites—an intensity that expands possibility. Nature itself: the pulling into and the letting go. He was a technician of silence. Rhythm. Silence in his compositions is music(al); not mere coloration or transition but silent spaces as units of an emotional continuum. Silence as shaped as tonal artifact, is what Monk captured. Undoubtedly, gospel taught him a lot— his music owes much to the human voice. It helped him challenge linearity; that is, he corrupted conventional sound— anticipation. His music possesses percussive truthfulness. A synthesis of conflict and beauty. A futuristic maturity. An opening out toward multidimensionality through simplicity . . . silence creates poetic tension and suspension. An exactitude defined by what's left out. Monk's music requires an active listener—someone who doesn't have to be told the whole story. A transmutation of mind and sound: a third something is created. He was a deep listener. And, yes, it was this quality of listening that helped him to create tunes like "Ruby, My Dear," "In Walked Bud," and "Misterioso." There's an emotional elasticity to Monk's world. Things that seem at odds with each other fit side by side: the human mind does the framing (inside and outside of conventional references). Clusters of chords. A woman's walk. A man's bluesy cry in the night. Expansion rather than construction. The listener helps to decide the music's shape—keeping it organic and alive. Always *becoming*. Monk listened to silence and respected it. Maybe his musical theory can be found in his title "Ugly Beauty."

From *Caliban* 4 (1988).

# Improvised Symmetry

When Knopf published Langston Hughes's *Fine Clothes to the Jew* in 1927, the *New York Times* called the volume "uneven and flawed."

Still, today, that critical phrase is with us, but it never fails to dismay me when I see it in print. What does it really mean? Is it like saying a suite of songs or a medley should be performed at the same tempo or that a dress must be cut from the same piece of silk? Is the human brain supposed to function like a fleshy metronome, with no highs or lows, with hardly any tonal or emotional or structural variance? Are poems supposed to be cut out like flawless rows of paper dolls and stitched between book covers? Or is each poem an experience in itself—with strengths and flaws?

Yes, I can easily see how a computer might be programmed to compose a very "even" book, but of artificiality. If we take a close look at pop music, we can see the impassive effects of drum machines—pure ennui.

Everything seems to be leading toward a kind of genetic engineering where human existence is a commodity and expression merely an anemic sameness. I realize that this is quite a leap from "uneven" books of poetry to the technological inbreeding of species, but I am only talking about a way of thinking today that seems to touch everything. We seem to desire draining the humanness out of art. But for me the so-called flaws often help to capture human action and depict improvised symmetry—the surprises in poetry, painting, etc. The surprises happen before the brain can wrestle with meaning and attempt to concretize the act of creation and

---

From *Caliban* 2 (1987).

contemplation, the flaws become the gems that truly communicate. These blemishes reflect and define the personality of a piece ... the poetic tension between yes and no, positive and negative, good and evil—the bridge that Passion walks between life and death.

# Poetry and Inquiry

Poetry is the primary medium I have chosen because of the conciseness, the precision, the imagery, and the music in the lines. I think of language as our first music.

My earliest experience with poetry probably has much to do with my methodical inquiry into those things around me: the wildflower, the Honeysuckle, the violent rituals of nature and people, the Mayhaw, the swim hole that had been recently dynamited to deepen it, and the images confronted in those little plastic viewfinders. For me those moments often became a visual and emotional composite, how things merge and how things bleed into each other have a lot to do with how poems are constructed. I wrote a poem in high school that was one hundred lines long, with rhymed quatrains. And I was too shy to read it. I remember how the poem celebrated and abstracted a "scary" future, which I assumed was quite unorthodox at the time. In retrospect I wish I had a closer relationship to the basic elements of the blues tradition and the fundamentals of the modernist aesthetic. Perhaps this would have given me a scaffold that would have supported the ideas that ushered me into manhood. I had very limited access to literature in Bogalusa, Louisiana, where I grew up. At first I read the works of Shakespeare, Edgar Allen Poe, Emily Dickinson, and of course a lot of Alfred Lord Tennyson. I think I liked best the poetry in Shakespeare's plays. I was introduced to African American literature in what was termed "the Negro History Week," which were brief moments in our education before we went back to the regular curriculum, which was the history and literature dominated by Europeans.

In the works of Langston Hughes I remember being struck by the surprises in his poetry, that it was so close to a spoken diction, with a blues, metric shape. It was so immediate, and it touched my existence in a complete way. In fact, his poetry comes out of what William Carlos Williams has called "an American idiom," though I didn't know that then. I also liked the fact these poets were different from each other. Brooks made me feel as if I were in an observation tower, surveying my neighborhood. Reading Johnson, I could play God inside my head as I recited "The Creation." And the poetry of Phyllis Wheatley was something I could meditate on. No, she wasn't as forthright and clear as Hughes, but I felt that there was a thread of language in her poems that invited me in and challenged my creative approach. For the first time I saw a glimpse of how the imagination could serve as a choice of weapons.

I grew up in a poor and impoverished neighborhood in the Deep South dominated by a Calvinistic work ethic. People around me believed that if they worked hard they could get ahead in the "American Dream." I didn't see it that way, which of course generated a few disagreements between me and my father, but, having been away from that part of my life for so long now, and in trying to establish some kind of intellectual equation, the American Dream seems to have been very much a myth.

There are six children in my immediate family, and there was always an energy surrounding me. Many times I would read poetry in order to establish a moment of contemplation, and other times I would go out into the wooded areas around our house to allow myself solitude. Those two escapes came together for me in ways that I'm only able to understand now with some distance. I don't know if my family thought my interests odd at that time, but in measuring my life against theirs, in retrospect, it must have seemed rather peculiar.

When I went to Vietnam, I carried a couple of poetry anthologies with me. I continued to read poetry but was not writing it. I was in the information field and was doing newspaper work. When I came back from the war, I found myself enrolled in a poetry workshop at the University of Colorado, and I've been writing regularly ever since. The first poem I wrote when I felt I could call myself a poet is titled "Instructions for Building Straw Huts." I realized after writing the poem that a certain number of worlds had come together to coalesce into a strange unity for me. The poem radiated with a number of surprises, and I realized I wanted surprises in my work from then on. If I don't have them, poetry doesn't work for me. Poetry is a process of getting back to the unconscious. Hence, I am always writing—even when I'm not facing the white space. I feel writers are like reservoirs of images. We take in what is around us. In the poetry classes I teach, I tell students to write everything down—not to think of the shape of the poem until the words are all down—and then revise, to be ready for the surprises, and to take them as gifts.

While in college, I wasn't able to take a class in African American literature, as so few were offered in the early 1970s. However, I did read everything in that area I could get my hands on. I felt cheated. Johnson's *Book of American Negro Poetry* became important to me and Clarence Major's *New Black Poetry* was a real surprise. Of course, much of this literature came after I'd read Lowell, Pound, Williams, Sexton, Plath, Ginsberg, Dylan Thomas, and hundreds of other voices in modern and contemporary poetry.

I feel everything is urgent, which is just the way my life seems to go. So in terms of what ends up in my poetry, anything and everything is subject matter. Often, one of the real problems in teaching creative writing, particularly to undergraduates, is that the students think there is something outside themselves, so distant from their lives, that is more appropriate subject matter. My tactic is to try and convince them that things that are very close to them are best to write about—it doesn't have to be an imagined experience in Italy or Japan. Many times people try to pull away from the center of their lives, but that is where the energy exists. We don't have to impose a superficial, invented subject matter in order to write. However, I do impress on my students the importance of reading everything—not just literature but also history, economics, psychology, philosophy—everything. And to observe everything around them.

In terms of my own creative process, I like working on scraps of paper—on discarded envelopes and pieces of junk mail. In this somewhat fragmented process I'm able to get everything down and then go about shaping the poem. I remember helping my father in his carpentering, and how he'd measure a board four or five times before he sawed it in two, and then how he'd just slip it into place. Impatient and wanting to go out and play, still it would surprise me how easy and tight the fit was. Precision. Symmetry. A rehearsed exactness that had everything to do with how well my father had learned his tools. He never rushed the work. I like to think that the precision with which he crafted shelves and tables and houses is the same kind of process I employ in my writing, particularly when it comes to revision.

There is automatically a psychological overlay for my poetry, as well as for who I am, when talking about blackness. I have never thought about the issue of blackness as subject matter for my poetry per se, but I suppose it has a lot to do with my perspective in terms of the shape of my emotional life. How I began to look at the world early on informed the shape of my adult artistic life, but I don't think I'd like to sit down and face the page and say: "I am now going to write as a black man." I don't entertain that thought, because I know who I am, and I don't have to face the mirror every day to remind myself. I've always accepted who I am and have hoped to let that direct my poetic vision.

I realize, by just going back and looking at folklore, that all along there have been hints of what we are dealing with today in terms of being black and male in our society. There have always been certain figures in the community whom we automatically categorize as what is often called "The Bad Nigger." I'm talking about the violent personae we see in our daily lives through popular entertainment. When a sense of Self has been undermined so dramatically and systematically, this is the reflection of impotence that is thrown back at us. Thus, we watch the Stagolees composed before our eyes—the mask. This mythical man is really a phantom, because, if we think in terms of folklore, he has no real power. There are numerous stories about a black killing another black man on Friday or Saturday night and being bonded out of jail on Sunday so that he appears for work on Monday morning. Only powerlessness fits into this historical equation. In terms of my own experience I had to sit down and have a talk with myself. It has not been so much about power for me as it has been about authorizing my sense of self. We are given vivid pictures of individuals who don't have any authority. And I think that these pictures might function as a psychological warfare. We need to remove these stereotypical images from our psyche—I'm talking about our collective psyche.

It's hard for me to dissect imagination and reality, because I realize that the two spring from the same subjectivity. They are constantly fighting and reshaping each other, so there is a chemistry and interaction going on that is informed by the "truth." I like the fact that there's this organic, evolving reciprocity going on beneath poetry and the need to write it. There has to be a need to write—if there isn't a need, then everything else becomes artificial. There are things moving along in our imaginative universe without us being able to define them, or to put any kind of logical shape around them. Consequently, we want to control all of the mysterious activity. Ultimately, we have to get rid of the mechanism of control and place our lives in the hands of who we are. Without boundaries. It is a scary venture, but, if it felt safe, it might become static or contrived. One has to realize that we only fill so much space. In filling that space, if there is any control involved, it is the control of one's ability to live in the moment.

It is difficult for me to write about things in my life that are very private, but I feel that I am constantly moving closer to my personal terrain—the idea of trying to get underneath who I am. I realize we are all such complex human beings and that there is a layered core in all of us. For me, and my writing, it is a process of removing those layers to understand what is at the core, and also realizing I can incorporate all of those layers into a clarified idea of who I am. The layers become overlays instead of obstructions. I know I've helped to create the layers, despite who I am as a thinking human being. Many times I try to push aside the easier things to write about, like my daily observations, and come back to them later, when there is more psychological debris to deal with.

I have never purposely written a poem for a select group of people. Generally, I just find myself writing a poem. There are certain poems I can read to young black men and women, and automatically they grasp the poetry. There are other poems that people have told me they had to reread numerous times before they could actually understand them. I like the idea that the meaning of my poetry is not always on the surface and that people may return to the work. Sometimes I may not like a poem in the first reading, but, when I go back and read it again, there is a growth that has happened within me, and I become a participant rather than just a reader. I try to encourage this sort of participation in my own poetry—I try to create a space into which a reader can come and participate in the meaning. For me a poem shouldn't have a resolution. I try to cultivate an open-endedness that invites the reader to enter, not merely to read the poem as an outsider but to experience it from within. I'm not talking about the physics of chance but about an enjoyment culled from hard work—a connection fused by interactive minds.

# Langston Hughes + Poetry = The Blues

And far into the night he crooned that tune.
The stars went out and so did the moon.
The singer stopped playing and went to bed.
While the Weary Blues echoed through his head.
　　—Langston Hughes, *The Weary Blues*


When we analyze and weigh the most innovative voices of the Harlem Renaissance, Langston Hughes—alongside Zora Neale Hurston, Jean Toomer, and Helene Johnson—remains at the axis. Where Countee Cullen and Claude McKay embraced the archaism of the Keatian ode and the Elizabethan sonnet,[1] respectively, Hughes grafted on to his modernist vision traditional blues as well as the Chicago Renaissance (Vachel Lindsay and Carl Sandburg).[2] So, as the other voices grew silent during the Great Depression of 1929—with modernism[3] and imagism[4] having taken a firm hold and reshaped the tongue and heart of American poetry—the 1930s found a prolific Hughes. From the outset an American-ness had been at the center of Hughes's work, which is one of the reasons he has endured. Even his benchmark poem "The Negro Speaks of Rivers" plumbs the "muddy bosom" of the Mississippi after its narrator praises the Euphrates and the Congo (i.e., after taking readers on a tour through African heritage, the poem focuses on racial tensions in America).

Like Walt Whitman, the pulse and throb of Hughes's vision is driven by an acute sense of beauty and tragedy in America's history. Arnold Rampersad says in *The Life of Langston Hughes* that "On a visit to Kansas City he became aware of yet another aspect of black culture on which he would draw later as an

From *Nexus* (1996).

artist and an individual. At an open air theatre on Independence Avenue, from an orchestra of blind musicians, Hughes first heard the blues. The music seemed to cry, but the words somehow laughed." Where Whitman had embraced the aria of the Italian opera (horizontal music), Hughes's divining rod quivered over the bedrock of the blues (vertical music).[5] The short lines of the blues poems create a syncopated insistence and urgency. Art has to have tension. And it is the simultaneous laughter and crying that create the tension in Hughes's blues poetry.[6] Hughes writes in "Homesick Blues": "Homesick blues is / A terrible thing to have. / To keep from cryin' / I opens ma mouth an' laughs."

In "Midwinter Blues" we find the same tension:

> Don't know's I'd mind his goin'
> But he left me when the coal was low.
> Don't know's I'd mind his goin'
> But he left when the coal was low.
> Now, if a man loves a woman
> That ain't no time to go.

Hughes also incorporates a jagged lyricism and modulation into his poetry by using short lines—a modern feeling that depends on a vertical movement that sidesteps contemplation but invites action/motion. There is confrontation in the blues. Stephen Henderson states in *Understanding the New Black Poetry:* "In oral tradition, the dogged determination of the work songs, the tough-minded power of the blues, the inventive energy of jazz, and the transcendent vision of God in the spirituals and the sermons, all energize the idea of Freedom, of Liberation, which is itself liberated from the temporal, the societal, and the political."

Hughes seems to have set out to take poetry off the page and toss it up into the air we breathe; he desired to bring poetry into our daily lives. In essence, he wanted his blues chants to parallel the improvisation in the lives of African Americans:

> To fling my arms wide
> In the face of the sun.
> Dance! Whirl! Whirl!

> Till the quick day is done.
> Rest at pale evening . . .
> A tall, slim tree . . .
> Night coming tenderly
>> Black like me.

Hughes speaks here about daring joy to enter black life. The poem, "Dream Variations," is more than the speaker day-dreaming about bringing images of nature into Harlem (the first black metropolis of the modern world): this is celebration and revolution in the same breath. Hughes addresses the future, forging through imagery and metaphor, the possibility of a new black culture in literature, music, and the arts.

To date, Amiri Baraka is one of the first names that light on the tongue if one were to ask, Who is the rightful heir to the Langston Hughes Legacy? This is mainly due to his long allegiance to jazz and the blues through essays and poetry. But some would argue that his most successful poems are informed by his Black Mountain School[7] connection (the poems in *The Dead Lecturer* are touched by a blues feeling). He says in his "Blues, Poetry, and the New Music" essay that "I begin with blues because it is the basic national voice of the African American people. It is the fundamental verse form (speech, dance, verse/song) and musical form of the African American slave going through successive transformations."[8] Undoubtedly, Baraka owes much to Hughes, as do many other voices—black and white. But some would say, What about Sherley Anne Williams? Just mentioning her name is enough to almost bring Hughes to life; her tribute to Bessie Smith underlines what Hughes was striving for in the blues idiom:

> She was looking in
> my mouth and I knowed
> no matter what words
> come to my mind the
> song'd be her'n jes as
> well as it be mine.

Sherley Anne Williams receives my vote. But one of the most recent voices associated with Hughes is Willie Perdomo. Claude Brown's blurb on the cover of Perdomo's book of verse, *Where a*

*Nickel Costs a Dime* (the title is a Hughes line), proclaims the following: "Langston Hughes has been reincarnated and lives in Spanish Harlem." True, some of the same anger is there; true, most of Perdomo's lines are short, with a similar jagged rhythm that is often linked to the blues; true, the urban subject matter might force the reader or listener to think of Hughes's simplicity with that which is simple. Yet Hughes's poetry is rather complex because it filters through the lenses of insinuation and satire. The laughter fuses with the crying, and the synthesis is affirmation. This is what Albert Murray seems to address in *The Blue Devils of Nada:*

> As for the blues statement, regardless of what it reflects, what it *expresses* is a sense of life that is affirmative. The blues lyrics reflect that which they confront, of course, which includes the absurd, the unfortunate, and the catastrophic; but they also reflect the person making the confrontation, his self-control, his sense of structure and style; and they express, among other things, his sense of humor as well as his sense of ambiguity and his sense of possibility. Thus, the very existence of the blues tradition is irrefutable evidence that those who evolved it respond to the vicissitudes of the human condition not with hysterics and desperation but through the wisdom of poetry informed by pragmatic insight.

NOTES

1. Cullen modeled his poetry on the verse of the nineteenth-century British poet John Keats; McKay's models were the seventeenth-century Elizabethan poets, including William Shakespeare.

2. According to Hughes's biographer, Faith Berry, Hughes's high school English teacher (at Central High in Cleveland), "introduced her class to the Chicago school of poets: Vachel Lindsay, Edgar Lee Masters, and—the poet Hughes admired most, and eventually his greatest influence in the matter of form—Carl Sandburg."

3. Modernist poets like T. S. Eliot, Wallace Stevens, and Ezra Pound broke away from poetic traditions of the nineteenth century, such as rhyme and "flowery" language, the kind of poetry Cullen and Claude McKay continued to write.

4. Imagism was a post–World War I literary movement that rebelled against nineteenth-century Romanticism and promoted the

use of free verse and precise, concentrated imagery. The early poems of William Carlos Williams and the poetry of H.D. exemplify this tradition.

5. The lines of Whitman's verse are very long, giving his poetry a horizontal feel. Hughes's lines are short, so the reader's eyes move quickly down the page, giving the poetry a sense of verticalness.

6. In a review of W. C. Handy's *Blues: An Anthology* Langston Hughes says the blues grew out of "the racial hurt and the racial ecstasy," out of "trouble with incongruous overtones of laughter [and] joy with strange undertones of pain."

7. The Black Mountain School refers to an artists' colony in North Carolina with which Baraka was associated during the 1950s.

8. Hughes said much the same thing about jazz.

# Improvisation / Revision

Poetry is an act of meditation and improvisation, and *need* is the motor that propels the words down the silent white space. For me the poem is an action that attempts to defy structure as container or mold. However, it does embrace control (an artist has to know and respect the instrument) in language.

Let's face it, images and metaphors are composed as part of the emotional schema—a melody that is vamped on. *Diversions. Surprises.* In the act of writing everything down, improvising, the poet can feel the language and nuances embracing each merger and connection, as if growing into a contract with the gods and goddesses of possibility—an act of faith brought to every trope. Tone is the poem's buried structure. Here I think of Charlie Parker as he played "Cherokee," incorporating surprised feelings into the composition.

Poetry is an act of non-mathematical creation that adheres to metrics embodied in language's natural music. It isn't a gush, but a felt and lived syncopation.

After I have written everything down, sometimes hundreds of lines that meditate on the poem's central subject, I begin circling words and phrases that seem to undermine the poem's emotional symmetry; I am eager to find the elastic pattern and tonal shape within the words. The surprises. A composite of surprises. Perhaps the true gods work in severe darkness. They don't care about constant gazing into the mirror for clues.

Revision means to re-see, and, at times, it seems more accurate to say re-live. The poem evolves from a body place. The intellect hums there in the juices and muscle of imagery, churning forth questions: Can it begin here and work back-

From *Inside Borders* (September 1998). Copyright © 1998 Borders, Inc. Reprinted by permission of *Inside Borders* magazine.

wards? How many ways can this tune be played? Bodily and intellectually, an image or linguistic nerve ending has to *feel* right, resisting any pre-cast mold. For me it is always a cutting back, a honing that compresses energy, as I hope for a last line that is an open-ended release. Working back up through the poem, listing all the possible closures, I search for a little door I can leave ajar.

# A Note to Bloom

July 13, 1998

Dear Professor Harold Bloom,
Caretaker of the Western Canon,
Master of Antics and High Jinx,

We have only met twice. The first time was at Washington University in St. Louis, November 1, 1996, when you delivered a rather passionate critique praising Jay Wright's poetry. The second time was in the green room at the Pierpoint Morgan Library, when you said that some young critic was using my work to lambaste you in an upcoming issue of the *Boston Review;* this was two hours before you delivered your keynote address for the 1997 awards ceremony of the Academy of American Poets. As I listened to your baffling speech, as you recited passages of Hart Crane, I realized that you were merely expanding your introduction (copse of rant and rave) from *The Best of the Best American Poetry* anthology—an auspicious tome in which my appearance remains in your debt.

I agree, for me, the best poets often attempt to embrace a system of aesthetics that searches for lyrical and imagistic truths. This isn't new. And, in many ways, we are really talking about taste. We can go back to Aristotle's *Poetics* (based on Plato's concepts of beauty); to Plotinus' conception of the sublime; to Horace's *Art of Poetry;* to the Renaissance, with Sir

---

"A Note to Bloom" is a previously unpublished response to Harold Bloom's introduction in *The Best of the Best American Poetry 1988–1997,* ed. Harold Bloom, ser. ed. David Lehman (New York: Scribners, 1998). A variety of poets/critics debated Bloom's controversial choices and omissions in *Boston Review* 23, no. 3 (1998).

Philip Sidney's *Defense of Poesie.* And after we have argued for days about Schopenhauer's "state of spiritual exaltation," we can then arm wrestle over what Tolstoy means by "personal aims of covetousness or vanity." But most of us poets are busy writing poems, and we leave it to others to stir the honey buckets as name-calling and hyperbole surge forth. We know that you critics and gatekeepers can get tough; we can hear Herakletios saying, "Homer should be thrown out of the games and beaten, and Archilochos with him."

We don't have to be historians to understand that human history is multicultural (from Dinknesh to the Sterling Professor of the Humanities at Yale University). This is plain and simple. Since you have been picking fights with paper tigers and straw lions, I don't think you're interested in a fair, mature, intellectual discourse on democratic arts and letters at the end of this so-called millennium (depending on which calendar). You're old enough to remember the social and cultural apartheid in our recent history. I don't desire to return to the good old days.

Now, come on, Bloom, you pride yourself as a thinker, as a scholar who's empathic and fair-minded, and as a man who cares about the industry of ideas and principles. How far back can you remember? Why all this erasure? Why all these contradictions? In your introduction to *Modern Critical Views* on Langston Hughes, before your quote from *The Big Sea,* you say that "it remains a strong testament," but I wonder if you fully comprehend the true gravity of Hughes's lines: "You don't know, / You don't know my mind— / When you see me laughin', / I'm laughin' to keep from cryin'."

Many minorities believe that whites *can't* understand them or their cultures. I believe that many of them *choose* not to understand. And sometimes there are calculated misunderstandings. Here, at this moment in the Northeast, physically distant from the Deep South, I'm thinking about how your argument against multiculturalism at times seems so close to the sentiment of the Southern Agrarians. Can you hear your own tune in these words by Donald Davidson? "It's art itself, as art, that is being attacked by an enemy so blind and careless that he does not know what citadel he is approaching." Or let us consider Athol Fugard's *"Master Harold" . . . and the Boys,* where two of the three characters, Hally and Sam, are having a heated exchange about the definitions of art, beauty, imagination, and entertainment to the point of exhaustion. Again, much of this has to do with taste and experience. The whole volley of verbal sparring between Sam and Hally coalesces around the merits of the fox-trot.

Bloom, old chum, in the early hours of this gray morning, why can't you consider Fugard's journey beyond an apartheid of the imagination? At this juncture in our history, in this country's divided psyche, we are hurting for critics who are determined to do more than gaze up at the sky for angels. We must demand that they remember with flesh and intellect, that they know in their guts what Sam means when he says, "You've hurt yourself, Master Harold."

# II.

# Poems

# Troubling the Water

As if that night
      on Fire Island
            never happened—the dune

buggy that cut
      like a scythe of moonlight
            across the sand—I see

Frank O'Hara
      with Mapplethorpe's
            book of photographs.

He whistles "Lover
      Man" beneath his breath,
            nudging that fearful

40th year into the background,
      behind those white waves
            of sand. A quick

Lunch at Moriarty's
      with someone called LeRoi,
            one of sixty best friends

in the city. He's hurting
      to weigh Melville's concept
            of evil against Henry

James. That woman begging
      a nickel has multiplied
            a hundredfold since

From *Urbanus* (1994). Reprinted in *The Best American Poetry 1995,* ed.
Richard Howard, ser. ed. David Lehman (New York: Scribners,
1995).

he last walked past the House
of Seagram. They speak
of Miles Davis

clubbed twelve times
outside Birdland by a cop,
& Frank flips through pages

of Mapplethorpe as if searching
for something to illustrate
the cop's real fear.

*A dog for the exotic—*
is this what he meant?
The word Nubian

takes me to monuments
in Upper Egypt, not
the "kiss of birds

at the end of the penis"
singing in the heart
of America. Julie Harris

merges with images of Bob Love
till *East of Eden* is
a compendium of light

& dark. Is this O'Hara's
Negritude? The phallic temple
throbs like someone

breathing on calla lilies
to open them: Leda's
room of startled mouths.

"Troubling the Water" is primarily improvisational, stimulated by some gut-level feelings from the Mapplethorpe exhibit four or five years ago in Cincinnati (I remember much heated debate about the collection of photographs). When I viewed the show, it seemed that it was the juxtaposition of the images, how the photographs were arranged and displayed, that created much of the visual tension and impact—black and white males and females in a kind of collective double-dare. The taboo and attraction had been aligned through the camera lens. But what was most provocative, for me, was the flower imagery, which suggested sexuality and invited the viewer in as an active participant. My own imagination could create the leaps and do some work. This is what I also want in my poetry: a collage/montage effect propelled by a certain fluidity. I feel that the desired effect has been accomplished with the three-line indented stanzas, a structure that invites voluminous data and various departures (inclusion). In fact, it is this same inclusion that makes much of Frank O'Hara's work so exciting; but I also wanted to address the conspicuous exoticism in some of his poems (especially about blacks). When the human body becomes mere object, this kind of voyeurism dehumanizes us. Until we fully humanize those images in our collective psyche, we are condemned to view many of the images that Mapplethorpe captures in his photographs as no more than a gelatinous sensationalism.

# Nude Study

Someone lightly brushed the penis
    alive. Belief is almost
        flesh. Wings beat,

dust trying to breathe, as if the figure
    might rise from the oils
        & flee the dead

artist's studio. For years
    this piece of work was there
        like a golden struggle

shadowing Thomas McKeller, a black
    elevator operator at the Boston
        Copley Plaza Hotel, a friend

of John Singer Sargent—hidden
    among sketches & drawings, a model
        for Apollo & a bas-relief

of Arion. So much taken
    for granted & denied, only
        grace & mutability

can complete this face belonging
    to Greek bodies castrated
        with a veil of dust

Images of black people have been caricatured worldwide, and
such a global attitude of ridicule has been accepted as almost

From *Kenyon Review* (1995). Reprinted in *The Best American Poetry 1996,* ed. Adrienne Rich, ser. ed. David Lehman (New York: Scribners, 1996).

natural. Not only is it accepted as the norm by whites (and others), but blacks have often been programmed to accept this abuse. So when I gazed upon John Singer Sargent's portrait of a black elevator operator, Thomas McKeller, the painting's grace and realism were striking. The golden-bronze had been brushed on the canvas with care. Thus, it wasn't hard for me to believe the two men had been friends, that McKeller had modeled for Sargent numerous times. What enraged me was to learn that the portrait had been unearthed in Sargent's studio after his death; it was hidden there because it embraced the true physical beauty of a black man. But what enraged me even more was to discover that McKeller's image had been cannibalized to depict Apollo and a bas-relief of Arion—other heads and hues grafted on to his classical physique. In fact, this can be viewed as a paradigm for the black man in Western culture. Hadn't this body been used to construct the economic foundation of America? Also, "Nude Study" addresses the fear associated with the myth of black male sexual prowess.

# Trueblood's Blues

They're on the edge
    of their seats, nodding
        heads up & down.

You know how the devil
    tortures the soul?
        He keeps them waiting.

Fat meat . . . Broadnax's wife
    steps out of the grandfather clock
        for the seventeenth time

& throws herself into Trueblood's arms.
    The bedroom fills with feathers
        again. He's Caliban,

savoring the punishment
    of their eyes like the last
        drops of a strong drink.

Yellowjackets blooming on the jaybird—
    this always grabs their minds. Yes,
        now, nothing can stop Zeus

in the astonishment of falling
    feathers. The dream woman's
        forbidden scent is deep

From *AGNI Magazine,* no. 40 (1995). Reprinted in *Ecstatic Occasions, Expedient Forms: 85 Leading Contemporary Poets Select and Comment on Their Poems,* ed. David Lehman (Ann Arbor: University of Michigan Press, 1996).

as his own. He craves
        the hex & lash, but his enemies
                reward his downfall with time,

cash, & plugs of tobacco.
        Norton, the philanthropist,
                meditates on his daughter

till she stands nude
        before him. He peels open a red
                Moroccan-leather wallet

& extracts a hundred-dollar bill,
        erecting his monument
                to someone "more delicate

than the wildest dream
        of a poet." Standing
                beside this sharecropper,

he pays for the look in her eyes
        before she started to fade
                in those ice-capped

Alps. But each sunrise
        the same question begs
                the wound raw again.

Trueblood is a Southern sharecropper (who impregnated his teenaged daughter one cold night when she slept between her mother and father) in Ralph Ellison's *Invisible Man*. This character is a classic storyteller and bluesy confessor and has been accepted into what we can call the Brotherhood of the Ultimate Taboo: these white Southerners, farmers and laborers, the equivalent of today's rednecks, are the "they" in the poem's first line. In essence, they have been willing to let Trueblood escape punishment for a certain crime: his attraction to Fat Meat, Broadnax's wife. In his dream she seduces him by walking nude out of the grandfather clock. She makes him betray himself. By copulating with this dream image, she has led him to violate his own flesh and blood. His other crime is that he realizes (after waking from the dream-trance) that he is having sex with his daughter—but doesn't stop until orgasm. The daughter is also guilty.

In *Invisible Man* the word *Daddy* underlines her guilt. Guilt is what also cements the relationship between Trueblood and the white men he confesses to. He has ventured to the most hostile territory to tell or retell his story. In fact, his confession is profane, which explains the name Caliban in the poem: "You taught me language," says Caliban to Prospero in *The Tempest*, "and my profit on't is I know how to curse." His confession is a scream, a cry for help, a blues he must sing to his enemies because they themselves have had similar thoughts and personal histories. The blacks are ashamed of him (especially those at the college). They want him banished and run out of town, and it seems that the whites want him to stick around as evidence for their ideas about so-called black inferiority. Trueblood knows that the white men are using him against himself: this is the agony and payment for his crime (he wanted his wife to beat him). Is incest a crime of only poor whites and rural blacks? No. When Norton, a wealthy Northerner who supports the black college, pays him to tell his incest story, we learn that this rich man has been frightened by the same terror inside himself when he speaks of his own daughter. Trueblood, a black man who has sung the old spirituals, now sings a relentless blues that he hopes can save him from himself. By using the three lines with staggered indentations, I discovered that I could incorporate information that enhances the text without undermining the poem's fluidity and music.

# Jeanne Duval's Confession

Because Charles couldn't
    dare beyond my breasts
        & berry-colored lips

saying "Madame est
    servie" in a short play,
        I never stopped seeing him

as some bouffant boy,
    with an armload of roses
        outside the stage door,

petals in Paris snow.
    Locked in his Babel
        of books, he quizzed himself

till he was nothing
    but a diseased root,
        till I was a whore

& Black Madonna,
    not a real woman
        beneath conjured cloth

& sheer lackluster.
    It wasn't my idea
        to garnish an apartment

with a blonde maid.
    I became Beatrice
        & Hamlet's mother

From *Black Warrior Review* (1996). Reprinted in *The Best American Poetry 1997*, ed. James Tate, ser. ed. David Lehman (New York: Scribners, 1997).

seduced with tropic fruit
between lion's den
& paradise. A bemused

lament, a brown body,
a good luck charm
found on Friday

the thirteenth. "Obi,
Faustus . . . ebony thighs,
child of midnights . . ."

Charles tried to work me
out of his heart & spleen,
but I'd been made into

a holy wild perfume,
a vertigo of bells in his head,
the oboe's mouth-hole

& only gold coins
could calm me down.
The most precious litany

dripped from his melancholy
quill. Even his red-haired
beggar girl possessed

my breasts. Charles
was hexed from head to toe,
but it wasn't my fault.

His mother said she
burned my letters because
I never said I loved

her son. He tried
to erase what he'd created
by mouthing Latin verses

beneath Wagner's piano.
As I leaned in an alley
on my crutches, behind

a pie shop, halfway
> to a pauper's grave, it was
>> then he seized a last breath

because I couldn't stop
> saying how much I loved
>> a man who could kill with words.

Having read Baudelaire's poems through the years, when I started thinking of his tormented muse, Jeanne Duval, she defined herself as natural subject matter. How could I not write about her, about the tension in these two lives? Their love-hate relationship became the foundation for much of Baudelaire's work, especially *Les Fleurs du mal*. His creativity makes us embrace Jeanne Duval as someone both virtuous and profane in the same breath. One can feel Baudelaire arm wrestling himself—there is a system of push and pull, moments of elation are etched out, almost like a tide, roaring in and rushing out. He worked with a canvas composed of foresight, enlightenment, and contradiction. Jeanne Duval wanders through his poems like a ghost that refuses to be subdued; one has a feeling that often she made Baudelaire drunk with words. I wanted to give emotional flesh to that ghost. I could not have written this poem in any other way because there she was speaking, through my mouth.

# Facing It

My black face fades,
hiding inside the black granite.
I said I wouldn't,
dammit: No tears.
I'm stone. I'm flesh.
My clouded reflection eyes me
like a bird of prey, the profile of night
slanted against morning. I turn
this way—I'm inside
the Vietnam Veterans Memorial
again, depending on the light
to make a difference.
I go down the 58,022 names,
half-expecting to find
my own in letters like smoke.
I touch the name Andrew Johnson;
I see the booby trap's white flash.
Names shimmer on a woman's blouse
but when she walks away
the names stay on the wall.
Brushstrokes flash, a red bird's
wings cutting across my stare.
The sky. A plane in the sky.
A white vet's image floats
closer to me, then his eyes
look through mine. I'm a window.

From *Dien Cai Dau* (Middletown, Conn.: Wesleyan University Press, 1988). Reprinted in *The Best of the Best American Poetry, 1988–1997,* ed. Harold Bloom, ser. ed. David Lehman (New York: Scribners, 1998).

He's lost his right arm
inside the stone. In the black mirror
a woman's trying to erase names:
No, she's brushing a boy's hair.

Now, as I think back to 1984, when I wrote "Facing It," with
the humidity hanging over New Orleans (a place raised by the
French out of swampy marshes) in early summer, I remember
that it seemed several lifetimes from those fiery years in Vietnam. I lived at 818 Piety Street and was in the midst of renovat-
ing the place: trekking up and down a twelve-foot ladder,
scribbling notes on a yellow pad. I had meditated on the Vietnam Veterans Memorial as if the century's blues songs had
been solidified into something monumental and concrete.
Our wailing, our ranting, our singing of spirituals and kaddish
and rock anthems, it was all captured and refined into a
shaped destiny that attempted to portray personal and public
feelings about war and human loss. It became a shrine overnight: a blackness that plays with light—a reflected motion in
the stone that balances a dance between grass and sky. Who-
ever faces the granite becomes a part of it. The reflections
move into and through each other. A dance between the dead
and the living. Even in its heft and weight, emotionally and
physically, it still seems to defy immediate description, constantly incorporating into its shape all the new reflections and
shapes brought to it: one of the poignant shrines of the twenti-
eth century.

Today I have attempted to journey from that blues moment
of retrospection that produced "Facing It" to this moment,
now, when I am a member of the advisory council for the My
Lai Peace Park Project in Vietnam. This project is also connected to the reflective power of that granite memorial in D.C.
Joined in some mysterious and abiding way, we can hope that
the two can grow into a plumb line or spirit level etched with
names and dates that suggest where we are and the distance
we have journeyed—something instructive that we can measure ourselves against.

# III.

# Interviews

# Lines of Tempered Steel

*An Interview with Vincente F. Gotera*

*Why don't we start with your background, biographical stuff, books you've written, and so on?*

Okay. I grew up in a place called Bogalusa. That's in Louisiana, about seventy miles out of New Orleans. It's a rural kind of environment, and I think a great deal of the bucolic feeling gets into my work. If not directly, then indirectly so.

I started writing in the military. It was a different kind of writing, of course—it was journalism. That was in Vietnam, between '69 and '70. I started writing poetry in '73 in Colorado, where I lived for seven and a half years—Boulder, Colorado Springs, and Fort Collins.

Actually, I had been reading poetry for many years; in fact, that's one of the things that kept me in contact with my innermost feelings when I was in Vietnam, because I took with me and would systematically go through anthologies such as Donald Allens's *New American Poetry* and Hayden Carruth's *The Voice Great within Us*. But I didn't attempt to write poetry then; I just enjoyed reading it.

*Were you writing any creative stuff at all at the time? Fiction, perhaps?*

I had started experimenting with short stories, in an attempt to emulate James Baldwin and Richard Wright, but I never really stayed with short fiction long enough to develop it in any significant way. Perhaps I'll return to that genre in the near future. I admire and love Baldwin, especially his *Go Tell It*

From *Callaloo* 13, no. 2 (1990): 215–29. Copyright © 1990 Charles H. Rowell. Reprinted by permission of the Johns Hopkins University Press.

*on the Mountain* and *Another Country*. And as an essayist, he can be meticulous and almost heartless with the truth. That is what keeps me returning to his *Nobody Knows My Name* and *The Fire Next Time*. As a matter of fact, I remember first checking out *Nobody Knows My Name* at the black library in Bogalusa that was really a bedroom-size building in the late '50s. I read that book numerous times.

Anyway, it took some time for me to actually start writing for myself. At the University of Colorado in '73, I took a workshop in creative writing, and that was my introduction, really, to imaginative writing.

In '77 I came out with a limited edition—a few poems— called *Dedications and Other Darkhorses*, published by *Rocky Mountain Creative Arts Journal,* which was edited by Paul Dilsaver. In '79 I had another limited edition, called *Lost in the Bonewheel Factory*, published by Lynx House Press.

Of course, I kept writing, and I went into the graduate program in writing at Colorado State in '76 with Bill Tremblay. Bill is certainly one of the most underrated poets in America— check out his book *Crying in the Cheap Seats.*

Well, okay, and from there I went on to the University of California at Irvine, studied with Charles Wright, C. K. Williams, Howard Moss, Robert Peters, and James McMichaels. There were also some wonderful student writers there: Garrett Hongo, Deborah Woodward, Vic Coccimiglio, Debra Thomas, and Virginia Campbell.

Then I went to the Provincetown Fine Arts Work Center— I was there in '80. That was an interesting time: a kind of semi-isolation in which I could very methodically deal with my writing. It was a close community of artists where I could get feedback; but mainly it was a place to develop one's voice, I suppose. Well, in essence, really, one's voice is already inside, but a sort of unearthing has to take place; sometimes one has to remove layers of facades and superficialities. The writer has to get down to the guts of the thing and rediscover the basic timbre of his or her existence.

*Where does your first book,* Copacetic, *fall into this process of unearthing and rediscovery?*

*Copacetic* falls into, or better yet, accumulates from many places, because it has some of my very first poems in it. The book covers a time when I had traveled around a whole lot: I lived in Panama, also Puerto Rico, Japan for a while, too. Along with all that, I had spent seven years in Colorado. *Copacetic*, however, was finished in Louisiana; I went back to Bogalusa in '81, after being away for many years. It was almost like going back to a hometown inside my head, to my own psychological territory, but in a different way, from a different perspective—hopefully a more creative, objective point of view. And also it was an opportunity to relive, to rethink some things.

Bogalusa definitely has its problems, and some of those are racial problems. At one time it was the heart of Ku Klux Klan activity, and consequently a lot of civil rights work went on. The Deacons of Defense worked in that particular area.

*And now, in Indiana, you're almost in the heart of that again. Just twenty miles down the road is a town, as you know, with the dubious fame of being the residence of a one-time Grand Dragon of the Klan.*

I realize that; I see it around me. [*Laughing.*] I can deal with it. I've learned to deal with it. Some of those things—some of the racial problems—surface in *Copacetic.*

*But a lot of* Copacetic *seems to be focused on South Africa.*

Right. There are parallels—definitely parallels. Even though we might not see those parallels on the surface, they do exist, I think. People are people, I suppose, wherever you are, and they definitely have their problems, things to work through.

And that's true for many writers—a good example would be Galway Kinnell. He worked near where I grew up, I think in the late '60s and early '70s. He was a field director for CORE [Congress of Racial Equality]. I remember some photograph—you might have seen it—on the cover of *Life* or maybe *Look:* it was Galway Kinnell with a bloody face.

*Etheridge Knight addressed a poem to Galway Kinnell.*

Okay, that makes sense. I know that the two appeared together at the Great Mother Earth Festivals with Robert Bly.

*What are you working on now?*

I'm working on some performance pieces, theater pieces. Which I've been writing since I've been here . . . able to have a distant, disembodied voice at times. You need that to work on certain kinds of monologues and soliloquies.

I'm also working on a book called *Dien Cai Dau;* these are

Vietnam-related poems. Also, a book called *Magic City*, about growing up in Louisiana: childhood experiences, observations. Trying to throw myself back into the emotional situation of the time and at the same time bring a psychological overlay that juxtaposes new experiences alongside the ones forming the old landscape inside my head. Trying to work things through, still; I suppose writers constantly do that.

*What about the book that's coming up?*

Well, it will be published in September by Wesleyan. It's called *I Apologize for the Eyes in My Head*. Actually, it's not really an apology, of course. [*Laughing.*] It's the opposite of that, in an ironic, satirical way. Once you look at the book, you'll see that I'm not really apologizing for anything.

*Have you found that living in Indiana has affected your work? Do you find that Indiana—the place itself, or the people you've met here, perhaps their speech—is that impinging at all on your work?*

No, not really. There's a sort of Southern tinge to speech here, perhaps even more than in Louisiana, particularly near New Orleans. Of course, Louisiana is a mixture of things—a mixture of people, of cultures. A different psychological terrain, an interesting place. Yet I don't know if I could really live there, especially since I'm on my way now to Australia, you know? The other side of the world . . . But, anyway, Indiana has been part of a growth process of sorts. Both in my personal life and in my writing—poetry and drama.

One effect Indiana *has* had is that I've had more time here to work on certain things. For some reason, I had been thinking certain poems, certain monologues and soliloquies, in New Orleans, but they never really got down on the page. Now I have the space, I suppose; it's not really a physical space but more of a psychological space to actually deal with certain things and put them down on paper. A space for me to go back to my early childhood. At one time, I saw all of my experiences in a negative context; that's probably true of most of us. But I see those now in more of a positive framework, and that's good for me. It's liberating, necessary for growth.

*Actually, you've had a similar effect on my work. For many years, I had been resisting certain memories, resisting my Filipino-American identity as a poetic subject. When you introduced me to Garrett Hongo's book* Yellow Light, *many things came together for me.*

It's interesting, the way Garrett is able to work those things through, you know, and I think he influenced me, especially in *Magic City,* to return to my childhood experiences and respect them for what they are.

*Let's talk about some larger, more universal issue. What's your definition of poetry? How do you go about writing it?*

My definition of poetry is, I suppose, grounded in everyday speech patterns. I really think the poem begins with a central image; it's not tied down in any way, not pre-defined. When an image, a line, develops into a poem, if it has an emotional thread running through it, when it can link two people together, reader and poet, then it's working.

I don't necessarily disagree with Wallace Stevens when he says that "a poem is a pheasant," but I think I feel closer to Coleridge's statement: "What is poetry?—is so nearly the same question with, what is a poet?—the answer to the one is involved in the solution of the other." In essence, poetry equals the spiritual and emotional dimension of the human animal.

Poetry is so difficult to define, I think, because it's constantly changing, growing. It's becoming something else in order to become itself—amorphous and cumulative until it forms a vision.

*When you say that an image or a line occurs and develops, does that mean you keep a notebook and let jottings or ideas percolate?*

I keep a mental notebook. I realize that I might write an image down that has reoccurred for four, five, or six years. And so I know where it came from. A good example is my Vietnam poems, where it's taken me about fourteen years to start getting those down. But some of the images go back to a time when I was writing more journalistic kinds of articles.

It's difficult to define what poetry is, and yet numerous people have tried to define poetry as such. I think it ties into the oral tradition for me, because I grew up with some strange characters around me. You know, storytellers and sorcerers. One of my first *Magic City* poems was about a gentleman who used to tell me ghost stories—it's about how he was able to pull me into those stories and create a kind of near-agonizing mystery. I'm definitely attracted to that.

*In much of your work, probably more so in* Lost in the Bone-wheel Factory *than in* Copacetic, *it seems to me that you strive for a tension between levels of diction. I see you yoking, for example, Latinate words with everyday ones.*

That's probably who I am. Fluctuating between this point over here and another strain over there: the things I've read come into my work, and also the things I've experienced affect my work at the same time. And both of these work side by side. I don't draw any distinctions between those two, because after all that's the totality of the individual.

It goes back to a statement by Aimé Césaire: essentially, he says that we are a composite of all our experiences—love, hatred, understanding, misunderstanding—and consequently we rise out of those things like, to use a cliché, a phoenix. We survive the baptism by fire, only to grow more complete and stronger. The way we are, perhaps today, might be entirely different tomorrow.

*It's interesting that you bring up the word cliché. In your Vietnam poems I see you doing something different from what you do in* Copacetic *and* Lost in the Bonewheel Factory. *You thread in clichés and then deflate them.*

Right, the kind of intellectual wrestling that moves and weaves us through human language.

*And that strikes me as something that's very hard to do.*

That's interesting, because, especially with soldiers, for some reason—individuals coming from so many backgrounds: the Deep South, the North, different educational levels—clichés are used many times as efforts to communicate, as bridges perhaps. And soldiers often speak in clichés—at least this is what I've found.

I've been using quotations a whole lot, as I remember them. Certain things in a poem will surface, and I can hear a certain person saying those things. And I can see his face, even when I cannot put a name to the face.

*That really rings true for me. I've been thinking about an Army poem and trying to hear those voices, you know? And I hear, "No brass, no ammo" and "Smoke 'em if you got 'em."*

Yeah, right. [*Laughing.*] Those *are* clichés, but they work in poems, mainly because there are real people connected with those words. I've been going through faces in writing these Vietnam poems, and I'm surprised at how few of the names I remember. I suppose that's all part of the forgetting process, in striving to forget particular situations that were pretty traumatic for me. Not when I was there as much as in retrospect. When you're there in such a situation, you're thinking about where the nearest safest place is to run, in case of an incoming rocket. You don't have time to even think about the moral implications.

*Does that mean that you find yourself psychologically resisting some of those memories?*

Yes, I did at one time. Now, it's more or less a process of recall. I had pushed many of those images aside, or at least attempted to. It's amazing what the mind can do; the mind does work like a computer, storing information.

And that's how poetry works as well: in *Magic City* I'm recalling images from when I was four or five years old. I've always been fascinated by certain plants, Venus's-flytraps, for example, their ability to digest insects. Of course, you know, something like that would fascinate a kid at four years old. Going back to that time . . . I was able to do that only a few years ago.

*Is poetry then some sort of need fulfillment?*

It's a way of working things out; it's a way of dealing with all the information taken in. I write every day. I'm probably writing when I'm not sitting down at the typewriter or scribbling the first draft of a poem on a pad. I think all writers probably do that.

*Yeah, I would agree. It's interesting that you talk about "working things out." Not all readers may see your poems in that light; in one review of* Copacetic, *the reviewer complains that you can tell a good story, but you're trying too hard for effects, and your poems are "too hip."*

Too hip? [*Laughing.*] I think, perhaps, he's talking about diction. And that's a similar thing: someone else accused those poems of being "too sophisticated," which is ridiculous. Going back to New Orleans as a composite of influences, the word *copacetic* for me conjures up a certain jazz-blues feeling. And many times, for the speakers in those poems, that's their psychic domain: a blues environment.

That was especially the case for me when I was in New Orleans, because there are so many layers to everything there. You have the traditional and the modern side by side; there's a xenophobia among New Orleanians, and it's all grounded in what the blues are made of. An existential melancholy based on an acute awareness. Those are some pretty hip characters, right? [*Laughing.*]

I admire that to an extent, because linked to it is a kind of psychological survival. How one deals with life: to be on this plane one moment and, the next moment, a different plane— the ability to speak to many different people. For example, I can more or less rap with my colleagues, but I have to be able as well to talk with my grandmothers, whom I'm very close to. They're not educated, and yet we can communicate some very heartfelt emotions. I'm still learning a whole lot from them.

We were talking earlier about Etheridge Knight; he, of course, belongs to a long line of poets, starting with Phillis Wheatley, the abolitionist poets Frances Harper and James Whitfield, and, later on, Paul Laurence Dunbar. Poetry for blacks, for the most part, has functioned as a "service literature." What I mean is that there has been a systematic need to define just what the essence of being black in America is about. But in a certain sense it has moved beyond that service-literature category, especially within the 1980s, where there has been more of an introspective poetry, a voyage inward, and my belief is that you have to have both: the odyssey outward as well as inward to have any kind of constructive, informative bridges to vision and expression.

*How does this double journey surface in your work?*

Basically, it's a recognition of history. It's almost like having one foot in history and the other in a progressive vision. The future as well as the past inform one another in possibility. A good example of this in action is Robert Hayden: in a work like "The Middle Passage," or an earlier poem called "The Diver," we find intense images that conjure up a journey *on* the ocean as well as *in* the ocean to a certain depth, touching the tangible as well as the unconscious in various symbolic ways.

*How have you been influenced by other black poets?*

Melvin Tolson is one poet who achieves much through language: he brings together the street as well as the highly literary into a single poetic context in ways where the two don't even seem to exhibit a division—it's all one and the same. Langston Hughes is another important poet because he celebrates the common folk—the true strength of black America—and his work clearly rises out of a folk tradition. Another poet who comes to mind is Sterling Brown, again a poet who celebrates the blues tradition. One of the most important voices is Gwendolyn Brooks, mainly because of her concern for language, forms, and content—all three of these come together to create a unique poetic synthesis.

Other contemporaries of Hughes also come to mind: Countee Cullen and Claude McKay, especially the poem "If We Must Die"—which is a challenge more than anything else. McKay also has a number of protest sonnets that display so much strength and control at the same time. Of course, we are again in the period of "service literature." During the same period as Cullen and McKay, Helene Johnson was also an important poet—there are a number of women, in fact, who are not often acknowledged as writers of the Harlem Renaissance, although they were an intricate, important part of the era.

After the Harlem Renaissance, of course, comes the time in which we see women as vivid presences: Margaret Walker and Gwendolyn Brooks. A later important poet is Nikki Giovanni, whose work arises out of the '60s and is really grounded in the oral tradition. Her poems are quite effective, but, let's face it, she is a popular poet. And we may wonder how popular poets will endure in terms of literary history. Gwendolyn Brooks is clearly an example of a poet whose reputation will continue to endure. And there are other significant black voices—I've already mentioned Etheridge Knight—also we have Ishmael Reed, Amiri Baraka, Michael Harper, Sonia Sanchez, June Jordan, Alice Walker, Rita Dove, Colleen McElroy, Quincy Troupe, Lucille Clifton, and many others.

*Etheridge Knight has clearly been influenced by the blues, in the same way that a poet like Michael Harper or Sonia Sanchez has been influenced by jazz. Do you find that the rhythms of blues and jazz influence your work?*

Yes, yes. I think we internalize a kind of life rhythm. The

music I was listening to when I was seven or eight years old and the music I listen to today are not that different. Because I listen mainly to jazz and blues, and some of the same artists are still around: B. B. King, Ray Charles, Nina Simone, Bobby Blue Bland, Aretha, and so on.

*Does teaching poetry as opposed to writing poetry involve that sort of resolution for you? What do you consciously try to do when you teach poetry?*

I like to listen to what different people are doing. I try to point out a poet's strongest points. Some may produce a baroque kind of poetry, while others may produce a "down-home" sort. Usually I can detect what the poet is trying to do and when that individual succeeds or when he or she falls short. What one has to do is look at the poem in its overall context, to see when the diction strays, when it's off the mark. The poem has to be believable.

What I look for is conciseness of language. Yet one can probably relate a given scene in a hundred different ways, and to an extent those hundred ways might work. I like to have an open-endedness in a class situation and yet still have a structure there. That's the space where people can grow; that's where I found myself growing. A relaxed kind of space.

*When you revise your own work, do you go about it in the way I see you approaching poems in a workshop: cutting words, superfluous language?*

That's what I do, yes. For the most part, I cut. I believe that we all over-write. As a matter of fact, in my own work, I find that I will go back to poems as they were originally typed, with fewer linear connections. I might have ten versions of a poem, and midway through the fifth version may work better than the ninth or tenth.

Some poems I write off the top of my head, and I realize I don't really have to revise those poems that much. But the writing of them has been a continuous process inside my head. I can pretty well see the poem in lines, and I can go back to it day in and day out, without putting it on paper. Usually, I'm working on five or six such poems at once.

*That brings up a question I've had about the way you break up your lines. When I have heard you read, it has seemed to me that the spoken chunks are quite different from the lines on the page.*

Many times that's the case, yes. I find myself doing that. For the simple reason that, when I first write a poem, I will confine it to its initial line breaks, but when I'm reading, I read basically according to how I'm feeling.

*Some people view the line break as a clue to the reader about how to read a poem aloud. Does what you say mean that for you lineation doesn't have that purpose?*

That can be bent. It's got to be flexible. I might have more of an improvisational feeling about me on a particular night. When I'm reading, I'm not always looking at the page, but I remember the words.

*Even if you read the lines as markedly different from the way they might have been published, do the line breaks nevertheless remain for you as entities in themselves?*

Yes, they still exist. I probably couldn't go back and change a line break on paper. That's definitely the line break for me, that's the way the end word falls, and there's no possibility I could break it any other way. There's a completeness about a line, a completeness and yet a continuation. It's the whole thing of enjambment, what I like to call "extended possibilities." The line grows. It's not a linguistic labyrinth; it's in logical segments, and yet it grows. It's the whole process of becoming; that's how we are as humans. There's a kind of fluid life about us, and that's how poetry should be. Say you're down to line 3—sometimes, I will cut a line. I would like to write poems that are just single lines. That is, a continuing line that doesn't run out of space because of the margin. I would like to write poems like that.

*In some ways, a prose poem may be described in that way. Do you see the prose poem as a different creature?*

Yeah. Incidentally, I was looking at Michael Benedikt's anthology of prose poems from years ago, and I was really surprised not to find Jean Toomer, especially excerpts from *Cane*. Essentially, it's a novel composed of prose poems. The chapter "Karintha" is a very beautiful compassionate prose poem.

But, yeah, the prose poem is different. What I mean by a continuing line is . . . well, it's the same way that García Marquez can write a thirty-five-page sentence, linking things without having strict categories. Where feeling becomes the connective. I see things as blending into each other, as a painter would do, blending colors to make a single emotional landscape. A kind of spatial elasticity. Lines should be able to work that way.

*Okay. You don't mean linearity as such, not just a string of words that extends only horizontally. But that there are vertical relations happening as well.*

Right.

*Samuel R. Delaney suggests in his criticism on science fiction that each word as you add words, affects all the other words, so that even he contends that the beginning* the *in a sentence is already a picture, and for Delaney that's something like a gray ellipsoid about a yard off the ground, if I'm remembering this correctly. And that an* a *or an* may *be pink. And then of course the first content word affects the overall picture in its own way. So there's a cloud of meaning, a valence, around each word that affects each other word, including spaces, or, in poetry, line breaks.*

Okay, yeah. Definitely. Language is color. All the tinges and strokes equal the whole picture; it is what converges within the frame of reference. The same as music and silence. And one doesn't need psychotropic drugs to see and feel the intensity of expression. After all, language is what can liberate or imprison the human psyche. Yes, all the parts are important; in that sense, language is like an organism. It's interesting what Delaney says about *the* and *a*, because I tend often to leave out articles. I feel that they're excessive baggage for the image and the line. Creeley and Ginsberg use a similar approach.

*Speaking of other poets, what would you say the state of poetry is in America, by any definition? Where do you see poetry going? And where do you think it should go?*

I've been kicking around the phrase *neo-fugitives* inside my head. What I mean by it is that there tends to be a fugitive sentiment that can be compared to John Crowe Ransom and Allen Tate. The creed states that basically the poet shouldn't get social or political. That he or she would do better to stick with the impressionistic and ethereal to the extent that true feeling evaporates off the page. That's much safer, and too often it insures a poet's empty endurance and superficial reverence in the literary world.

There's a sameness about American poetry that I don't think represents the whole people. It represents a poetry of the moment, a poetry of evasion, and I have problems with this. I believe poetry has always been political, long before poets had to deal with the page and white space . . . it's natural. Probably before Socrates, in Plato's *Republic,* banished poets from his ideal state—long before South Africa, Chile, Mississippi, and Marcos in the Philippines suppressing Mila Aguilar and others. There seems to be always some human landscape that creates a Paul Celan. Too many contemporary American poets would love to dismiss this fact. Of course, there are exceptions to the rule: Michael Harper, June Jordan, Forche, Rich, C. K. Williams, and Baraka. But still, if you were to take many magazines and cut the names off poems, you would have a single collection that could be by any given poet; you could put one name on it, as if the poems were all by one person. True, a writer can say almost anything in America and have it completely overlooked, yet I think we should have more individual voices.

*Would you say that this situation—a milieu that fosters a "poetry of the moment" or, we might further coin, a "poetry of fashion"—is attributable to the writing workshop system that's developed in academe, the MFA industry?*

That brings up another point: for the first time, there is also a rather healthy community of readers and poets. There are probably more poets writing today than [*laughing*] . . . there are more poets writing than reading. We can look at the amount of books written and the number that are sold, for example, and see that.

Anyway, on one hand the poetry community is healthy, and on the other hand it is unhealthy. There are very few individualistic voices. We tend to emulate each other and also imitate success. You might have someone writing in a unique voice, and, before you know it, you have twenty, thirty, or forty clones. I think we are so easily influenced without realizing we have a unique voice that we can improve, each of us. That is, if we're willing to take risks and reach deep enough into ourselves and touch the true passion. Yes, there's a vacuum that our waste economy has created that reaches into the arts . . . a cultural hedonism that touches everything.

What workshops do many times is they will attempt to undermine that which is different. Consequently, there's a kind of threat: if it's different, people ask "do I really understand that?" or "shouldn't I have some kind of objection?" There's often censorship against so-called taboo or inviolable topics and uniqueness, creating a kind of taciturnity.

*Do you think this fosters a kind of "missionary" mind-set? That there's a "correct" way to write poetry?*

Correct, yes. But without realizing that what is considered wrong today is often right tomorrow. That's happened to certain writers. Ginsberg is a good example; in the '50s, the literary world said no to him, and now it's "Ginsberg, yeah, we know exactly what you were doing, and we agree with it." It probably has something to do with endurance and tenacity as well. If the risk taker and innovator survives, he is then accepted in the academic realm.

*Who would you classify these days as having that sort of individualistic voice you're talking about?*

I admire all of Alan Dugan's work. Also Michael Harper. I think C. K. Williams is another. If you look at Williams's work, in his recent books *With Ignorance* and *Tar,* he has long lines. His images and phrases are strung together with commas. He was doing something like that in his earlier two books, *Lies* and *I Am Bitter Name:* short lines with slash marks. A continuous voice.

Who else? Ai has a unique voice. A sense of hard reality. At times, however, I wonder if it has really been earned. I don't know how long she can carry on that kind of voice. Let's see. There's something different in Denis Johnson: a straightforwardness in some of his work. I think Garrett Hongo is different; he's able to weave things together in a unique way, and his sense of history is almost flawless. There are also a number of high-energy poets I like a lot: Jayne Cortez, Larry Neal, Wanda Coleman, Sherley Anne Williams, Anne Waldman, Dionisio Martinez, the Japanese poet Kazuko Shiraishi, and others.

*What about the place of rhyme, meter, form? There's clearly more and more of a movement toward that kind of formality.*

There's one poet who does that quite well, I think, and that's Marilyn Hacker. It's not obvious that she's using rhyme because she does it in such an offhanded, very effective way. You don't know you're reading a sonnet or a villanelle even if she puts *villanelle* or *sonnet* in the title. And I admire that in her work. I also love her political breadth and depth in formalized structures. She has some of the same surprises and playfulness as Brooks and Roethke, especially in her earlier works.

As a matter of fact, there's a book that I've been slowly working on called *Black Orpheus and Other Love Poems*. This book is made up of poems with traditional structures, and it's something that's going to take me a long time to write, partly because of the forms dictating the tone indirectly. I think form does that, and a poem does not really fly off the page like it's supposed to . . . it doesn't stay with the reader.

*What you say about inherited form not staying with the reader, at least in a contemporary context, reminds me of Hayden Carruth's* Asphalt Georgics. *In that book he's taken enjambment to even further lengths. He achieves his rhymes by hyphenation—quite a tour de force. But it's the other direction from Hacker, where you think of her rhymes as being natural and subtle, instead, Carruth's rhymes are broken . . .*

Automatically drawing attention . . .

*It's like Hopkins taken to the furthest extreme. But it* is *technically interesting, perhaps even significant.*

Carruth has done so much—he's really prolific. I think he started with a formalized structure. I also like what he's done with jazz and blues. I've been working on an anthology off and on for a number of years now—a jazz poetry anthology. You'd be surprised at the number of poets who have been influenced by jazz. There are some wonderful poems by Hayden Carruth on jazz musicians—and, of course, there are some important poems by William Matthews, Al Young, lots of people.

I'm interested in all the things a poet can do in a single poem. Tolson comes to mind; if you look at his book *Harlem Gallery*, you'd be surprised at what he can accomplish. I partly agree with Allen Tate's statement that "Tolson out-Pounds Pound." If you want to really see things coming together from so many places and points of view without clashing, look at Tolson.

*Well, speaking of Pound, what about experimentation today in American poetry? You mentioned Robert Peters as one of your teachers, and I'm reminded of his books on single people, like* Kane *and* Hawker.

Robert Peters is very prolific and inventive. He has an amazing talent, which, I think, is often underestimated. I admire especially "Gauguin's Chair" and what he did with the Shakers. Which I understand is an impromptu rendering, where he's actually taken over by voices and things of that sort. I admire that capacity, especially since he's trained as a Victorian scholar, and yet he's able to go on these voyages and imaginative tours de force, using different voices.

What's happening in experimentation . . . Well, the language poets like Michael Palmer and Ron Silliman and others on the West Coast, mainly San Francisco, and of course the people associated with Colorado's Naropa Institute, the Jack Kerouac School of Disembodied Poetics. I think Anne Waldman and Laurie Anderson and Tom Waits are others . . . And yet there is a resistance in the academic community when you bring up these names. Perhaps that resistance is what we should look at: why? I've been asking myself that question.

*I recently read an article written by a photographer that addresses the issue of conflict of interest in the world of art—how any single person may be asked simultaneously to be artist, critic, curator, collector, and so on. One wonders how that affects the objectivity and ethics of the artist.*

Yes, the artist can be easily forced into the position of demigod . . . catering to a number of factors that have little to do with artistic merit and talent . . . controlled by others and divided against himself or herself. That can take the passion and need out of the artist, who can become Faust overnight. Yet I would like to believe that such multifarious persons often meet the challenge in maintaining objectivity and ethics, but I know that too often that isn't the case. What we lose is art, and what we get is only a ghost of possibility.

In rejecting Walter Benjamin's stern analysis and contempt for Baudelaire, Ernest Fischer says this: "For the vulgar hypocrite and anaemic aesthete, beauty is an escape from reality, a cloying holy picture, a cheap sedative: but beauty which arises out of Baudelaire's poetry . . . is like the angel of wrath holding the flaming sword. Its eye strips and condemns a world in which the ugly, the banal, the inhuman triumphant. Dressed-up poverty, hidden disease, and secret vice lie revealed before its radiant nakedness. It is as though capitalist civilization had been brought before a kind of revolutionary tribunal: beauty holds judgment and pronounces its verdict in lines of tempered steel."[1]

NOTE

1. *The Necessity of Art,* trans. Anna Bostock (1959; rpt., Harmondsworth, U.K.: Penguin, 1963), 68–69.

# An Interview with Muna Asali

*Dien Cai Dau seems consciously focused upon the experience of a single, black soldier and not the experiences of black soldiers as a group in Vietnam. Other than the obvious decision to begin with one's own experiences, how do you achieve this careful balance of self and community in a literary atmosphere that tries to classify individuals? How do you attempt to keep yourself from being ghettoized?*

I think the idea of ghettoization is imposed upon certain people, and that it is a pigeonhole the artist attempts to traverse by all means. But we cannot crawl out of our skin, even when we try to lie to ourselves or say that race doesn't matter, that art and artists are color-blind, which is no more than an empty, delinquent illusion. This illusion has nothing to do with art or artists, though many of us would love to turn history on its nose and erase hundreds of years of cultural and social oppression.

*What about that soldier in your book?*

That elusive black soldier? I don't know, but perhaps he isn't different from all those other black faces half-hidden in history. Hardly any different from Simon Congo or Big Manuel brought from the Dutch West India Company to Colonial Manhattan. He is maybe a descendant of someone who fell in the shadow of Estevan, Crispus Attucks, York, Du Sable, or Stagecoach Mary. A distant relative of a Buffalo Soldier or member of the 761ST, which liberated Buchenwald and Dachau. He's just one black face connected to a parade of others who have risked their lives for this enigma we call America. This black soldier in Vietnam, however, seems rather uncomfortable with his role. Maybe the agent of freewill lurks like a specter in his psyche. Or perhaps he feels guilty, because he

From *New England Review* 16, no. 1 (winter 1994).

has a sense of history and he knows that he's merely a cog in the whole contradictory machinery some might call democracy or even manifest destiny. Maybe he has singled out himself because he feels responsible. After all, we are condemned to carry the weight of our own hearts. Indeed, this soldier seems limboed in a kind of existential loneliness.

In fact, I realized about a year after I completed *Dien Cai Dau* that I had been very lonely in Vietnam. I was even lonely in a crowd, and spent most of my time trying to make sense out of the whole damn thing. I was very conscious of what I was doing and what was happening to me. Though we were responsible collectively, we were also responsible as individuals. I had to write *Dien Cai Dau* as a witness. And I couldn't escape the prison of my skin, which has also been the source of my strength.

*You mentioned the idea of being a "witness," and I'm thinking of the violence that permeates many of your poems. Although you mention your own anger a number of times, it is rarely the "I" of* Dien Cai Dau *or* Magic City *who is the violent one. More often, he is the witness to or even the survivor of violence, and this somehow informs his identity. I was wondering about the connection between violence and spirituality.*

Growing up in a rural environment, one is very close to violence. Violence is accepted as a natural process, woven into everything, in every way possible. Within the context of a rural environment, there are different levels of violence, and we are able to view, in its natural stance, a praying mantis . . .

*Or a Venus's flytrap.*

Human violence is different from that of a predator. We have the capacity to say yes or no. Conscience and freewill. The capacity to reason. Of course, this is shaped by one's environment. But in most cases, except the most severe, even the psychopath knows right from wrong. We also have the capacity to lie to ourselves, attempting to escape censure or guilt. Human violence has a lot to do with power, or the lack of it. And, of course, we admire power in this country. Who are our folk heroes? Too many of us envy Rambo and the gunslinger. Perhaps mass murderers in the back of their minds know that we have the warped capacity to worship killers—so they attempt to kill their way into the collective psyche of

America. They want to be important, to be a part of the national mythology. Respected. Exalted. This might be the clue to why mass murderers in this country are mostly white males. An instant symbolic power. Ego. A violence wielded by those who think that power is their God-given right. Their inheritance. This is perverted thinking, yet such thoughts are handed down—almost to the extent that one might wonder if they are not woven into the evolutionary process whereby nature itself has been perverted and corrupted.

Of course, all this has a lot to do with classic fears also. Fear consumes the national spirit. It's deadly. For the most part, this is often what wars are about. One sees that violence is always there and begins to incorporate it into his or her imagination.

For me, when I went to Vietnam, I did not fear the land. I realized a kind of beauty in the overall landscape. And many times that is what we have, beauty and violence side by side. We have been taught to see that as a contradiction, but, to me, contradiction is a sort of discourse. You have this push and pull in everything. It's underneath everything. That's what nature is about. And that is what creative energy is about. That's what the chemistry of the mind is about as well.

*And it also seems to transform our way of perceiving images. I'm thinking of "Initials on Aspens," where the speaker's perception of words carved into a tree is transformed into a vision of the branding of slaves.*

Yeah, it's the way the mind plays tricks on you, but it's a wonderful trick, especially for the audience, because they realize images are more than their static component. There's an emotional and psychological association. And coming to terms with dreams is important. We cannot be afraid to dream. The horror is there beneath the imagination—depending on what we bring to those images. Our sense of history.

*"Mismatched Shoes" begins with a dream image, moves on to a compressed genealogy, and ends up at a sort of redemption or return to origin, the "mismatched shoes" of the "I" in the poem, an American identity and an African one. What is the significance of that return for you beyond taking the name Komunyakaa?*

There's a need to take that voyage. In order to make oneself whole there has to be this journey back so the future can exist, because the past and the future are all part of the same man. I had to go back and accept my history in order to take steps forward.

*Well, actually, my other question was about the mismatched shoes of the title. They are the grandfather's shoes, one a man's and the other a woman's. That image of someone who has a foot in both worlds . . .*

A boy and girl!

*Yes, a boy and girl . . .*

My mother related this story to me about fifteen years ago. When my great-grandmother slipped into this country from the West Indies, with my grandfather and his brother and sister, she was too poor to afford proper shoes for her young son. I never met my grandfather, but the image of those mismatched shoes guided me to the poem. It became a cosmology of the past, the future, and the present when I wrote the poem; it created a bridge between me and my grandfather. I grew up with a big, oval-shaped photograph of my maternal grandparents, side by side, as if they were deeply in love, staring from the wall at the foot of my grandmother's bed. I was awestruck by this icon. I never asked questions about my grandfather. He was always out there somewhere—ethereal and intangible, and beyond my grasp. He was dead. Beyond me and my imagination. The poem helped me to know him in some unspoken way. He wasn't any longer revered to the extent that he was less than a name in my mouth; now he was a dead man I could love. Someone I could pose questions to, though I answered them myself. Finally, he was an affirmation of my heritage and all its ambiguity.

*I see, but because the image is of a man's shoe and a woman's shoe, does the issue of gender enter into it?*

No, not exactly. It's more of an empathy for the other, and that empathy is what makes us complete. Sometimes, there is a merger of the opposites that can save us from ourselves. To me, the image has a spiritual dimension, but this wasn't true in the beginning. Gender dominated the picture: why was he wearing a girl's shoe, and why did this detail magnify and become so important in his personal history? I had met his mother, my great-grandmother, once, when I was about three or four, but I visualized those mismatched shoes clearer than I remembered her face. They seemed so mysterious, and yet the reason had been so simple. It says so much about their

79

lives. In fact, often when I see photographs of those lopsided boats filled with Haitians, I think of those mismatched shoes on my grandfather's feet.

*In* Copacetic *there are a number of poems about South Africa and blues music, and, with the exception of the speaker in "Family Tree," there isn't much in the way of an "I." Was it necessary for you to provide a sort of context for yourself before you ventured into the realm of personal recollections from childhood in* Magic City?

That first "I" is a celebration of others. It's an "I" that's filled with tribute. I think what's happening is that the initial "I" is trying to negotiate something within himself. He's trying to find out who he really is because he's linked to all these other people. He cannot stand apart from them. He has to recognize their existence, and in doing so they become his foundation.

*Does this imply that this "I" is able to come into his own as a result of this recognition?*

He's establishing a sense of history. That earlier "I" is trying to grow into the speaker's skin. He's trying to build a bridge to his future—edging toward the person he's willing to become or negotiate.

*This issue of growing into one's skin seems related to the Vietnam poems in which you speak of Asian soldiers' attempts to convince black soldiers that they are fighting a war for white men. What about the issue of doubting the value of one's actions?*

I think those doubts are there in the poems, but at the same time the need to create stability is weighing itself against those doubts. In the moment one cannot stop and think about the action being taken, because taking that break could mean that one will not survive. It took me fourteen years to actually excavate that whole terrain, to explore the involvement of the speaker, because perhaps beneath it all there is a cryptic guilt. Guilt. If you have time to think about what you are about to do, you may not do it, but also you may not live to talk about it. There's a weighing of all this, a battle within the psyche.

*Is this the battle the lone soldier fights in "The One-Legged Stool"?*

Yes, and in a way that poem is a diagram for the rest of the book. He's imprisoned within a paradox. His body is imprisoned in a cell but also in itself as well.

*You've mentioned the loneliness of war, of life, but in* Dien Cai

Dau *you also talk about the people who were not in Vietnam whose images were brought there to help those who were there. For instance, in "Combat Pay for Jody" the speaker brings his lover's picture to the war in order to get through the experience, but when he returns he realizes that it was only her* image *that was there.*

Right. The strange debts that we owe others. But not only that, the strange debts we owe ourselves, our imagination.

*Because it is really he who sustains himself.*

Yes, not by a thought-out, systematic plan. It just happens that way. Life is a process of growing into oneself. An external journey that parallels that journey within, and each mirrors the other to try and make itself whole. The drama of that poem was a daydream solid enough to rest my head against. A phantom lifeline that kept me breathing and fighting to stay alive. At the time it was happening I couldn't realize I was walking across a false floor because, if I had, I would have fallen into an abyss. But poetry helped me to articulate the anguish. It surprised me. In that sense, we can't map out the journey because our lives become the map. And what we see isn't always beautiful. In my poetry I desire surprises. Of course, those surprises can hurt. Good and bad—that's what I think life happens to be about.

*So, was the ending of that poem a surprise to you?*

In a certain sense. Not that it's a resolution, but it told me that I had reached the end of the poem. I couldn't go any further.

*You mentioned earlier that you had not been afraid of the land when you were in Vietnam, and you also talked about the very frightening possibility that your own thoughtlessness or thoughtfulness could be lethal. How was the terrain capable of feeding you spiritually and working against your internal conflict?*

Well, essentially I did not see the land itself as a threat. There was a beauty that I could accept in the same way I accepted the raw beauty of the land on which I grew up. Maybe this familiarity was something I imposed on Vietnam in order to survive. In a certain way, Vietnam connected me to the place and people I had come from. Of course, I only realized this in retrospect. I could identify with the peasants and their rituals.

*In light of the ideas of making connections after the fact and of growing into one's skin, "In Praise of Dark Places" seems to be an effort to create your own metaphors for the significance of darkness as a person whose identity is called into question by the standard connotations of darkness.*

That's where life accumulates its energy, its essence—out of darkness. That's probably where all life comes from. For some reason, built into the Western psyche is this great fear of darkness, of the unknown. Darkness is negative. In the dictionary most words that begin with *black* have connotations of death. So, for myself, I've been forced to turn around the definitions that we accept, to reverse them and turn them back on themselves, and also to turn language back on itself. I think we have to be responsible even for those connotations buried within the context of the language. We have to be very aware that each word has a social history.

*You combine a number of levels of diction in your work. How did you come to develop your voice and have confidence?*

I began to listen to the music of the language around me as I began to listen to the music of the language I was reading. There was a difference, but I felt one could join those two together to create a more exciting diction.

*Does this connect with your idea about the tension of opposites?*

Yes, and through music and this tension one can create new ideas, new continuity.

*Does this mean that for you continuity is wholly created?*

I suppose that my first exposure to poetry came in the form of the blues. And it was not so much about the story but that even if you were very far removed from the voice you could still pick up the music without understanding it. It made me realize that there was chemistry at work in the music that allowed these people to be who they were in relation to the land, to possibility, to dreams. I suppose what I'm talking about is creative energy. And I was able to listen. Nobody told me that I should be listening. It wasn't a planned thing, but many times I would find myself listening to things while there was great activity around me. I would key in to certain things. I think we are influenced by how we listen more than what we listen to. Do we listen with our heads, or do we listen with our whole bodies? I would like to believe that ultimately I listen with my whole body.

*How is the way we learn to listen related to the way we learn to read?*

For me it is in the discovery that each word leads to other words and images. Each word is important on its own but it is also given meaning by the word before it and the word after it. That same idea of connection and continuity. For instance, one of the first human activities was to name tools we used, and that made a connection between the hand and the brain. We are able to make great leaps through language, and these leaps might yield private aspects of language, each person's familiarity with the language and personal metaphors. And this allows me to transform darkness at least for myself, but also in an attempt to penetrate someone else's language.

*You have a number of Australia poems, and while you have mentioned a recognition, albeit in retrospect, of Vietnam's landscape, I am wondering what you recognized about Australia.*

Australia was initially very difficult for me to deal with. In many ways it is similar to the United States. Of course, I began comparing the experience of the Native American and the black Australian—down to the distribution of smallpox blankets. I am amazed by how the two groups of indigenous people feel that the land has been entrusted to them, and that each one is a part of the natural landscape. I've traveled to Australia four times, beginning with a yearlong stay in 1986. But only this year was I able to really connect to the place, because I went there without expectations. Also, in the past few years it seems that there's more of a multiculturalism there. Maybe the young Australians are attempting to remove the blemish of the "White Australia Policy." When many Americans think of Australia they think, "Oh yeah, England." Anglophilia kicks in. Or they are only familiar with the place through Bruce Chatwin's novelistic misrepresentation. Seldom do they know the works of black Australian writers and poets such as Colin Johnson, Kath Walker, Jack Davis, Kevin Gilbert, etc. These voices bring us closer to the land and its people. There is an elusive spiritual dimension. There are also complexities and contradictions. Surprises. I remember hearing a pure-blooded Aboriginal singing Leadbelly in Kings Cross. He knew it exactly. I think he could interpret the feelings. Maybe that was the moment I realized I wanted to connect to these people. Because this young man had connected in such an important and visceral way, I wanted to complete the connection. I need to understand the landscape. I began looking closer at the hills and valleys, birds and animals, at clues wherever I could find them, and it was then I realized the poetic significance of the people and their totemic gods. The taboos and rites. I think I am coming closer to understanding how forty thousand years have woven the people into the landscape. Why this is sacred. Why there's so much pain and laughter in the faces of these people. I just want to learn more. Ironically, it has been my connection with black Australians that has made me realize the deep and complex relationship of Native Americans and blacks in this country. Down Under has helped to bring me to names such as Pio Pico, Edmonia Lewis, Kitty Cloud Taylor, Diana Fletcher, and Seminole chief John Horse, and so forth. Thus, my personal landscape—psychologically and spiritually—is evolving into a more panoramic one. I feel like I am still growing. Of course, that's all one can hope for.

# Hotbeds and Crossing over
# Poetic Traditions

*An Interview with Kristin Naca*

*Let's start off talking about process. Recently, there have been collec-tions of essays available on poets writing about their process.*

Essentially, my process involves writing everything down. When I work on a poem, there's virtually, I should say, a number of brainstorms. Then there comes the organizing— what lines create certain connotations, or become the basis for another line. So it really becomes a sort of juggling act. It seldom comes out whole, complete as a poem. I write every-thing down and then I cut back. Furthermore, I'm able to extract words, phrases, lines, even whole stanzas, that seem rather extraneous—so I'm able to strike those. But I do think process is greatly affected by reading, for me that is. If I'm reading history, an article on science from *Scientific American,* some kind of historical or scientific information might end up in the poem—so that's all part of the process as well. Finally, what I'm trying to get at is a layering, so that everything has a full quality. The layering influences the tone, the rhythm. I think about the rhythm. Richard Hugo talks about the neces-sity for writing with long and short lines—influenced by Swing music. He's stated that he's able to bring Swing into his process. So I'm thinking about how the poems actually sound, and this goes back to the "oral" tradition. I come out of a tradition where people tell stories. But I'm not really reaching for a linear narrative. I prefer the lyrical narrative where there are certain leaps in the poems. So the process focuses on really drawing them out.

*When I think about the leaps that happen in say "Venus's Fly-traps," in the narrative, where you're practically looking through the boy's eyes, walking through the field, and the images collapse or they leap onto you, is this what you mean: the images becoming very magical, very surreal?*

When we think of magical realism, we usually think of South American writers. But then it's also important to note that the South American writers are somewhat Faulknerian, and of course Faulkner was shaped by the cultural and social landscape—that marriage of beauty and terror side by side, especially with that tepid "dialect." There's danger and terror. So I grew up realizing that beauty is connected to terror, that it can really turn against one—life itself. It's something I learned through observation, though of course I didn't realize it at the time when I was living it—not until about twelve years ago.

*So when you were studying as a young man in that place, in Louisiana, you were influenced, maybe, by Southern texts, but their value has or does increase as you are able to go outside and read South American works and then come back to that idea of magical realism in your own place?*

Yes. I don't know why, but there comes a time of psychic closures because there's this great boom, and everything flies back together—except there's the first moment of intense disorientation when one realizes, "this is what I came out of," and then all of a sudden—"this is something I should know."

*It's also hard for people to recognize and accept this. And there's a great power in accepting one's culture, even when it means coming back to the elements of being from the South, its roots in the Faulknerian.*

Yes, it is continuously, because everything around one is attached. There are clear moments, that we accept with certain details, a reality, and we realize there are other realities attached to this one.

*So have your processes been different when you're writing from a loosely autobiographical perspective, striving toward the lyrical narrative, like in* Magic City *or* Dien Cai Dau?

It isn't. It still entails writing everything down and trying to make some sense out of the narrative. Everything isn't—I think, in a certain sense—conceived as a strict narrative structure. There's an internalized phonology, and it's sort of put down that way. And yet one has to realize that certain things are extraneous to the story and that they pretty much take energy away because their contexts affect the whole chemistry of the piece. The poem is a kind of organism that grows, it has natural phrases of maturation.

*So you're saying, the poem cuts off pieces of itself until it becomes whole?*

Yes.

*On the back cover of* Magic City *the word* autobiographical *appears.* Autobiographical *is such a strange word; it appears in so many different ways and is used perhaps to catch the attention of or get more people interested in reading a book. What's your idea of an autobiographical poem?*

I suppose for me it's a poem that comes together, fusing a number of facts—in this way it is autobiography, though it is constantly changing. I asked my brothers about moments we experienced, and often they see them entirely differently than I do. So autobiography is also filled through with a number of hallways, like places on a map—sometimes there's a kind of clarity; rights, wrongs—that make themselves known, other times there's a more blurred reality.

*In some essays on process I've read, authors might refer to the word* truth. *Maybe your truths are musical truths, imagistic truths, things that attach themselves to each other for a reason? And so when I look at* Magic City, *I don't necessarily say, "Oh that happened" or "This guy's got twenty different people running through his head."*

Well, autobiography becomes a kind of beaded necklace of possibilities. There's evidence for that as well. Sometimes I have an idea that this is the poem I want to write, but if the poem turns into something else, it turns into something else. Say, if I might have written twenty lines and I get to the twenty-first line, and that twenty-first line becomes a line that should be a different poem altogether, though it's loosely connected to the cadence of the first twenty lines—I might go with this new direction—without taking away from the emotional makeup of the poem.

*When editing, then, you're not too attached to the emotional weight of say single lines?*

Sometimes one can put the line in a box and try to get some distance from it, so that, when editing, one can be vicious.

*So then as an editor, it's a different process, a different stage. Does this play over into when you're looking at other people's poems?*

In workshop, let's just say, I don't want to see everyone

writing the same poem. I like the fact that there are different voices, styles, subject matter. At first, it seems oppositional, but then we realize they're not really oppositional to each other—that they are informing each other as well. Often, I wish I could do that in a poem or in a book where one has numerous styles. That would probably be the most ideal for me. And yet I realize that there is a tone in books, they have an almost seamless quality. But, I think, the real challenge for me would be to write a book that contains a number of styles or aesthetics with each influencing the other.

*Almost what* Neon Vernacular *is, but, instead, the book wouldn't take its work from different books, because you can see how the poems in* Neon Vernacular, *their styles, are so organically connected to each other within each section. So when you're writing poems, or say organizing a book of poems, do the poems that "don't fit in" not make it into the book?*

Many of them. When I think about it, a lot of those poems, well those poems that are actually finished, I try to hold onto. But there are some, there are hundreds of poems really, that don't arouse me any longer, and so I can abandon them. But then there are others that I keep coming back to that I'm *never* going to finish—some poems I've been working on for ten years, and there's something about them that keeps me curious, because it's not happening.

*Maybe if you put the poem down for ten years and then come back to it?*

Well, it's just an obsession really. An obsession and a determination to make it work. But at the same time, there's a certain invincible distance to them.

*Recently you've had eight poems in* American Poetry Review. *And these are poems that are historical/literary moments—very different than say your "autobiographical" poems, though they contain the same deep and heavy voice that guides the reader through the moment. Could you say something about these poems?*

There's a book I've been working on, *Remembrance of Things to Come*, it's a three-part book; maybe it's really a trilogy contained under a single title. I realized that there are so many historical facts I seem to be aware of, some things I've been reading through the years, and other people are not made aware of these facts or exposed to these points of view. For example, for years I've been reading "A Rose for Emily," and one thing that's interesting to me is that the character Tobe doesn't have a voice—it seems as if it were impossible for Faulkner to give him a voice. Maybe silence is a voice. Maybe that act of walking out at the end of the story, going into the woods, can be the only act of defiance. For me, I've always heard a verbal voice for that character. The first time I thought about it, I had my students write a monologue in Tobe's voice, with what he would have said, living and coming to that house as a servant, as a cook, as an individual, shocked—what would he have said. So finally, I got around to writing a poem called "Tobe's Blues," a poem from Tobe's point of view.

Or I might have a fact in my head and I improvise on it. For example, when we think about Russian literature, we think of Pushkin as the father of Russian literature. But I'm also drawn to Pushkin's African background, and he was very much aware of it as well. So I wanted to write a poem about Pushkin and how he served as a muse for Anna Akhmatova.

*I think in "Homage to a Bellboy" I was impressed to see moments, and a voice, of someone whom we're not usually made aware of, that we don't ever hear his voice, and nobody knows about these things that happen to him.*

It's a strange moment in *Black Boy*, that moment when we're confronted with invisibility, where the bellhop goes into a room, I think he's serving whiskey to this typical white southern man and woman, and they're nude in the bed. And he comes in, and it's if he doesn't exist or as if he doesn't have the freedom to acknowledge what he sees. In the same way Tobe doesn't have a tongue to speak in Faulkner's story—it's this kind of severe invisibility that, think about it, also Ellison addressed, Michael Harper addresses in his poems. So many people address.

*It is, as well in recognizing maybe even the reason for it.*

Think about that Richard Wright epigram "It startled as no more than a blue vase or red rug." One has to disappear. Because if you don't, if you acknowledge, then you lose your life—that's the situation, so you don't have a freedom to acknowledge. It's almost as if some kind of strange pact has been made with the devil, that defines your invisibility, that you're participating in your own invisibility, which in this way is doubly tragic.

*It's difficult for people to understand how some people don't have the ability to come out and say who they are. Is this a choice, do you think people allow it to happen?*

I think they don't have the freedom. Especially in that particular story, at that particular time, these bellhops in a Southern city. You know, the whole idea of "looks that weren't looks."

*Then, as well, it's a difficult process for people who decide to go from invisibility to visibility?*

Yeah, it's a hell of a risk.

*Has your process changed at all over the years, say, maybe how you read?*

One way I read poems is that I try to read them over and over. It's very important to me to take them out and look at them at different times because it depends on what's happening around you, or happening to you, because it will lead you to see something else. That's what really attracted me to poetry: that I could continually come to a poem and get something different from it. Whereas in prose—I like reading short stories, novels—it's different.

*Maybe with prose we're perhaps influenced or directed more by plot?*

Yes, the whole thing about attempting not to resolve a poem. You know, where one hopes the reader can continually come into the poem and there's not a clear-cut resolution— that it's somewhat open-ended.

*I notice in reading either* Copacetic *or* I Apologize for the Eyes in My Head, *especially in the latter, the speaker's voice comes through from a specific moment in time. We come into that moment and we exit from that moment not very far apart in time, and so there's discreet or subtle changes. The speaker does not say, "I've made these large changes in my life, living what I have been for a number of years, or months, or days," and so we come back to those poems over and over, they have a tendency, an inherent quality to turn and change, and in that way they never end.*

Yes, I don't think this was ever a conscious strategy, but I realized that this is something I wanted to do in poems, that I didn't want them to end. It's the same way that I often read poems, that I don't want them to end.

*It's very attractive to step back into that moment, but then it's difficult to ever say what the poem's about because you come into it different each time. I think that this quality is very distinctive in your poetry, say, for instance, in "Facing It," when the speaker realizes that the woman is brushing the boy's hair, or maybe in* Magic City *too, the main speaker is obviously very full-voiced, and he as a person or character is going to keep going on. It makes you want to follow him on further.*

It's a strange place, going back to that landscape I realize there are so many things I didn't write about, and perhaps I'll never write about—that's alright because it's really a sort of hotbed. I was very much aware of language early on, when I say hotbed I can go back to a moment, which portrays hotbed, where you plant seeds, and you pluck the pepper seedlings or whatever out of it, or you transplant the greens. And I realize that that's a place where things begin to grow. So, in that way, Bogalusa was sort of a hotbed.

*And some hotbeds have seasons, and some don't.*

It depends on how you enclose it.

*I wanted to ask you a little bit about the* Jazz Poetry Anthology *(1991). You've finished collecting and editing poems for the second edition that will be published this year,* The Second Set. *Was there anything specific you were looking for when you decided which poems to use in the second collection?*

We, Sascha Feinstein and I, realized that there were a number of poems we wished were included in the first edition. A good example would be some of Gwendolyn Brooks's poems. And, in a way, I'm glad we didn't originally include her work. That makes the second book so much more important. A number of voices were influenced by jazz in a complete way, and so the second anthology is an attempt to go back and take a look at other jazz-related poems and poets who had written about it. A poem by Yevtushenko, an important Russian poet. And once we finalized *Second Set,* we kept thinking, "Is there a third set?" And of course there's a third set. The reason why there's a third set is that jazz has a real international scope. So, obviously, if there's an international scope, there's some other Russian poets besides Yevtushenko; there are some Japanese poets, Scandinavian poets. Impulsively I surmised that yes, and already there are so many. For instance, the popularity of jazz in Japan—why wouldn't jazz influence their poetry as well? It's very popular in Russia and at times it was forced underground—why wouldn't it influence the poetry? And what I'm finding is that, yeah jazz did, at least in the poets' individual voices. I'm thinking about Lorca's *Poet in New York*. Borges loved jazz, and now I'm wondering if he ever wrote a jazz-influenced poem.

*Who were the jazz poets who influenced you the most?*

I began to realize maybe about 1980 that there were certain poets who wrote about jazz a lot. And I think I started with Michael Harper, Jane Cortez, and William Matthews, those were the poets who came to mind. Then I started to look around and realize that there are a lot of others. And of course Langston Hughes, writing blues-related poems, and Sterling Brown's poems. All those poets were there, and then in retrospect I realized that even some of the poems written by Gwendolyn Brooks have a jazz base or a jazz feel. But those voices didn't have an immediate influence on my work. The music itself did have an influence.

*I think there's a great musical allure in some poems that you're exposed to as early as high school. And you ask why is this poem so great, and at the time your teacher can't explain it to you because she or he has no clue.*

I think I've said that lately I've been equating language as music—and the body as an amplifier.

*As well, maybe the poem I was drawn to earliest was "Theme in English B," not consciously by the music but by the subject matter.*

Well, Hughes at the time didn't seem as close to traditional blues; he wrote "English B" because of subject matter; it's closer to traditional American/European expression.

*A music that attracts your ear, and then it's what leads you back to that poetry or that music. Like a kind of bridge from one tradition to another. Gwendolyn Brooks's work is another example of that.*

Yes. With Gwendolyn Brooks, it's also the way she reads her poems. It's the music and rhythm in her voice. And she's influenced by traditional literary pursuits, but she's very conscious of the spoken quality informed by the community.

# Still Negotiating with the Images

## An Interview with William Baer

*During the Vietnam War you saw combat and were awarded the Bronze Star. You were also an information specialist, a reporter, and an editor for the* Southern Cross. *What exactly did you do in those roles?*

*Information specialist* is a military term for reporter. For my first six months in Vietnam, I was pretty much out in the field every day. Whenever there was any engagement, I'd be ferried out on a helicopter to the action—to the middle of it—and I had to report, I had to witness.

*Was there an expectation that your reports would tell things the way the military wanted them to be told? You've written poems like "Touch-up Man" and "Re-creating the Scene," which deal with how the truth gets known or not known during wartime. Did you feel pressure in any way?*

Not really. At least, I didn't feel that kind of pressure at the time, yet I think the pressure might have been there. But I pretty much reported things as I experienced them or saw them. I also had a column "Viet Style," which was about the culture of the Vietnamese. So I was doing both side by side.

*Do you think that any of the wartime journalism had an effect on your poetry when you eventually got around to writing it?*

Yes, especially since I knew a good deal about the culture. I'd started reading about Vietnam and the Vietnamese culture even before I went over there. And when I arrived, I was especially struck by the land itself, the terrain. It was such a vibrant landscape, especially during the rainy season. There's

From *Kenyon Review* (fall 1998).

vegetation everywhere, and I'd grown up in a similar atmosphere in Louisiana. When one drops a seed on the ground, something automatically grows, so that kind of vibrancy in the landscape didn't frighten me.

*Your poems always have a powerful sense of place, especially the Vietnam poems. But you've wondered in the past whether your efforts to comprehend and appreciate the Vietnamese landscape were just a defense mechanism for dealing with the difficult situation that you found yourself in. How do you feel about that now?*

Well, the overt appreciation was in retrospect. But I do remember I had a certain feeling about it at the time, and I suppose that if I'd come from an urban environment, I would have been frightened, definitely frightened, of that terrain.

*The various fears and horrors of these poems come not just from the startling almost hallucinatory images—a burning woman, underground tunnel searches, night ambushes, etc.—but also from the nerve-wracking psychological torment within the mind of each GI. The poem, "Jungle Surrender" decides that "the real interrogator is a voice within," and this internal dialectic informs all of the Vietnam poems. These poems aren't just written from the perspective of a vet looking back at Vietnam but, as Don Ringnalda puts it, a vet "watching" himself as he looks back at Vietnam. Was this concept with you from the beginning?*

I don't think I was fully aware of the tactic, the concept, itself. It was sort of unintentional; it just expressed where I stood at that moment in history—where I stood inside my body. Let's face it, we internalize everything, and that which is internalized informs the future and how we actually experience and see things later on.

*Some of the poems, especially "Starlight Scope Myopia," portray a real compassion for the enemy. Was this true at the time, or was it an attitude that came only after years of trying to deal with the whole experience?*

I'm not sure if I felt that when I was there. I was quite aware of Vietnam's history, and I think that fact had a lot to do with my feelings. A crucial bond was the concept of the Vietnamese "peasant." I, myself, came from a peasant society of mostly field workers, and my father always believed if one worked hard enough, he or she could rise to a certain plateau—a black Calvinism. So I saw the Vietnamese as familiar peasants because that's what they are, and, consequently, I could have easily placed many of the individuals I'd grown up with in that same situation—especially the sharecroppers.

*No poem shows the interrelatedness of human beings in war-time more effectively than "Tu Do Street" in which the black soldier, after being rejected in a "white" bar, finds a "black" bar and temporary solace with a Vietnamese prostitute. Then he reflects:*

> *Back in the bush a Dak To*
> *& Khe Sanh, we fought*
> *the brothers of these women*
> *we now run to hold in our arms.*
> *There's more than a nation*
> *inside us, as black & white*
> *soldiers touch the same lovers*
> *minutes apart, tasting*
> *each other's breath,*
> *without knowing these rooms*
> *run into each other like tunnels*
> *leading to the underworld.*

*This is an amazing image of our connected humanity, but is the connection with "the underworld" just a harsh reminder of death that should stir us to behave with more kindness, or is it a pessimistic reflection of the human propensity to divide and destroy ourselves?*

It was one of those endings that, once I'd written down, just stopped where it was. There were many symbolic underworlds in Vietnam, the underground tunnel systems, some of the bars, and the whole psychic space of the GI—a kind of underworld populated by ghosts and indefinable images. It was a place of emotional and psychological flux where one was trying to make sense out of the world and one's place in that world. And there was, relentlessly, a going back and forth between that internal space and external world. It was an effort to deal with oneself, and with the other GIs, the Vietnamese, and even the ghosts that we'd managed to create ourselves. So, for me, this is a very complex picture of the situation of the GI—going back and forth, condemned in a way to trek back and forth between those emotional demarcations while trying to make sense out of things.

*In poems like "Hanoi Hannah" and "Report from the Skull's*

*Diorama"* you've described the racial psychological warfare targeted at the black GI. How prevalent was it? Was it constant or occasional?

Occasional, but at the same time, the Civil Rights Movement was going forward back home, along with the anti-war movement. So the problem was very much alive for black GIs, and there was always a discourse.

*Was it very alienating, or was the overall situation so overwhelming that you didn't have time to think about it?*

The overall situation was extremely overwhelming. When you were out in the field in an ambush situation, you didn't have time to think about such things. You were keenly sensitive to surviving, and you knew that you had to connect to the other American soldiers. But when you saw friends getting killed or wounded, all kinds of anger would flare up, but let's face it, if you're placed in that kind of situation—and you've been trained—you're going to fire your weapons. You are going to try to stay alive. You're going to try and protect your fellow soldiers, black or white. But at the same time, there were those vicious arguments with oneself. One would feel divided.

*So it had its effect?*

Yes, it did. But it wasn't the first time black Americans have encountered such dilemmas. Black American participation in combat goes back to the Revolutionary War. I think there were at least twenty-five hundred who served. During the Civil War there was the participation of several black regiments, and, afterward, there were those four black regiments in the west that escorted the wagon trains westward. I believe the Tenth Cavalry was responsible for the capture of Geronimo. And then there was the peculiar case of James Beckwourth, who was war chief of the Crows, had dealings with the Cheyenne, and was also implicated in the Sand Creek Massacre. Then there was World War I. As a matter of fact, my first connection with war happened through my great uncle, Uncle Jesse, who'd served in World War I at the age of seventeen with the Ambulance Corps. When he came back home, he used to have horrific dreams, and other grown-ups refused to talk about it. I must have been about six years old at the time, but I eventually realized that his experience in World War I informed his whole personality later on. He became a professional gambler, and I'm talking about in the rural South! He came back, visited the Turpentine camps, and gambled.

*What were the Turpentine camps?*

They were camps where groups of blacks collected the resin from trees to distill turpentine. I can still remember my uncle wearing a suit coat, overalls, and carrying his .38 Smith & Wesson Special. But when he came to my grandmother's door, he would take out the gun, wrap it in a white handkerchief, and then give it to her. It was a ritual.

*You saw this as a boy?*

I did. I also remember that he always had a pocket full of dimes, bright silver dimes, which he gave away to the neighborhood children. But he would still have those terrible dreams, so one morning I cornered him and said, "Why do you have those nightmares?" and he told me a haunting war story. He said that so many soldiers were getting killed during the war that they had to bury the bodies in trenches. As they did so, they'd take the dead soldiers' two dog tags, and one was placed in a collection bag, and the other was placed in the mouth of the corpse—so they could identify the soldiers when they came back to dig them up. It was a horrific story to tell a young boy, but I think, in a way, he was trying to tell me about war. It was a story that was supposed to teach me something about how to look at war.

*To be prepared?*

Yes, to be prepared.

*Eventually, in 1990, you returned to Vietnam. What was it like going back?*

I went with five other veterans, fellow Americans, and when we landed in Hanoi, I was quite shaken. I'd never before considered the possibility of actually being in Hanoi, and, for a while, I realized I didn't feel safe. But, eventually, when I began to talk with the people and make friends, I felt more relaxed.

*So, it was a matter of getting over the initial wariness of actually being in Hanoi?*

It was definitely that, and it was also the knowledge of what had been done to the Vietnamese people and trying to place myself inside their collective skin. It was quite difficult, and I felt that, if it had happened to me, I'd be very angry. So I was very affected by how forgiving the typical Vietnamese happens to be toward Americans—especially toward the American veterans, for some reason. It's still difficult for me to fully understand that special connection, but I think it has to do with the idea of the "shared experience," even if that experience was horrific and negative. It makes me think of that statement of Baldwin's where he says that, in the South, whites and blacks are closely connected—almost like kissing cousins.

*Are you planning to go back again?*

I'd very much like to go back, and I was supposed to return last year, but I didn't make it.

*A number of commentators have praised your Vietnam poems for not offering facile solutions—for being, as Bruce Weber puts it, "achingly suggestive without resolution." Yet many of the same reviewers have found a "redemptive," "salvic" quality in the same poems. Do you think that these are fair characterizations?*

It's difficult for me to say what's fair because I think I'm still negotiating those images. I'm still dealing with them. I don't know if I'm going to write any more Vietnam-related poems. I feel that I won't be writing very many, if at all, especially since I have a section in my forthcoming book, *Thieves of Paradise*, about Vietnam. The section is called "Debriefing Ghosts," and they're prose poems about returning to Vietnam—but there are a few other kinds of ghosts as well.

*In 1981 you returned to your hometown of Bogalusa, Louisiana, after an absence of over a decade, and you later told the* Times-Picayune *that your life had been a "healing process from the two places"—meaning both Bogalusa and Vietnam. Yet many of your poems about your childhood, especially in* Magic City *and the "New Poems" section of* Neon Vernacular, *portray a generally pleasant childhood of sports, music, mischief, and rites of passage—a place where you could always "depend" upon certain relatives' "love to get us out of our trouble." Have you gradually come to have a greater appreciation of your youth in Bogalusa?*

I'm always re-thinking my youthful rituals in Bogalusa. Recently, I was shocked by the realization that growing up in Louisiana there wasn't any place that I couldn't walk in the middle of the night—and I'm talking about two or three o'clock in the morning. But at the same time, there was an unspoken fear lurking underneath that youthful sense of freedom that greatly affected us all, especially the adults. I think I personally connected with my environment because, early on, there was a youthful investigation going on. I would investigate pretty much everything, especially the terrain, and the social demarcations as well—even though I never crossed those boundaries. There was so much to look at, to query, within the context of my own environment, that it kept my imaginative life very much alive. I was also, constantly, projecting myself somewhere else in the world. I would easily daydream about Mexico, Africa, or somewhere in Europe, and I later realized that those daydreams were actually connected to where I was growing up—that there was a unique space, an eminent silence, from where I could project myself to other possibilities.

*Was it because you wanted to get away, or was it the natural, imaginative daydream life of a future writer?*

I think it had mostly to do with the quality of invention because I always could come back to that temporal space, that physical territory as such, and deal with it. I didn't have any problem about wandering for miles out into the woods, or things of that sort.

*In your memories of Bogalusa the symbol of the paper mill is especially significant, and it appears in your poems—with its "acid fumes" and "chemicals / That turn workers into pulp." Yet even the factory is the source of financial security, camaraderie, and satisfaction about one's work.*

Yes, I've realized that growing up was intimately involved in the broad significance of "work." I started working very early on, physical labor. I had definite responsibilities, and, as a teenager, I realized that it had somehow become a competition between my father and me—probably because he respected physical labor so much.

*Yes, the most important aspect of these poems is the young narrator's complex relationship with his father. Maybe the most telling of these is "Songs for My Father," in which the dying carpenter father, who never approved of poetry as a vocation, asks his son to write a poem about him. Is this a true incident?*

It actually happened. He wanted a poem for his birthday, and it's strange to think about it now because within less than a year he was dead. So, even if he hadn't received proper medical attention, he surely knew that something serious was happening. So I tried. It was probably the most difficult assignment I'd ever been given, and I couldn't write the poem. But I tried, and I can still remember reciting certain lines to him, although I'm not sure if any of those lines actually ended up in "Songs for My Father."

*But even though you were never able to produce the poem while your father was alive, it does seem that, at that point in his life, he'd accepted your vocation as a writer?*

Yes. But I think that what my father really hated wasn't the writing so much—it was the disconnection we felt when I left home. Early on, there had been a very deep trust between the two of us. I remember, at about twelve years old, that he came to me around Christmastime, and he asked me to hold all of his money—and for me it was a lot of money, a couple thousand dollars. He could always trust me in that way; so, there was a special kind of connection that I still don't fully understand.

*You were the oldest son?*

Yes, there are four brothers and one sister, and I'm the oldest.

*Another meaningful character in your narrator's search for identity is the grandfather—a man who'd once emigrated here from Trinidad and given up his "true name." Eventually, you took his last name, "Komunyakaa," as your own. Was this a problem with your father—or with other relatives?*

It upset my dad quite a bit, but it didn't bother my mother or my grandmothers.

*It was still a family name.*

That's right, but it still bothered my dad a whole lot, even though the rest of my family embraced me and dealt with it. In my youth the very name itself was like a family secret, and I'm still trying to understand it. My great-grandparents had come to Florida as stowaways and slipped into the country. I can still remember visiting my great-grandmother, and there's a kind of pleasant mystery associated with it. I was probably about three or four years old, and I can still remember her and her house, which was raised on stilts above the water. But that's the only real-life image I have of her, and neither the name Komunyakaa nor my great-grandparents themselves were discussed very much in the family. So, one day I cornered my grandmother about it, and she began to tell me a bit about my grandfather. But mostly, I remember my grandparents from a very large, framed photograph of them in my grandmother's bedroom. Often, as a child, I'd sort of meditate on that photograph because they were such grand-looking people.

*Do you know where that photograph is today?*

The large one got damp, and, since it was old, it deteriorated. As far as I know, that was the only photograph of my maternal grandparents together, but I've been told that smaller versions of it were given to older members of my family, so maybe there's still one in existence. I'm not sure. But I still have this mental picture of them together, just married, in that oval photograph.

*During your youth in Bogalusa, racist Klan activities were still present, and they're tellingly described in "The Whistle" and "Knights of the White Camellia & Deacons of Defense." How active were they? And did you see actual conflicts with the freedom marchers?*

Yes, I saw some of the conflict; the Klan activity was very much above ground. Yet, as I mentioned earlier, I'm still amazed by the fact that I would walk anywhere I wanted alone. Maybe that had a lot to do with the direction I would generally walk, because I liked to head straight down the tracks, the railroad tracks, at any time of night. When I think about it, it probably has a lot to do with the ritual of one of my great aunts, my maternal grandmother's sister, who lived to be about ninety-five. Up until her death, she would rise and walk to the Post Office on Wednesdays, which was about five miles away. She lived in a very wooded area, a very closed off area, and, when she went to the Post Office, she would always walk straight down the tracks.

*Was it a passage of safety?*

It could be. The railroad tracks were the demarcation in the South between black and white communities. But it represented another kind of "safety" as well because, when we thought of trains, we thought of Pullman porters and individuals who were able to move freely from North to South. So, maybe that's all part of it too—and related to the fact that I would meditate on the passing trains. Often I'd count the boxcars and think about where they might be going.

*A less safe subject and theme throughout your work is the evil of sexual betrayal and the desperate need for meaningful love. For example, your poem "Boy Wearing a Dead Man's Clothes" ends with the uneasy child remembering the dead man from a few weeks ago:*

> I saw him & Mrs. Overstreet
> kissing in the doorway,
>
> & Mr. Overstreet drunk
> with his head on the table.

*And "The Heart's Graveyard Shift" describes a man "Between loves" who's so desperate for love he might actually "go off his rocker." Are these related problems especially significant in our contemporary times, or are they just inevitable facts of human behavior?*

Given the complexity of human social interactions, I see these realities as products of the whole social fabric of the society. I grew up seeing all kinds of things happening within the context of that society—unspoken things—things that were not talked about, just accepted, and that's how I began to understand the adult world—by examining the things that weren't talked about.

*Walcott considers his poetic vocation both "votive" and "sacred," and you've described the spiritual in various ways in your poetry—the prayers of a Simeon-like grandmother; the "something" that saves the narrator's life in two of the Vietnam poems; and, more recently, the spiritual dimension of the Australian landscape. Could you discuss this aspect of your writing?*

I grew up with the Bible. It was the first book I read through from beginning to end. Several times, in fact. I was quite taken with the Old Testament, and I think I've said somewhere that perhaps the Old Testament, in a way, brought me to a clearer understanding of surrealism because, within surrealism, I could fire up my imagination again—as I'd done with some of the biblical images that are frightening, rather horrific—like visualizing mythic animals with nine heads. And the Bible and religion got me very close to the language itself. I especially remember the phrase "In the beginning was the Word, and the Word was God." That phrase really stuck with me and seemed relevant to both the rituals I observed in nature and the rituals between individuals. I was also greatly affected by the fact that through language, especially poetic language, we can speak for others as well, members of my family, or members of the larger community. Not that one should speak for them, but to share something they have touched in a certain way and that has also touched one's life—informed it in some way.

*Do you see that use of language as having spiritual dimensions?*

Yes, I think it does have spiritual dimensions.

*And how about the Australian landscape, which you've often described as having a spiritual significance?*

Spending so much time in Australia has taught me that my own rituals, my early rituals in Louisiana—like going out and looking at the landscape—weren't really chosen; they just happened to exist in the context of my own personality. I've talked to my brothers and sister about this, and even though we grew up in the same place, they always say that their memories are entirely different than mine—even though we were looking at the same things! So, my experience in the Australian landscape, especially after talking to some of the Aboriginals, has helped me to understand how they looked at the landscape, and it's also taught me something about my own early experiences in Bogalusa. For example, it seems that, as contemporary people, we're very fearful of silence. But why? Why does every moment have to be filled with some kind of external vibration coming from the radio or television or some other technological device? I don't know, but I now realize silence is not an endurance test for me, and it never was.

*Over the years you've been involved, in various ways, with theatrical or dramatic writing. What have you been working on recently?*

Most recently, I was commissioned by ABC, the Australian Broadcasting Corporation, to do a piece on Bird, on Charlie Parker, and I thought this was such a challenging request that I agreed to do it. When Chris Williams of ABC first suggested the project to me, we talked about the traditional libretto—the conceits of the traditional libretto—and I thought I could negotiate those forms. But once I started looking closely at Parker, I decided not to do a traditional libretto but, rather, fourteen symmetrical pieces under the title *Testimony*. So, I sent Chris Williams part of the text, seven of the fourteen pieces, and he was initially concerned that it wasn't in the form of the traditional libretto. But when he talked it over with the composer Sandy Evans, she said, "I don't see how we can do it any other way!" So I finished *Testimony* a few months ago, and they're going to use a thirteen-piece band and four singers to actually perform it.

*For radio?*

Yes, for radio, but I believe that they're going to make a video as well, and I think it might even come out as a CD. A few years ago I'd been asked to write something about Vietnam to be set to music. But I was so busy at the time I couldn't do it. Then, a few months later, someone sent me a news clipping announcing that a piece called *Fire Water Paper: A Vietnam Oratorio* had been done by the Pacific Symphony, commissioned by Carl St. Clair, and performed with Yo-Yo Ma and some others. This past April the recording was released by Sony, and on April 13, I got to see it performed at Kennedy Center by the Boston Symphony. It contains only two of my poems, along with excerpts from the *Stabat Mater,* Vietnamese folk poetry, etc., and it's really a compiled text, set by the composer Elliot Goldenthal, who often does movie scores.

*Are you working on anything at the present time?*

I'm working on something that began a few years ago when I visited the La Brea Tar Pits. At the time, I thought it would be interesting to write a piece to be performed in the enclosed glass space at the Tar Pits. So I'm now writing it for the Glass Ark section in my next book, *Thieves of Paradise.*

*So it's a dramatic piece?*

Yes, it's spoken between two people, a woman and a man. They're paleontologists, talking among prehistoric bones, but actually talking about something entirely different.

*In a 1990 interview in* Callaloo, *you said that you were slowly working on a collection of poems in traditional forms called* Black Orpheus and Other Love Poems. *How's that project coming along?*

That project is coming along very, very slowly! It's one of those projects I want to savor—that I really don't want to finish. I remember when I was a kid slowly nibbling on a candy bar, for days it seemed, saving it, prolonging it, so it's like that.

*Does it include sonnets and ballads and couplets?*

Yes, all of those. That's how I first started. That was the kind of poetry I first started reading, poetry informed by traditional forms and structures.

*You've often mentioned your early love of Poe and Tennyson.*

Yes, interestingly, I recently wrote a series of songs for a jazz singer called *Thirteen Kinds of Desire,* and I relied on traditional rhymes in the songs. In my youth the other way that I came to poetry was listening to the radio. My mother always had the radio tuned to stations in New Orleans, and my impulse, as a child, was never to sing the actual lyrics, but to make up my own. I can remember, at six or seven years of age, creating rhyming lyrics.

*What else are you working on?*

Well, the way I work is that I simultaneously compose several collections side by side, so presently, along with *Black Orpheus and Other Love Poems,* I'm working on *Thieves of Paradise,* which will probably come out next; *Talking Dirty to the Gods,* which is a longish book composed of sixteen-line poems, each with four four-line stanzas; and *Remembrance of Things to Come,* which really started out as an excavation of history. Over the years I'd read a great deal on African American history, but also on black history throughout the world. So the project began as an excavation of specific historical individuals such as Ira Aldridge, who played Othello—there's a bust of him at the Royal Shakespeare Theatre—and James Beckwourth, and other individuals whom I'd never, in the past, really thought about writing poems about. But once I started writing them, it made perfect sense to me.

*Do you usually compose in your head?*

I do. I see this as a kind of meditation for the most part, so, in the beginning, I try not to impose a shape on the poem. For example, I know that I want to write a poem entitled "Ishi." Ishi, a Native American, was the last member of his tribe around Oroville, California, which is close to Paradise, California. Ishi ended up as a kind of museum piece in a way, and I've been meditating on what it would be like to be the last living member of your tribe. I've been meditating on this for about eighteen months now, and I know I'll have to write in the near future, since it's a section of *Thieves of Paradise*. So I'm getting very close to actually sitting down and doing it.

*So, in general, you're meditating on several poems at a time, and you write them down when the time comes?*

Yes, they sort of choose their own direction.

*How often do you work at your poetry?*

Not as much as I'd like to, but I can still read on the road.

*You're a firm believer in a poet "unearthing" his true voice. How does one go about that? What do you advise your students?*

Well, the first thing I want to know about my students are the things they really care about—things that might not have a direct link to poetry, but which they're really passionate about. They have to have a need. Poetry, I believe, has to be informed by a need. Otherwise, it becomes a kind of artificial apparatus that the poet straps on, and it becomes more of a burden than a telling moment—a poem is both confrontation and celebration.

# The Body Is Our First Music

*Interview with Tony Barnstone and*
*Michael Garabedian*

*Barnstone:* The epigraph to Toni Morrison's *Song of Solomon* reads, "The fathers may soar / And the children may know their names," and the book is very much a quest for authentic naming. As one of the characters says about Malcolm X: "his point is to let white people know you don't accept your slave name." Here's a passage from the book, an internal monologue by the protagonist, Milkman Dead: "Surely, he thought, he and his sister had some ancestor, some lithe young man with onyx skin and legs straight as cane stalks, who had a name that was real. A name given to him at birth with love and seriousness. A name that was not a joke, nor a disguise, nor a brand name. But who this lithe young man was, and where his cane-stalk legs carried him from or to, could never be known. No. Nor his name. His own parents, in some mood of perverseness or resignation, had agreed to abide by a naming done to them by somebody who couldn't have cared less" (17–18). In your poetry, and in your life, naming seems to be a major issue as well. I'm thinking particularly of the poem "Mismatched Shoes," which is a poem that explains your act of self-naming—a kind of act of self-invention. Would you mind talking about that poem and about naming in your life?

*Komunyakaa:* Well, actually, it comes from a secret within the context of the family, my grandfather having come to Louisiana. I think first they landed in Florida, and then came to Louisiana, and they sort of slipped into the country as stowaways.

From *Poetry Flash,* no. 227 (June/July 1998).

*Barnstone:* When was this?

*Komunyakaa:* This would have to have been a little after the turn of the century.

*Barnstone:* In that poem you talk about the name Brown and the name Komunyakaa, and changing to Komunyakaa as a connection with an elided past. Am I getting that wrong?

*Komunyakaa:* Well, I think in a certain sense because it was like a secret—it was a dare more than anything else, and in the context of the dare there was a kind of liberation. And I'm talking about a personal liberation as opposed to a political statement; one has to feel a certain freedom within the context of one's name.

*Garabedian:* I'd like to move from the subjective naming to your naming of reality. In some of the poems there is the suggestion that humans or human senses are flawed, as in "Jonestown: More Eyes of Jadwiga's Dream," where "reality bleeds into fiction." In "Audacity of the Lower Gods" the search for the truth via science is inadequate: "I'd rather let the flowers / keep doing what they do best," says the speaker, as opposed to calling the poison oak "Diversiloba," for instance. The suggestion is that categorizing tends away from the natural or the real. How is poetry as an alternative "mode of perception" more adequate? Is it more adequate?

*Komunyakaa:* Well, I think what happens is that the naming of a thing, things in nature being named by human beings, is a way of branding. Emotional branding. There's also a kind of claiming more than anything else. A good example would be the instances where American Indians ventured into the mountains—Pike's Peak, particularly. And yet those places such as Pike's Peak (there are a number of other places) do not really bear the early names . . . there was an attempt to claim the places by renaming them. As far as poetry goes, I think it's a naming and renaming. It's a constant ritual of trying to get it right. That is really the energy—that is really the urgency—of the poem. That's why I think refrains are interesting, because the poem becomes a motor—not of conquest as much as a motor for direction. In that process there's a kind of renewal . . . in that kind of naming, something is being observed, and in that observation, let's assume and hope that there is a connection, and that there is a naming that has to do with celebration, not the naming to dominate.

*Barnstone:* And for you science is more as a naming to dominate?

*Komunyakaa:* I think often so. It's a naming to divide and . . .

*Barnstone:* Categorize.

*Komunyakaa:* Yes.

*Barnstone:* It's interesting. I was recently reading William Carlos Williams's *The American Novel,* and he was talking about just this—about scientific naming and how it nails everything down and kills it, and how this is a source of suicides and trips to the North Pole . . .

*Komunyakaa:* Right! It is a naming that lays claims to the land and its people. In regards to the North Pole; automatically, I think of Matthew Henson, whom I would like to dedicate a poem to. Usually, we think of Admiral Peary, of course.

*Maki:* I'd like to know what kind of role poetry plays in talking about these things that are considered insignificant.

*Komunyakaa:* The things we tend to overlook—the things we see as insignificant—I don't think of them as insignificant at all, and that's the reason I attempt to embrace these things. There's a celebration in those things we tend to overlook, when, in fact, it's all part of a kind of immense unity. I was very curious, like science, how we see into things in the same way Aboriginals do paintings—we call them "X-ray drawings." They look inside of things, and look into things. I was interested in that cosmology . . . I think about the poem as layered with images (it's a composite of things that we might see as insignificant), which are there to illuminate us. Or if not illuminate us, at least force us to pose questions. And sometimes those are rather silent questions—we are posing questions without even being aware that we are posing them.

*Barnstone:* I have a lot of questions about *Dien Cai Dau,* but, first, could you translate the title for us?

*Komunyakaa:* It means crazy. That's what the Vietnamese would call the American soldiers. *Beaucoup, dien cai dau:* Very crazy. So it made perfect sense that I would use this title, because it pretty much nailed things down.

*Barnstone:* The other question I was going to ask returns to this issue of nature. It seems to me that nature is used in very interesting ways in this book. There's a kind of pattern of nature imagery—I'm thinking of the first poem in the book, "Camouflaging the Chimera," in which the soldiers "wove / ourselves into the terrain, / content to be a hummingbird's target." The poem ends:

> We weren't there. The river ran
> through our bones. Small animals took refuge
> against our bodies; we held our breath,
>
> ready to spring the L-shaped
> ambush, as a world revolved
> under each man's eyelid.

This proliferates connections with the deep image poetry of Robert Bly and James Wright, or classical Chinese poetry, about connecting with nature—the poet as Taoist sage. And so, when I think about the world revolving under each man's eyelid, I keep thinking of Emerson's "transparent eyeball." But it seems to me there's some kind of ironic transcendentalism going on here, where connection with nature is not to connect with the oversoul, but simply some kind of survival in a Darwinian sense.

*Komunyakaa:* Well, camouflage is part of it, the fact that there is a need to blend into nature—to almost become nature. But I think the reason the soldiers almost become nature at that moment has to do with a kind of severe fear more than anything else. And let's face it, if we go back to the reason why animals camouflage themselves, it is out of fear. Predator and Prey. Often, nature is a beckoning, but also a warning.

*Barnstone:* So it seems a kind of total connection that undermines the discourse of the connection with nature.

*Komunyakaa:* I think there's something else going on here as well . . . There's a certain kind of fear, and it has to do with the fact that one hasn't been initiated. So, in that situation there's a certain kind of initiation going on, even though it might not be a conscious initiation. There's an unconscious situational initiation going on.

*Barnstone:* To follow this up, in other poems nature is terrifying. In "Somewhere near Phu Bai" the soldier on guard is desperately trying to read the shapes of the night, trying to see which might be the Viet Cong, and in his mind "The moon cuts through / night trees like a circular saw / white hot." And in "A Greenness Taller than Gods" again a soldier is trying to read the enemy through a gorgeously unfamiliar nature, monkeys jabbering in flame trees, torch birds burning through the dark-green day. In *Paradise Lost* Milton speaks of how Adam must read God through the book of nature. It seems to me that the soldiers here are trying to read this unfamiliar book, this unfamiliar nature. But also, in some peculiar way, that makes the unseen enemy almost like a god, who is known only in the moment of death.

*Komunyakaa:* Yes. My feeling is that often the soldiers were more afraid of their surroundings than their so-called enemy. And I'm not just talking about vipers and tigers; I'm talking about how nature becomes part of the disguise. I think it was very difficult for the soldiers to deal with that. I think those coming out of urban—or small towns even—hadn't been fully initiated into that which we define or classify as nature. Nature not as precious or as commodity, but nature as part of oneself. In order for that to happen, there has to be a certain trust. So they had not really reached the place of trust.

*Barnstone:* And, of course, how could they in that circumstance?

*Komunyakaa:* Yes.

*Barnstone:* I'm also interested in the ways in which in your imagination or memory of Vietnam, nature becomes a terrain in which you have this extraordinary beauty, but it's also described in mechanical or technological terms. In "Hanoi Hannah" "Flares bloom over the trees" like flowers, while "Howitzers buck like a herd / of horses." In the next poem, "Roll Call," seagulls are a "metallic-gray squadron." So, nature is technology, and technology is blossoming—it's a very interesting connection. There's even a moment where a human being is reduced down to a rifle in that poem, in an image in which an M-16 is "propped upright / between a pair of jungle boots / a helmet on its barrel / as if it were a man" . . .

*Komunyakaa:* Which is ritual. When a GI was killed, often they would have ceremonies. Sometimes out of a platoon one might see five pairs of boots and five rifles, sitting there, as icons.

*Barnstone:* It also seems to me that it turns the man—and—nature into a kind of weapon; something that might go off at any moment in ways you can't know.

*Komunyakaa:* I think that's really the essence of guerrilla warfare—to turn nature into a weapon. To make nature at least an ally.

*Garabedian:* This seems almost contradictory: an alliance of opposites. Dr. Barnstone was reminded of Emerson, but, when I read a lot of the poems, I note a particularly Whitmanesque quality. Whitman is wholly inclusive in his poetry and writes rather graphic descriptions of death, violence, or ugliness, which, though these things seemingly contradict, attain beauty of their own. He writes, "Very well, then, I contradict myself." This idea plays out in several of your own poems. For instance, in "Praising Dark Places" the speaker finds beauty in the scorpion and the insects revealed beneath an old board. You have said in another interview with Muna Asali that you are interested in contradictions, like Whitman. Why are you interested in contradiction, particularly between the beautiful and the horrific?

*Komunyakaa:* A good example comes from growing up in Louisiana. Being conscious of English and what's buried within the context of the English language—I'm particularly thinking of that which is dark, that which is always defined as horrific, always mysterious—98 percent of words, phrases, prefixes about darkness would probably be regarded as negative. And yet when I looked at nature, going back to childhood experiences, I always saw those places of darkness as places of a celebration of life, an embracing of life, the making of life. In the same way of Theodore Roethke's poem "Root Cellar," you know, this down in the intense murky existence of things, going back to the basic concept of life. As a matter of fact, probably sunlight, especially immense, intense sunlight, would destroy.

*Barnstone:* . . . I think you can take it back to the Zoroastrians, when you begin to separate a god of light from a god of darkness, and say that the god of light is the god of good and the god of darkness evil, as compared to Taoism, where you have yin but also have yang, and they're interconnected.

*Komunyakaa:* But we—as writers, critics, whatever—have sort of embraced the contradictions.

*Garabedian:* Do you think this negativity associated with darkness is a particularly Western convention?

*Komunyakaa:* It seems more apparent as a Western condition. It's all woven into the language, and I think it has a lot to do with the Western psyche.

*Barnstone:* And not only the language but also the images. Was it *Newsweek* or *Time* where the image of O. J. Simpson was darkened to make him look more threatening?

*Komunyakaa:* Yes, it's amazing—the technology.

*Barnstone:* Or the other [image] that jumps out in my mind is Sadaam Hussein during the Gulf War. I believe it was a *New Republic* cover, where they shortened his mustache so he would look like Hitler. Talk about disinformation!

*Komunyakaa:* I have a sense that these individuals—beyond the airbrushing and so forth or coloration—know exactly what they're doing. And it's amazing that they would know what they're doing and we, often, as audience, are not aware. I would rather think that we are aware of all this baggage.

*Barnstone:* As Orwell writes, I have the quote here, "political language—and with variations this is true of all political language from conservative to anarchist—is designed to make lies sound truthful, and murder respectable, and give the appearance of solidity to pure wind. One cannot change this all in a moment, but one can at least change one's own habits, and from time to time one can, if one jeers loudly enough, send some worn-out and useless phrase into the dustbin where it belongs."

*Komunyakaa:* Let's hope so! This whole thing with praising darkness—why not praise darkness along with light?

*Garabedian:* A sort of all-inclusiveness.

*Komunyakaa:* Well . . . we cannot define one without the other.

*Garabedian:* I would think that generally violence is regarded as negative. But the representations of violence in some of the poems seem to attain a contradictory status of good, and, if not good, then neutrality in the matter-of-fact presentation. Instances of sex are often treated in a similar manner, and, in fact, they (violence and sex) are sometimes allied; for example, in "Woman I Got the Blues," the woman lies "Half-naked on the living room floor; / the moon falling through the window / on you like a rapist." If I could go back to Whitman—he celebrates sex and violence because he is a transcendentalist; there is an all-inclusiveness where everything is good. How does the neutral exposition of violence or sex function in your poetry?

*Komunyakaa:* Well, first of all, I think it's not the fact that the country is so violent, or "the making of civilization" is so violent—one war after another, one army conquering the other. For me, in looking at violence, we recognize its extreme in order to go past it. We deal with it. We break it down to its elements and deal with it in that way. We take it apart. I've been fascinated recently about how we talk about mass murderers in this country. We have a profile today of such murderers: a Midwesterner looking a certain way—not exactly like James Dean, but coming pretty close. And I think it's taken us some time to recognize this image. Maybe in recognizing this image we can deal with it. Because violence is not new, as all civilizations can attest to.

*Garabedian:* Thinking about civilization, do you see a distinction in the type of violence related in the corpse garden in "Blasphemy" from *Copacetic* as opposed to, say, the goat's slaughter in "Happiness" from *Magic City?*

*Komunyakaa:* When we think of violence in this country, we think of urban violence. How about rural violence? My tendency is to think of rural violence as the most severe. And, interestingly enough, the whole thing with the ritual of the goat killing or the hog slaughter is associated with the rural violence that we take for granted. I'm particularly thinking of the child who internalizes this ritual. Getting his hands bloody as well. And this is something we accept.

*Barnstone:* My understanding of *Dien Cai Dau* is that it is a kind of extension of the kinds of dramatic monologues and third-person story poems that your first two books were engaged with, in which you blend together autobiography with speaking in a more general way as a universal soldier. When you move to *Magic City,* are you fully in autobiographical mode, or are you still speaking in dramatic monologues? Do you worry about the boundary between fiction and autobiography?

*Komunyakaa:* Not really, because when I wrote the first of those poems, "Venus's-Flytraps," I realized that here I had re-introduced myself to a certain terrain—and it was a necessary terrain to deal with. I had very systematically written around this, in the same way I had systematically written around the Vietnam experience. It became important to write about things I had dismissed from the territory of poetry.

*Barnstone:* That's interesting, because so many writers today feel that they can't get past their lives and their childhoods as the territory for poetry, and yet it took you a long journey to come to this point. It's an interesting journey, and in a lot of ways it mirrors a lot of the confessional poets—people like Robert Lowell, Adrienne Rich, and others who started off formally and moved toward the more personal.

*Komunyakaa:* Yes.

*Barnstone:* I have a more nuts-and-bolts question about the poems. As an aside, I should say that I love the fact that they are such visual poems, and short-line poems. Do you really see yourself as a poet of the eyes—of the visual sense—and do you think that is one thing that makes you write shorter lines, because it tends to frame those images more clearly?

*Komunyakaa:* I think so. It has a lot to do with growing up in a rural space. Oftentimes I found myself as a child attracted to wooded areas, attracted to the rituals of the birds and insects. If I hadn't become a poet, I'd probably be a painter. Often I wish I could paint, but that might be something I can attempt later on.

*Barnstone:* The follow-up to this is that John Engels, in what's otherwise a positive review of *Magic City,* complains of what he calls "obsessive simile-making." Certainly, throughout *Dien Cai Dau* simile dominates the rhetoric, and is the primary form of figurative speech. It seems to me, however, that this use of simile is quite self-conscious, particularly in one poem, "You and I Are Disappearing," which is wholly structured around a proliferation of similes. I'm wondering why this is so relentlessly a book about what war is like. Is it something about the ineffability of the violent sublime of war that you can't name it directly?

*Komunyakaa:* Well I think what it is, is an attempt to name it. Because I do think it is a composite of so many things—

history, culture, and so forth. So, it's always something that seems to escape naming. One reason is that we don't want to believe what we have witnessed. Some people say, "No, this can't be true—it has to be this." And then we say, "It's this— no! It can't be this, it is something else." So, it is that kind of journey—a journey into the mystery.

*Barnstone:* Is it also a kind of mending? I'm thinking of one moment in "A Greenness Taller than Gods" where the soldiers are breaking the landscape, as they walk they're breaking spider webs, and "the spiders mend [the] webs [the soldiers] march into." It seems like the similes are doing this mending somehow.

*Komunyakaa:* It's an attempt to suture that which has been disturbed, that which has been cut into and cursed by the presence of the outsider.

*Garabedian:* In *Dien Cai Dau*'s "Hanoi Hannah" or "Tu Do Street" (and some extent "One Legged Stool") you deal with the African American experience and Vietnam. I was interested in the presentation. You are African American and a Vietnam veteran, and both of these groups have been marginalized in many ways at various points throughout American history. Other African American poets and writers—Langston Hughes, W. E. B. Du Bois, Naomi Long Madgett, Audre Lorde—in addition to veteran poets and writers like Randall Jarrell and Amiri Baraka, tend to manifest in their works particularly angry sentiments, perhaps because of this marginalization. I find in your poems a greater objectivity. I was wondering what you hope to achieve through this objectivity.

*Komunyakaa:* I think it had a lot to do with the fact I waited fourteen years to write about the experience. Consequently, there is a certain kind of objectivity. I wanted the images to do the work—I wanted to avoid statement, if possible.

*Barnstone:* Is there an influence in your work of Chinese poetry—I know that there is the wonderful poem about Li Po: "Everyone's Reading Li Po." But the reason I say this is because there seems to be this ability in Li Po and Du Fu to blend an absolute crystal-clear objectivity of vision—of the self, the body, and the world—with quite extraordinary statements of countries destroyed in rebellion and warfare.

*Komunyakaa:* Well, I've read some of the classical Chinese

poets, some of the classical Vietnamese poets as well, and I think it has to do with an attempt to understand—to have a sense of a place. That is, not to reap any kind of domination, but in a sense to try to cultivate celebration.

*Garabedian:* I was going to ask if this objective presentation called into question some of the issues that these images might suggest. For example, the absence of anger calls anger into question.

*Komunyakaa:* I don't know if I could say that anger has been totally erased from the canvas. I do think there's a certain kind of anger there, and it has to do with the ability to present the whole of the picture. It's not cut off in any way, and I attempt to show every little corner of the picture, if possible. And in that sense, the reader or the listener enters in as an active participant of meaning, definition.

*Barnstone:* In some ways it's harder to preach to people than it is to show them.

*Komunyakaa:* Yes. I think, automatically, because what I hope I'm doing is trying to activate participation.

*Barnstone:* As in "Reflections," it seems to me that what we're talking about is how you put the second person—the you, the reader—into his shoes.

*Komunyakaa:* Such a long-ago poem! That sort of surprises me.

*Garabedian:* I kind of saw a progression in the four books, sort of getting darker and darker from *Copacetic* to *I Apologize for the Eyes in My Head* to *Dien Cai Dau,* but then in *Magic City* there is a sort of rebirth. Did you perhaps need to go through the experience of writing *Dien Cai Dau* to get to the "Happiness" or "Glory" of *Magic City?*

*Komunyakaa:* Well, it's not so much the happiness—it's a different landscape. But it's still a part of my psychological landscape. I do think, yes, the writing of the Vietnam poems helped me to get to *Magic City.* If I hadn't written *Dien Cai Dau,* I probably wouldn't have written *Magic City.*

*Barnstone:* I have a follow-up to that question, about *Dien Cai Dau.* The book goes through some pretty awful places but seems to end surprisingly upbeat. It ends with poems about boat people daydreaming about "Jade Mountain," about the half-American and half-Vietnamese children who were the product of so much death, and with an extraordinary poem about memory, emotion, and loss. And also that extraordinary poem "Facing It," which ends ambiguously upbeat: "In the black mirror [of the monument] / a woman's trying to erase names: / No, she's brushing a boy's hair." It's both a kind of erasure, forgetting all this tragedy, and at the same time a gesture of either comfort or affection. It seems to me that the book is moving toward some kind of resolution through emotion, affection, maybe even forgetting. Was the writing of the book itself that kind of resolution for you, or did it help?

*Komunyakaa:* No, not really. It wasn't an erasure. It was more an attempt to gain a certain clarity, because I wanted to understand the experience, and I think that, in writing the book, I understood the steps through the ritual.

*Barnstone:* The ritual of war?

*Komunyakaa:* The ritual of war through reflection.

*Barnstone:* The Argentine writer Jorge Luis Borges was once touring the Midwest and was asked by a member of the audience, "Mr. Borges, could you tell us whether there has been one woman in your life who has been your muse, and your great love?" And Borges thought about this in silence for a minute before replying: "Yes, as a matter of fact, there was, but the strange thing about it is that she kept on changing her name." In *Dien Cai Dau* you also seem to be creating this universal woman, a kind of anima figure, who is simultaneously prostitute, betrayer, lover, mother, fighter—all these things. In a number of poems you talk about her always appearing in different wars in different places. I'm interested where the female resides in your wartime imagination, and where does sex and motherhood and generation come into this activity in which, for the most part, men kill men?

*Komunyakaa:* Well . . . on the boundary, on the periphery, of every war, there seems to be the spoils of war alongside an industry of sex. But it's more than that, because often there's a kind of cleansing going on as well. People are getting killed, and people are being born on the periphery. This has always been the case, and so I see it as a kind of natural presentation. Because the same men who are killing, the next day are loving. And often risking their hearts. So there is all this contradiction in their personality and perception. And I suppose we need that kind of complexity in order to make ourselves whole—you'll find all the contradictions.

*Barnstone:* There are also a lot of moments in the book where the men fighting with each other are described as lovers. There's that moment in "Sappers," where the sappers with dynamite wrapped around their naked bodies are throwing themselves into the arms of the GIs; there's a moment where the speaker in a poem is shooting a soldier who's swaying in the grass as if dancing with a woman at that moment, and at the end of the poem turns him over so that he's not kissing the ground, but kissing the sky like in "Purple Haze." So, there's a kind of erotics of death going on, too.

*Komunyakaa:* I suppose we might go back to Alexander the Great. When Thracian soldiers paired, they fought harder, they defended each other to the death, I suppose. That might at least be the background.

*Barnstone:* Achilles and Patrocles.

*Komunyakaa:* Yes.

*Garabedian:* You talked before about including the contradictions—presenting it all. It seems perhaps that you want to present "the truth." In fact, many of your poems are concerned with what one might call "the search for truth." Here I'm thinking of poems like "Safe Subjects" or "Gift Horse," or even "Instructions for Building Straw Huts," where it becomes imperative "to understand" and "to know." To some extent "Tunnels" from *Dien Cai Dau* might be thought upon as the tunnel rat's own search. There is also the notion that what is real has been hidden for whatever reason; again and again there are allusions within the poems to masks, which both hide the wearer and obstruct his or her view.

*Komunyakaa:* One is reminded here of Dunbar's "We Wear the Mask." But it's more than that. It's the fact that we often find ourselves masked against history. Or, more completely, hoodwinked.

*Garabedian:* "Let truth have its way with us" the speaker in "Safe Subjects" implores. Can poetry be employed as a method to arrive at truth?

*Komunyakaa:* Well, at least an approximation of truth—truth with a small *t.*

*Garabedian:* Then again, in "Venus's-Flytraps" the child

wants to know—he's so very curious. At one point, he says, "I can hurt you with / questions / like silver bullets." Is poetry such a silver bullet?

*Komunyakaa:* Not really a "silver bullet" as much as . . . well, let me think about this. Because when we think of silver bullets, it is in a negative way. That is, to kill the werewolf—the predator at night. But if we think of the poem, we think of the poem as a place where we're trying to get to an approximated truth. And this involves our search into our own psyches that is an attempt to align the external with the internal. So, truth is always taking a step back—and it keeps us moving ahead—and there comes a point where what we really discover is, in essence, our own selves.

*Barnstone:* It's interesting, particularly if you think of the tunnel rat as digging for truth, since, if he finds the truth, he finds the enemy—it's kill or be killed. An uncomfortable truth!

*Komunyakaa:* Yes.

*Barnstone:* I'd like to shift subjects here and talk about your interest in music a bit. I'm thinking about the book *Copacetic. Copacetic* is a book with many dramatic monologues, often spoken in a very interesting idiom, by characters who have street names. And a lot of the poems are called "blues poems"— there's "Untitled Blues," or "Jumping Bad Blues," or "Woman, I Got the Blues." I'm wondering, do you come to this dramatic monologue tradition—as I said earlier, I came to write dramatic monologues myself after reading Browning, Masters, Robinson, Ai, and others. Ezra Pound. Do you come then from the blues or poetry, or both?

*Komunyakaa:* I grew up where the radio was always on, and consequently I internalized the blues to an extent. What I mean by "the blues"—I don't mean, you know, melancholy. The blues is really a combination of many different feelings. So, when I got to New Orleans, I would often have the radio turned to WWOZ—traditional blues, jazz—and in a way it connected me to those early experiences being four or five years old, listening to the radio. In some way I think it really helped me to write some of those poems. And I do see the blues as confrontation. I'm not talking in a strict political sense, but confrontation with one's mortality, confrontation with the essence of just being human. Pain, celebration—all those things mixed together—not creating a flotsam but creating a kind of relation, if possible.

*Barnstone:* The blues poems are also joined with a smaller number of poems about jazz, and about jazz greats—Monk and Mingus, for instance. Also, you've co-edited an anthology of jazz poetry. My question is whether the jazz poems versus the blues poems—whether you're trying to do something different in terms of mood, or rhythm.

*Komunyakaa:* Mood, yes. But essentially I think we cannot really have jazz without having the blues.

*Garabedian:* I'm thinking about the melancholy of your utterances—that "cruel happiness." A lot of times in *Magic City* this negativity in the text—or ostensible negativity— informs the present, and redeems it in that manner. Do you get that at all from the blues? It seems to me that there's a similar process happening in the blues.

*Komunyakaa:* In the blues, if you listen to the lyrics, they're singing about heartbreak, failures. But you realize that they're singing from the point of view of witness, of experience, but also an attempt to get beyond the pathos by singing about it, by laying it out, by "putting it on the line," as they say. It was, in a way, a departure into another day.

*Barnstone:* And structurally? In a poem that is structured as a jazz or blues poem, do you find yourself doing more repetition?

*Komunyakaa:* In a blues poem I think automatically you have to have—if you think about the classical blues—at least a refrain. Often what I'll do is I might write a poem with a refrain in it and then take it out, because a refrain pushes an intuitive imaging.

*Barnstone:* It becomes the underpainting.

*Komunyakaa:* Yes.

*Audience Member:* How do you try to get the oral quality of your poems across when you write them down? Just the way you spoke them carried its own meaning.

*Komunyakaa:* I'm quite conscious of spoken diction. But I also think the poem has to function on the page as well, and, for me, the white space is silence. Think about silence. We wouldn't have music if there wasn't silence, because we wouldn't have modulation. We wouldn't have tension or the space for tonal contrasts.

*Barnstone:* William Carlos Williams used to like to quote from Gertrude Stein: "a poem is made up of words, and the space between the words."

*Komunyakaa:* Yes.

*Barnstone:* I noticed when you were reading there were a lot of interesting pauses syncopating the sentences. I was wondering—because I wasn't following on the page—whether those correlate with line breaks?

*Komunyakaa:* Sometimes they correlate with line breaks. Other times what I do is I like to tell myself that I want to surprise myself in reading, if possible. And I do that because there is flexibility in language. It's elastic, you know. You can pull it this way and that, and it can endure that kind of tension, push-pull. In the same way I think musicians work. I'm not talking about Coltrane's idea about sheets of sound, but a kind of blues modulation.

*Barnstone:* One of the things the critics are tied up in knots about is what on earth Williams's "variable foot" actually means. But one of the most sensible explanations they've come up with is that it's essentially the same as musical notation. That any line or partial line in the triadic stanza of a Williams poem can be read incredibly slowly like a whole note, or many words will be eighth notes, and so that way you can expand or pace the poem. Do you see that happening in your poetry? Do you work with a variable foot, do you work with some kind of metrics? Or is it visual poetry, as some people say?

*Komunyakaa:* Early on—my very first poems—were over-controlled, traditional. A good example: The very first poem I wrote was in high school, and it was one hundred lines long, traditional rhyming quatrains—I remember being too shy to read it. So, somebody has it somewhere. As a matter of fact, I'm the one who has it. It's a well-kept secret.

*Audience:* [*Laughter.*]

*Komunyakaa:* But, I used to count out the metrics of the poem. Now, I read everything aloud to myself. The ear is a great editor. Even when poems are published I'm still revising. But one doesn't want to polish the heart out of the poem.

*Barnstone:* It's interesting. I usually think of metrics as a good training device to develop the ear; once you have the ear, you can dispose of the metrics.

*Komunyakaa:* That's right, but one has to be conscious of the poem's musical tensions or possibilities.

*Audience Member:* When you were writing that one hundred–line poem in high school, do you think of yourself then as a poet? When did you know?

*Komunyakaa:* I'll tell you exactly when it happened. I had been teaching at the University of New Orleans, and I said (I'd been teaching four sections of composition for a few years): "Okay. What I'm going to do is apprentice myself to a cabinet maker. And I'll become a cabinet maker in order to have time to do my writing." That's when I knew!

*Audience:* [*Laughter.*]

*Ayame Fukuda:* My experience tonight listening to you read was as if I was being amplified through your words. It was the most physical poetry reading experience I've had. I have heard other poets who have been influenced by jazz, but, for some reason, my head was the drum, and my body was full of insects, and it was the jungle, and I think the lack of finite resolution at the end allows the reader—or not the reader but the receiver, I guess—to reverberate back with you. Something like that. There's a reverberation happening.

*Komunyakaa:* Well, that's interesting because my idea is to— if possible—create a situation where the listener or the reader can be co-creators. And if possible, whenever that happens, we can say it's working. Often that's how I read poems. I'm very taken with poems that I can enter in as an active participant. Everything hasn't been told to me, it hasn't been resolved, it hasn't been neatly tied up.

*Ayame Fukuda:* A lot of your endings kept me on edge, awaiting, as if I were about to take that next physical step. I know I'm speaking sort of vaguely . . .

*Komunyakaa:* No, no! That's the same thing I feel with certain musicians. There's a certain kind of phrasing.

*Ayame Fukuda:* A phrasing that you had and that I would complete. I almost felt like humming with you or completing your phrases, or I would pick up on a rhythm that you dictated and I'd go "da-da-da-da" in my head. I really heard the stuff in my head.

*Komunyakaa:* That's interesting. I would like to know . . . can I have a dictation?

*Audience:* [*Laughter.*]

*Ayame Fukuda:* It was a very musical experience.

*Garabedian:* You preface parts 1 and 2 of *I Apologize for the Eyes in My Head* with quotes from Aimé Césaire's *Poetry and Knowledge* and Czeslaw Milosz's "Dedication," respectively. Césaire contends that the poet's "entire being [and] experience should become the poem," while Milosz suggests that "poetry which does not save / Nations or people" is deficient. The first poem seems to endorse a more esoteric or cathartic type of poetry; the second advocates a more exoteric, possibly didactic poetry. I'm wondering which of the two types—the reflective or the instructional—is more important for your poetry? Are the two necessarily distinct?

*Komunyakaa:* I think they're interwoven. I think I can't have one without the other. But I don't quite necessarily see Milosz as didactic. I see what's happening there as a presentation of a certain reality that embraces images that are often beautiful, frightening. I don't see at all how the attempt to get to the truth is didactic, the attempt to say "I witness this" is didactic. It's more presentational than anything else—this is what happened, so consequently you don't have to go through it. You only have to use your imagination to get there, necessarily.

*Garabedian:* Does this at all inform whom your audience is—those who haven't experienced these types of things?

*Komunyakaa:* No, I think all of us experience all kinds of negative things, and there's a whole commodity of distractions in which we try to escape them, and we realize that's impossible, finally. So I think maybe what I'm saying is that we have the capacity to have a certain empathy for those who come into contact with that which is horrific. We have the capacity to measure out the horrors against their existence. At least I hope so.

*Barnstone:* And the words in the poems, as I am understanding you—again, I'm thinking here of William Carlos Williams—there's a moment in an essay about Shakespeare in which he sees Shakespeare as one who didn't write *words* so much as write *actions,* and this is what he thinks a poem should do. Not print a copy off the face of the world, but make a world for people to walk into.

*Komunyakaa:* Yes. To not show them through it, to not guide them through it, but the world is placed there, you enter at your own risk and necessity.

*Garabedian:* You are located to some extent in academia. One friend of mine contends that academia is a means by which issues that society deems "radical" or controversial might be marginalized. Do you think this is true? This would depend much upon what you see as the purpose of your poetry, but do you find your position in this setting hindering at all?

*Komunyakaa:* Well, I don't think so. For the most part, it keeps me close to what I like doing. Reading is one thing; I think it's important, and I think it has a lot to do with my own creativity. We have spoken about science. I tend to tell people to read texts in literature, science, history, philosophy, etc. The reason for science is that there's a line between beauty and terror, and it creates artistic tension. Poetry has to have tension. That's probably the only thing I embraced from John Crowe Ransom—the Fugitives.

*Barnstone:* For the last year I've been obsessed with chaos and imagination—where the two intersect. Often what I find myself doing for myself and my students is to—rather like having your students read history and science—is to show them that the brain is much better at making connections between two already-present objects than it is about taking one object and imagining what sort of connection might reach out to another, as yet undetermined, object. So, if you randomly fill your brain with a chaos of words from another discourse—science, physics, whatever it may be—while you're writing about making love, driving your car, whatever it may be, then you'll suddenly find a language for it that is utterly unexpected.

*Komunyakaa:* Surprise.

*Barnstone:* Yes.

*Komunyakaa:* The surprise is very important. That has a lot to do with the composition of a poem. One wants to surprise himself or herself, and consequently when that happens, often we say, "Where did that come from?" It came from some little place within the context of the psyche—some little door. That's the joy in the imagination, and it has a lot to do with possibility.

# Yusef Komunyakaa on
# Etheridge Knight
*Interview with Tom Johnson*


*I suppose I'll begin by asking you to characterize your personal relationship with Etheridge Knight and to explain how you came to know and admire his work.*

I had read his work in the late 1970s and I had been really taken with his poetry and experiences, especially with the fact he was born in Mississippi and I grew up in Louisiana, so I saw at least a parallel there. In 1981 I wrote a letter to him in Indianapolis, and I requested a jazz-related poem, and he responded with a kindness I was quite taken with. I sensed a connective tissue that was just there. We never really sparred in any way, which is great because I have heard all kinds of stories, different stories . . . I was telling someone recently that one can actually go across the country and collect a whole body of stories on Etheridge. So, that says a lot about the complexity of the man. I was intrigued by the fact that Dudley Randall and Gwendolyn Brooks had connected with him in such a direct way. It said a lot about an extended community. So, I saw Etheridge as part of my community, and it was one of those flexible communities. Etheridge could drift in and out of places, and I liked that a whole lot, that ability to deal with so many different people.

*In 1993 you wrote a piece on Etheridge called "Tough Eloquence" for the* Trotter Review. *In that essay, which is for the most part a praise piece, you talked about the authenticity and naturalness of his poetic voice and the tremendous pathos that it is able to achieve, and*

---

Originally appeared as "Double Takes on Etheridge" in the *Worcester Review* 19 (1999).

*you also discussed the ways in which he uses irony and the art of signifying.*

Yes. Well, I think Etheridge, as I have said before, is connected to a blues tradition, and it is something I was connected to early on. I was also mystified by the blues, just coming through the radio from New Orleans. And that way, I was connected again to Etheridge, because I think somewhere he said he wished he were a blues singer.

*Yes, I've seen a number of interviews where he has said the same thing. Just for the record, I thought I would read his comment in the back of your* Jazz Poetry Anthology. *I think it is my favorite one . . .*

Well, he wrote that in a letter.

*Really?*

It is an excerpt from his response to the letter I had written him.

*So, it is more of a personal communication . . . I believe I like it all the more now. I think I'll go ahead and read it:*

> *The influence of Jazz in my poetry is natural. Like most black people—especially those of us who are born in the south—I grew up in an atmosphere that was permeated with music: blues, gospel, and jazz. I was conceived in the Great Song of the Universe. And before I was born, I boogied in my mother's belly while she sang her songs in the country churches and clubs in northern Mississippi. So jazz is not an abstraction to me, it is a physicality (so is all music really). We speak rhythms, ask anyone who stutters. Our speech patterns—the intonations, inflections, nuances—are to a larger degree determined by the music of our lives. We talk jazz and we walk jazz. I came of age with jazz. Got my first "piece" listening to Cooty Williams in the background. And when I die I hope Coltrane is played at my funeral, 'cause Jazz has been very important in my life, and therefore to my poetry.*

He came out of the Southern tradition and consequently, he remained in the Southern tradition, even when he was in Indianapolis and elsewhere.

*And there is also a definite urban feel to his poetry. It's difficult to distinguish the prison metaphor and have it complement the Southern feel, but, underneath even his most streetwise poems, there seems to be this lyricism . . .*

I think it is in the lyricism, it is in his directness, and the metaphors linked to the earth itself. You know that poem of his where he is praising his father about the bones in the delta, "The Dry Bones of My Father." It is really, in a way, a spiritual.

*Definitely . . . In fact, he seems to be overtly playing off of the dry bones passage in Ezekiel.*

Yes.

*Now here's a rather large, loaded question for you. Could you characterize Etheridge's place in the continuum of African American poetry for us?*

Shew! [*Laughter.*] That's a good question because when we think of Etheridge in the '70s, and all the poetry coming about in the '70s, his seems to be more grounded. I think Gwendolyn Brooks says, "Art is that which endures," and that's what has happened with Etheridge's work. He produced a body of work that definitely endures. It is aligned with oral and literary traditions. Etheridge, I would say, has been influenced by all of his experiences, but also by everything he read. And there is a gentleness in his work, and at the same time, there is a kind of hard-core, jagged edge to Etheridge as well. He is a person who has everything to do with survival. I am sure his persona was actualized even before he went off to prison, but it was really, I would say, refined, within the prison environment. But just growing up, particularly as a black male coming out of the rural South—the history of Mississippi— Etheridge knew that history, he had internalized it. And at the same time, it was an internalization that tempered his work, but he didn't really become an embittered individual, and I am quite mystified by that, and, matter of fact, I respect it. But I think it has everything to do with the temperament of an artist.

*It clearly meant a lot to him to be an artist . . . much more, I would say, than a lot of other good artists. It was an identity that he wore with tremendous pride. I think you encapsulated Etheridge's spirit when you spoke of survival and his sense of endurance without bitterness. He was angry to be sure, but there was still love.*

There was still love there, and that is important in his kinship to the blues tradition, because you have all the sacrifice, tempered with anger, but at the same time the immense capacity to love and endure through grace.

*A fine line between rage and healing.*

Yes. And it is a kind of ongoing healing. I think his poetry has everything to do with an attempt to heal the psyche.

*I have sent away for his exact military service records, so I should be receiving them in . . . who knows . . . a few years* [Laughter.] *But he was actually in the service twice. He enlisted before he was eighteen, and the story is—and I have heard this from a couple of different sources—that they found out he was too young and kicked him out. He then rejoined after he turned eighteen, and his second period of service was only eleven months long, and that was right when the Korean War began. But it is odd, and you mention this in your* Trotter Review *piece, that he never wrote about his war experience.*

He didn't really write about it. I am quite sure that was a troubling moment for him because, let's face it, any kind of presence on a battlefield, especially with the sensitivity of Etheridge, would have been traumatic.

*Yes, and since he didn't talk much about it, there is some fairly equivocal information out there about his experience, but, again and again, what you do hear are statements of mental duress and psychological extremes.*

And especially if one served as a medic. I would think that would have been very difficult. It is my understanding that that is when the drug addiction began—morphine, I think.

*That's certainly the official line, but I have also heard that he had an addiction before the war; so, as with so many Etheridge Knight stories, it seems to have become something of a myth.*

If he had an addiction before, I don't see how he would have gotten into the military.

*Yea, I don't know. That's why I have sent for his military records. He was also known for his Free Peoples Poetry Workshops, and again and again, in interviews and letters, he talked about how important it was, to him, to keep poetry in the streets. He thought that academia oftentimes co-opted the vitality of the artist. I know that you were a "poet in the schools" in New Orleans and have had some experience teaching poetry to children, now you are off to Princeton, so I was hoping you could shed some light on the influence of academia on art.*

What is rather important when you think about it, children are very vibrant and imaginative. I'm particularly thinking of third-, fourth-, and fifth-graders, and they are rather amazing. They are constantly surprising themselves, and they are not afraid to surprise themselves. But there is that moment when they are in the sixth or seventh grade, they seem to begin to really question creativity. And peer pressure, I think, is part of it. Especially with boys, I know this is true. But, for the most part, children are great when it comes to poetry. They seem to automatically create some strong metaphors and similes.

*I think there is a parallel to be drawn here between that kind of consciousness that is open to different metaphors and Etheridge's practice of conducting his workshops in prisons, bars, and basements, as opposed to classrooms.*

Those are the places, I think, Etheridge could identify with. I think he was threatened by formal education. And yet I think he respected it, but he didn't really come out and say so because he hadn't been formally educated himself. I think that is the reason he felt threatened by it.

*I did come across a statement he made once where he likened being an artist and not having tenure to castration. I should also point out that he said this at a time when he was having some serious financial difficulty.*

If you think about it, some of Etheridge's close friends were connected with institutions. In particular, I am thinking of Galway Kinnell, Donald Hall, James Wright, and Robert Bly. They were educated, and Etheridge educated himself. So, it seems like something he admired, but he hadn't really matriculated through an institution himself.

*I think he knew the source of his strength was his self-education.*

Yes, I think so.

*But that he did, as you say, respect more formalized education.*

Because he read books.

*It seems as though he just emerged on the scene with a fairly disciplined poetic voice. You would have to attribute some of that to Gwendolyn Brooks and Dudley Randall and other influences, but at the same time his mind was certainly already rigorous.*

*Etheridge was reading books!* [Laughter.]

You see? I think, again you get into this whole male persona—especially in prison—is it cool to read books?

*Exactly. Actually, he was put on the spot by an interviewer once who said, "I hear you are a closet reader," and Etheridge started talking about books that he had read, and indeed he had read Faulkner and . . .*

That's right. And he had plenty of time to do that in prison.

*Another thing that Etheridge brings to mind . . . Have you seen the new* Callaloo *issue [vol. 19, no. 4] that contains some of Etheridge's letters . . . ?*

I haven't seen it yet; Charles Rowell, the editor, is supposed to send me a copy.

*Anyway, some of them are letters he had written to Sonia Sanchez while he was still in prison, and it is obvious that he had really been fed and fueled by the strong rhetoric of the Black Arts Movement. And when he came out, I think it was Don L. Lee who criticized* Poems from Prison, *saying that he had adopted European patterns and forms of poetry, and I think Etheridge found himself in a really tenuous position. I mean he was almost groomed, in a way, to be an articulate, representative voice of the prison experience as a black male from the South and so forth, and then, at the same time, he got some flack for befriending Donald Hall.*

It was an interesting moment in the 1970s, because, if you think about Robert Hayden, he got the same kind of criticism. And as a matter of fact, spoken by people who were just full of contradictions themselves, such as Haki Madhubuti, who later goes to the University of Iowa to get an MFA. So, it shows how people were speaking off the top of their heads, without thinking. Yes, an attempt to stereotype Etheridge in a way that he could only be of the streets is just ridiculous.

*In interviews Etheridge had a wonderful way of evading questions with narrative, which was sometimes more informative than if he had answered the questions. But at one point in a particular interview, the questioner pinned him down and said, "Look, what was your relationship with the Black Arts Movement? You have been criticized by . . ." and Etheridge just said, "Man, those just ain't cool questions." And that was that.* [Laughter.]

I think with the Black Arts Movement, Etheridge was really on the sidelines of that movement. His poems are a lot more grounded than the voices coming out of the Black Arts Movement. Etheridge is not reactionary in his poems. He is confrontational, and he is also seeking a level of truth that pretty much defines the essence of him—an individual, an artist. Same as a blues singer would, same as a Robert Johnson would. Coming to his own voice and technique, and yet knowing the overall tradition. I think he knew the blues tradition, the black folk tradition, but also the European tradition, probably through reading in prison. Moreover, he was also closely respected by people such as Gwendolyn Brooks, who had also come through that tradition. As a matter of fact, I think when Gwendolyn Brooks aligns herself with the Black Arts Movement her poetry loses a fundamental ground, except the book *Into the Mecca*.

*So, you think, in a way, she maybe ideologically wanted to embrace something that wasn't so much of herself as her earlier poetry?*

I think so. But again, she is reaching out for a community. Reaching out to those individuals who would have denied her existence unless she co-opted herself.

*I would like to know a little bit about your position during all of this. You were just coming back from a war, so you obviously had some other issues to deal with that required immediate attention. Michael Harper wrote some Vietnam poems in* Debridement, *and he told me that he has been asked, "How can you be clear about this [war] when you were not there?" And his reply was, "Anyone can understand when your only option is either victim or executioner." So, you come back from Vietnam and are faced with this same kind of polarization back home, not just surrounding the war but also with race relations and the Black Arts Movement.*

The polarization actually was in Vietnam as well, when I think about it, especially when you talk about black and white troops. Not so much in fire fights as much as when people were on leave and R & R—rest and recuperation. But I remember reading very closely the voices associated with the Black Arts Movement, and I have gone back and looked at my own work, my earlier work, work that I haven't collected, and I can see the beginnings of the voice that I have now. But, for the most part, I would say 90 percent of it was just imitative of the Black Arts Movement. I knew I wanted a certain musicality in the poem, and I knew that each line was a musical increment in the overall piece. And I knew that I really wanted to have images in my work more than statements, but I found more statements in the poetry of the Black Arts Movement. It was more political philosophy.

*Less art, more ideology?*

Ideology, yes.

*Something else you mentioned about Etheridge, again referring to the* Trotter Review *essay, sounds a bit like what you are saying about your own work, and that is Etheridge's ability to cut deep, but without really moralizing.*

Well, I like the idea of not really resolving the poem, leaving the poem open ended so a reader or listener can get inside, if possible. I am not telling people what to think or how to feel, but I hope I can write poems where a listener or reader can immerse him- or herself in the text. That's how I like reading poetry. So that taught me a great deal . . . what I lacked, you know? That is why I admire Robert Hayden, because he is such a technician. I wish he had written more, because his work is brilliant. But I remember when some associated with the Black Arts Movement really came down on him.

*I read Michael Harper's letters to and from Hayden—they were published in* Callaloo *as well—and he always talked about that, and, virtually every time he mentions a reading, he said that the "bloods" were there and that it was a bad experience. And, as you say, here is a man who was an incredibly deft poet.*

Well, I don't know if it has anything to do with the restlessness of youth, maybe the inability to really stake oneself down and think about things from many angles. Poetry isn't to answer anything. Poetry for me poses questions, and I think that's what it is in the best of Etheridge's work. These are poems that pose questions.

*In your opinion, what happened to the Black Arts Movement? What happened to its momentum and the aggressive side of its rhetoric? Etheridge once said that "the people who were in the forefront were no longer getting kicked in the ass as hard," that their voices diminished, and that the next generation didn't quite pick up the same head of steam.*

For the most part, I think a maturity of the imagination kicked in. However, a lot of the rap culture is directly linked to the Black Arts Movement.

*What about the New Black Aesthetic?*

Up until recently, black Americans wrote a service literature, and that service literature had everything to do with defining the essence of blackness, just by imperatives of history. What has happened recently, I think, is that for the first time black writers have the freedom to delve into their own individuality—individuals who are not condemned to write a service literature, individuals who are willing to say, "I am going to write as a person, I am going to write as a man or woman," and stand his or her ground. This is something, interestingly enough, that Hayden and a number of others have done. One individual whom I really admire is Helene Johnson, a poet of the Harlem Renaissance. She was one of the younger voices in the Harlem Renaissance. Looking at her work, it seems different from most of the Harlem Renaissance poets. As a matter of fact, to me she is the most talented of those voices, and even as far as her poetry is concerned, perhaps more talented than Langston Hughes. Langston Hughes is, of course, associated with the blues tradition, and I see him as a modernist in that sense. There are very few Harlem Renaissance poets that we can say are actually modernists. Perhaps someone such as Jean Toomer, because of his book *Cane*, but, looking back at Helene Johnson, I really see her as a modernist.

*With the New Black Aesthetic and, as you say, its fierce individuality, is there any fear that this new generation of black writers is not going to preserve the literary and historical heritage that was so painstakingly won by its predecessor?*

Oh no, I think there are writers preserving it, but they are not really, as I said, condemned to write a service literature; they are writing from their own personal histories. I think it is something they have wrestled with. It's an achievement. Langston Hughes embraced the blues tradition. The blues is very political, but the poet is perhaps condemned to write one kind of poem. In comparison, when we look at Etheridge's work, you know, he wrote many different kinds of poems.

*And I would say the same is true with your work as well. Your poetry is fiercely individual and introspective, but, at the same time, you can speak extremely eloquently about being a black male in America.*

One has to, as an artist, attempt to do that, you know. Attempt to look at things many different ways. Poetry is really distilled empathy, and in order to empathize one has to have the capacity to place him- or herself in different situations at different times.

*Then, in a way, the empathy takes care of the responsibility.*
Yes.

# Notations in Blue

*Interview with Radiclani Clytus*


*In a recent interview Charles Wright asserts that besides himself, you are one of the only poets working with the "true tradition of nonnarrative, Southern imagistic, agrarian poetry." Could you discuss your role as a Southern writer?*

Well, I don't think of myself especially as a Southern writer. However, I do realize that one pretty much internalizes a terrain; I've talked about this a number of times before. Automatically, in my early experiences, I suppose I had the misfortune and luck to have grown up in rural Louisiana. I would venture out into the wooded areas; I knew all the creeks and contours in the landscape. I think in doing that it led me to the psyche of the Southern people. I see myself, basically, as a product of a tradition of farmers and peasants, people who were very close to the land.

*Are there any Southern writers or specific cultural art forms that have influenced you personally? Is there something else other than the rituals of rural life, say, something more literary, that affects your craft?*

In the literary sense? Of course, I read Faulkner early on and that type of gothic, magical realism that takes place in his work, a good example would be in his *Light in August* and *Sound and the Fury*. Everything that he wrote pretty much, I think, had to do with the South and how its tradition seems to want to hold on to a sense of its history and also its pathos. But, if I think about other writers, well, there is also Paul Laurence Dunbar. Dunbar was born in Dayton, Ohio, but there is something quite Southern about him that I believe has a lot to do with the fact that his parents were former slaves and were born and raised in Kentucky. He probably knew the

South by their stories and their memories. Very early I grasped on to Dunbar's voice because of the sense of history in his poems. I especially liked the fact that he was able to do dialect but could perfect standard English poems as well. Importantly, Dunbar agonizes over the fact that most critics and readers of his work were drawn to the dialect poems.

*I think what I hear from Wright when he prides himself as a Southerner is not entirely what you claim as your South.*

Perhaps history?

*Yes.*

It's an interesting situation because, automatically when I think of the South, I think of the South as a place of oppression, and I think of the South as regressive. So, I'm fighting with the South and embracing it at the same time.

*Yes, I agree, and without misconstruing Wright's own cultural imagination, how can we come to understand the concept of a Southern literary tradition beyond the exclusionary nature of its "understood" aesthetic iconology. Confederate history, plantations, John Crowe Ransom, and so forth.*

Well, I don't think of that apparatus as such. I can usually put faces on individuals I respect and love. And realizing that they are very close to me and that they represent people who are survivors, people who came up against hardship and were also able to exist as men and women and not just with their lives intact, but also with a certain kind of moral structure intact. So, the South for me is a place of opposition and therefore a place of birth for the black writer. He or she has to claim his or her birthright. I think Ernest Gaines, James Alan McPherson, and Zora Neale Hurston accomplish that. You claim the oppression along with the moments of severe beauty and elegance. One cannot claim one over the other. One has to take the whole "wormy" package.

*What has been your impression of Charles Wright's craft since you've left the University of California, Irvine?*

When I read Wright's work, *The Grave of the Right Hand, Hard Freight, China Trace,* those were the books I think I'd read before I actually studied with him. I thought that he was doing something entirely different. And what's interesting to me is that not only is his voice different from any other Southern writer, I think it's also different from any American writer. In effect, it's almost as if translating Montale and Campana was very important in getting his own voice honed into a mechanism of imagistic expression.

*What do you identify as particularly Southern about Wright's work?*

Well, there are place names in the work; other than that I don't see his work as really Southern. It is an acquired tableau. There isn't a sense of region. I think it has everything to do with those years that he was reading Pound and living in Italy translating Italian writers.

*Has your view of contemporary American poetry changed since your last unflattering comment regarding its condition?*

I think I said something to the effect that one could take a magazine of poems and cut the names off them and have a single collection of poems as if written by one person. And to an extent that is still true, but there are those individuals out there who have all along been doing new and different things. Someone such as C. K. Williams, whose voice has always been rather different, and his horizontal reach of the line on the page fascinates me. Also, Rita Dove has a unique way of illuminating the concerns of everyday people. And I think Jorie Graham is doing something fascinating; however, I'm more attracted to the early poems, for instance, *Erosion,* not necessarily the poems in *Errancy,* her latest book.

*How important is the relationship between individuality and experimentation?*

I think individuality is very important. Wallace Stevens said that every poem is an experimentation. I don't necessarily agree with that but I know what he's talking about. The fact that if one confronts the page and says to him- or herself that I am writing a poem suggests that the poet is experimenting in that sense. And if the poet experiments, he may become.

*You have mentioned in passing that sometimes experimentation embodies a sense of evasion. Can a poet evade voice through his rejection of a particular form?*

Well, it depends on what are one's experiences and observations. I think that, within the structure of the poem, the structure can be experimental, but how about the content? Does the experimentation erase or reject the content of the poem? The point I'm making is that one should be able to experiment and write about anything. My problem is when the experimentation becomes a process to disguise or erase the content.

*How important is William Matthews to your understanding of contemporary American poetry? His voice seems to resonate with a number of your own poetic projects.*

I've been reading Matthews for a long time. I think the very first poem of his I read was in *Partisan Review* in the mid-1970s. I think it was a poem on Coleman Hawkins, and I was quite taken with the poem. One reason was because of the subject matter, but also because of the finely tuned voice in the poem and an authority that wasn't "puffed up." It was stated matter-of-factly. So, I admire that. It was a voice that I could really believe and trust. Sincerity came through and also a great knowledge of poetry, language, innuendo, and understatement for the most part.

*Where do you see him, within the American continuum?*

I'm very much interested in that fact that he, in his work, was able to embrace jazz and blues, but also those everyday things, those everyday rituals in life. I think that is how he has influenced American poetry—basically saying that those everyday things, such as washing clothes or whatever, are important and that they can be placed alongside those moments of philosophical and political inquiry. So it's a different mental map for the most part, and his poems give sanction to writing about any and everything—writing about one's pets if necessary.

*Do you see any similarities between the reasons why he has written so many jazz-related poems and your own work? Is there something different that brings you to the music?*

I think there's a love for the music. Bill loved the music, I think he played clarinet for a while, and I think it was at seventeen that he marched over to Mingus and established a conversation. He had been close to the masters for some time.

*You have been working on a number of poems that are restricted to sixteen lines at four stanzas each as well as investigating some prose projects. Could you talk a little more about your relationship to form, particularly the sixteen-line approach?*

Well, at this moment, it's rather instructive. It tells me that I can write about anything and basically collapse whatever my observations and meditations are into a structure—if it's on metaphysics, a scientific principle, or the ritual of an insect or an animal—I can collapse it into that sixteen-line structure and, hopefully, through that compression be surprised. I'm saying more than I could say in thirty lines, at least that's the way I'm reading these poems at the moment—making every word speak for itself.

*How does this idea of more from less correspond with the recent experimentation with prose in* Thieves of Paradise?

Well, the prose poem has always interested me. I wanted to have those long lines but I wanted it to stay very close to the language and imagistic patterns of poetry. I didn't want those poems to veer away from that which is important for poetic expression. If you read those poems closely you will realize that they are rather economical. So in that sense there is a relationship between the two structures.

*You are now writing another libretto; can we assume that this new interest in structure is related to your experimentation with dramatic form? Or could it better explain your recent adventure into songwriting?*

As far as songs go, they were the first things I began to experiment with as a child. Just the fact that songs came to me through the radio prompted me to sing out loud or at least sing in my head. As far as drama goes, I have never given up that part of my life. It has only become another creative voice for me to consider on paper. Baraka says that every poet should be a playwright. And I've been thinking about that a long time. It becomes an interesting question because there is that story about Edward Albee giving W. H. Auden a sheath of poems and Auden saying later, perhaps you should be a playwright. But also I've looked at the poetry of Tennessee Williams and realized that his poetry informs his drama. The same thing is true of Beckett. The poems perhaps inform his plays, and so it is with Baraka.

*How is the writing of poetry similar to the creation of drama?*

Well, the language has to be exciting, not overly provocative, but exciting. There has to be a certain kind of conciseness within the language or risk taking in order for your characters to rise to the occasion. But also, when we think of characters, we think of them saying things that are particular to their character. Each, as a person, is an inventor of life, elation and chaos.

*Since your poetry has overwhelmingly been the type of lyric poetry that shapes the reader as speaker, have you found the actual writing of characters a difficult enterprise?*

Often the poem becomes a dramatic monologue, so my having written a few dramatic monologues has moved me closer toward the play. And I think a play always consists of dramatic monologues. Let's face it, the characters are always speaking from somewhere within themselves. And sometimes it is an unconscious design and even the characters are surprised by the words that flow out of their mouths. Not that one wants the characters to speak poetry, but there can be images woven into the dialogue.

*In that case, what do you expect to accomplish with* Slip Knot, *the libretto you are composing along with T. J. Anderson?*

Well, the main character, Arthur, is pretty much a challenge. He is a slave born in Massachusetts in 1747 and dies in 1768. He's a controversial figure who seeks refuge amongst American Indians but always returns home, to his detriment. I'm quite taken with an expression of his when he says, "I'm almost free." There is something about him that is modern. Overall, I want to present aspects of his life as entertaining, but also as intellectually sound. This is the great difficulty I face at the moment.

*Should we expect to see more theater from you in the future?*

Yes, I've been thinking about a number of ideas for plays. And I've had these ideas for some years, but I've never had the time to commit them to paper. I'm attracted to the possibility of theater, characters getting up on stage and coming alive, saying things that surprise us, but also parallel the ideas and feelings within our own minds and bodies.

*What was the motivating factor in your recent collaboration with jazz musician John Tchicai? Is there an overriding artistic purpose to your CD,* Love Notes from the Mad House?

I said yes to that project when I was called by Tony Getsug. He said he wanted to bring poetry and music together, and I said, "Great, why not?" But I knew that I didn't want to present poems that would mimic musical expression because music itself does a good job. So, I wanted something that could contrast and create tension in the performance. I wanted the poem to complement the music, and vice versa. I knew what already had been done, and I knew where the failures were. If we think about the 1950s, we think about the typical Beat scene. You know, somebody pounding on the bongos and bases or maybe there's a horn in the background. Black berets, specs, and turtlenecks. What happened there is that there was a kind of mutual disrespect. So, I wanted something that was the opposite of that. Of course, we began by rehearsing. I don't think that one can rush to the stage and say this is going to be a "happening." As a group, there must be rehearsals, and out of that rehearsal time is where respect develops. The musicians respect the words and the poet respects the notes and all those surprises and collisions occur.

*So, what is it musically that you are interested in effecting while reading poetry with jazz? I would presume it is somewhat different from the poetic processes that you become aware of after writing a poem.*

I wanted the two forms to come together and create a third space, a very different musical space, one where the pieces become an active collaboration in themselves.

*Are you satisfied with the overall project?*

Yes, quite. When one is on the stage, he or she doesn't hear all of the things occurring on the stage itself. There are so many things happening and so many people—not to mention the moments of improvisation.

*One of the things I noticed while reading* Thieves *was how much your earlier works seem to inform the various sections of the book. There are remnants of Vietnam, the various instances of complex desires tackled in* Copacetic, *and a rather urbane rendering of the blues and jazz related, which all of your previous collections investigate. Was there a conscientious effort on your part to return to these themes, or was this something you had no control over?*

I knew I wanted seven sections to the book. And I pushed for that structure. I knew I wanted those sections to stand on their own and at the same time complement the other sections. I wanted them to be in concert with each other—not in a direct way, but in more of a tonal signal between the different sections. I wanted to deal with some of the same themes even, but deal with them in a different way. The prose poems, for instance. I had thought about writing a book called *Debriefing Ghosts,* a whole book-length manuscript, and, before I knew it, I was inserting that section into *Thieves,* and things started working that way. I began to arrange things and shift things around to create a kind of balance.

*Yes, I was particularly struck by your prose in the book's fifth section, "Debriefing Ghosts." Although the images merge into one another, they always appear to suggest a coherent narrative.*

In this section I didn't want a traditional trajectory. I wanted a narrative space where we are transported through the images and consequently there are little doors left all over for us to walk through and find ourselves in the design of the book. I also think that this could be an interesting mechanism to develop in a novel. I'm not afraid of letting the images create the narrative. I start with images and I improvise on images, so while in the act of improvisation, if an image informs me in some way, then fine. Everything doesn't have to be seamless, things can be disconnected, or at least they appear disconnected. Form is only an increment of the overall cosmology of what the poem is becoming.

*So you do not advocate controlling the narrative through imagery although it is the central organizing principle?*

I think the way the human brain works, it imposes its own order and structure, and in that sense the book has numerous substructures because each reader will bring something different to it. I think the most exact kind of communication is when the reader or listener isn't being guided through the poem or the novel. I suppose this is one reason I have a continuing argument with television and typical Hollywood movies. I'm more interested often in the European film because there is more of a space for the imagination to get involved with the text.

*I'm under the impression that "The Deck," which is also from "Debriefing Ghosts," is a highly autobiographical poem. In fact, its sentiment reminds me of* Magic City, *but its form suggests a later birthdate.*

Well, "The Deck" came to me when I was in Bloomington, while teaching at Indiana University. I had actually been working on a deck. But when I went back into the house, and this is about a year after my father died, there was an immense presence. I felt like he was there, almost as an instructor in a kind of way, or there to embrace what I was doing because he was a carpenter. It was as if, by the act of using tools, I had reconnected with him. He always told me, "If you know what tools can do, then your job will be a lot easier." And only in retrospect did I realize that he also taught me something about the act of creating poetry. He would measure a board five or six times, back and forth, and when he cut the board it was always exact. I understood later that it had a lot to do with economics; once you cut a board and it doesn't make it, it's lost. [*Laughter.*] But also it had a lot to do with the fact that as a carpenter, he was very meticulous, and for everything he did, he demanded precision.

*What is your primary motivation for opening with "Memory Cave"?*

Well, initially I was fascinated with the idea that bears were once seen as images of gods or godlike figures. So, I thought that it would be interesting if the individuals who celebrated the bear entered the caves when a bear was in hibernation and therefore had an opportunity to touch the god—that is, they sort of sneak up on them and in that way have an illusion of being in control. I suppose my interest in the chronology of history, however, is what prompted me to open with "Memory Cave."

*Can you account for the subdued quality of some of the poems in* Thieves of Paradise?

Well, I wonder if they are subdued. I like the idea of dealing with silence through poetry. I'm taken with moments of meditation and not so much with the notion of entertainment.

*How do you perceive the boundaries of poetry as a genre?*

I don't think about boundaries. I think that all things are connected. Although categories are easily constructed, I am always pushing against the walls they create. I will always do this—success or failure. Theater and song won't be the last of me.

*What is poetry?*

Poetry is a kind of distilled insinuation. It's a way of expanding and talking around an idea or question. Sometimes, more actually gets said through such a technique than a full frontal assault.

# IV.

# Explorations

# Tenebrae

In the fall of 1990 Professor William Roberts, who teaches percussion at Indiana University, asked me to consider writing a tribute poem in memory of Richard Johnson. He laid out the facts: Johnson, the first black tenured professor at Indiana University, received the Bachelor of Music degree from Indiana University in 1950 and from 1948 to 1950 served as an undergraduate assistant in percussion in the School of Music. He also attended McGill University in Montreal and the Julliard School of Music, where he studied with Saul Goodman, tympanist with the New York Philharmonic Symphony Orchestra. From 1950 to 1951 Johnson attended the Conservatoire National de Musique in Paris, studying with Felix Passerone, tympanist with the Paris Opera Orchestra and Société de Concerts du Conservatoire.

I was already enthused with numerous images in my head. And then Roberts said that Johnson had problems in Bloomington, that he had difficulty finding "accurate" housing, etc. He had grown paranoid and rented a room in the IU student memorial building. Roberts paused, finding it difficult to continue, and then he finally said: "He killed himself there. Right there in the student union, and I replaced him here at IU."

Did he shoot himself? Did he hang himself? How? When? I can't remember if Roberts shared any of the details. Yet I felt a great loss for someone I had never known. I could feel that some part of my imagination had known him.

Weeks passed. Months. I felt I had said yes to something I wouldn't pull off. I walked around Bloomington—maybe crossing paths with this phantom I'd inherited—with only a refrain for "Tenebrae" in my head: "You try to beat loneliness / out of a drum . . ." These few words grew into the tonal muscle that threaded itself through an elusive imagery, that tied every-thing down. It was as if the refrain had conjured the rest of the poem, had pulled it out of my psyche.

I didn't worry about meaning. I just wanted the words to jostle each other, with an undertone of praise and surreal agency. I wanted to see if I could get close to Johnson's psycho-logical hardship, but also avoid melodrama.

Why was this poem so damn elusive?

And I kept wondering if art had failed Johnson. If so, would it likewise fail me? Would I fail it? At that moment, it seemed to me that the (existential) blues had tracked and cor-nered him in Indiana.

Finally, late one Saturday night, after playing Art Blakey and the Jazz Messengers and sipping merlot, "Tenebrae" came forth. Hundreds of lines. Then I spent days revising, cutting the poem down to its structure. A week later, one Sunday morning in late December, a couple of days before William took off for his home in Denver for Christmas break, we met at the Uptown Café for breakfast.

I felt nervous. After ordering Earl Grey tea and pancakes, I handed William the poem. He sat there, reading it over and over, as I convinced myself that I had failed. I would try again—maybe there was some bit of information I needed. Then I glanced up and saw tears in this man's eyes. He nod-ded. "This is it," he said.

I wanted words that could spark and signify percussive ele-ments, but without competing with the musical instruments. So, when I strolled into the hall for our rehearsal that morn-ing in mid-February, I was shocked to see so many instruments on stage. I was scared. My poem seemed to diminish itself. Since my instrument was only words, the mere timbre of my voice to give definition and register, I feared the poem would sound like a whisper in my throat.

I thought about all those failures of jazz with poetry in the 1950s during the Beat era. Those "happenings" didn't work. It takes mutual respect, and little can happen without rehears-als. We worked out spaces and time, bending the structure till it was what we wanted. The music and musicians were great. We were having fun. The poem seemed to expand with each note, and it was then I felt like a deprived philodendron had been given the life of water. Voice and wood, metal and touch, ivory and brass thronged with leather, electric, and acoustic, it felt as if I were trying to raise the dead. It was working.

*Tenebrae*

"May your spirit sleep in peace.
One grain of corn can fill the silo."
                                        —the Samba of Tanzania

You try to beat loneliness
out of a drum,
but cries only spring
from your mouth.
Synapse & memory.
The day quivers like dancers
with bells on their feet,
weaving a path of songs
to bring you back,
to heal our future
with the old voices
we breathe. Sometimes
our hands hang like weights
anchoring us inside
ourselves. You can go
to Africa on a note
transfigured into a tribe
of silhouettes in a field
of reeds, & circling the Cape
of Good Hope you find
yourself in Paris
backing The Hot Five.

You try to beat loneliness
out of a drum.
As you ascend
the crescendo,
please help us touch what remains
most human. Your absence
brings us one step closer
to the whole cloth

& full measure.
We're under the orange trees again, as you work life
back into the double-headed
drumskin with a spasm
of fingertips
till a chant leaps
into the dreamer's mouth.

You try to beat loneliness
out of a drum, always
coming back to opera & baseball.
A constellation of blood-tuned
notes shake against the night
forest bowed to the ground
by snow & ice. Yes,
this kind of solitude
can lift you up
between two thieves.
You can do a drumroll
that rattles slavechains
on the sea floor.
What wrong makes you
loop that silent knot
& step up on the gallows-
chair? What reminds you
of the wounded paradise
we stumbled out of?

You try to beat loneliness
out of a drum,
searching for a note
of kindness here at the edge
of this grab-wheel,
with little or no dragline
beyond the flowering trees
where only ghosts live,
no grip to clutch the truth
under a facade of skylarks.

# Shifting Gears

When I was five or six, I never sang the lyrics as they floated from the magical box of the radio. The words I sung were mine, and I remember feeling empowered by their buoyancy. I discovered that I could have fun with words.

By my eleventh birthday, I had stopped singing along with the radio, even though I admired some of my friends who doo-wopped and harmonized all the popular R&B tunes word for word—all the vocal antics and gestures. As I listened, the words in my head were different from the ones that poured from their mouths like slow, honey-filled notes of seduction. Their renditions weren't surprising to me. At the time, however, I didn't realize I craved words and phrases that had an imagistic urgency through raw energy. It seems I was already reaching for an imaginative voice by merging acquired images with those culled from experience (an untutored surrealism). But also the images had to mean something: I wasn't just interested in wordplay and puns.

Years later, a half-lifetime from Bogalusa, after the war in Nam, I found myself listening to Bob Dylan. His lyrics surprised me more than the ones that had come out of my own mouth. I liked the poetry in his songs, that mystery even his voice couldn't kill. I listened to every word. His lyrics, my mind refused to tamper with them. Matter-of-fact, I think, Dylan's lyrics had muted my desire to write songs. I kept hearing his "I Shall Be Released," "Just Like a Woman," and "All Along the Watchtower." And, of course, Taj Mahal, Richie Havens, and Nina Simone always fired things up if and when Dylan backslid.

One night in early 1995, after reading "Rhythm Method" to a bluesy piano (played by Cathy Hartley) at the Kiama Jazz Festival, a singer, Pamela Knowles, walked over and asked me if I could write lyrics. I said, "Yeah," that I believed I could pen lyrics that would challenge a listener. Also, I thought that the writing process would lead me to the tone and structure I envisioned. I said I wanted to write something that would take me beyond the commercialization of sentimentality. I heard in my head a refrain that could embrace ideas and integrity. I desired a jagged symmetry in the songs. For me, a poem is formed around my own voice; a song lyric, however, seems to be shaped around a voice outside of myself—a singer's voice in performance.

When I began writing *Thirteen Kinds of Desire,* the song lyric seemed easier than the typical poem. I would walk around humming the words for days, would sit and scribble the phrases down, and then let my wife, Mandy, read them. And I'd stand nearby, eagerly awaiting her response. A smile. A grunt. Yes. No. Maybe so. I could see that some of the rhymes surprised her. She's my greatest critic for poems and lyrics.

*Thirteen Kinds of Desire:* "Satyrs and Dryads," "Take Me Home, Lock Me Up," "Styling for the Letdown," "Flying High," "Shot Down," "New Blues," "Incantation," "You Know," "Shake on Shake," "Mirage," "A Grown Woman's Love," "Otherwise," and "Joie de Vivre." I wanted to toughen up the songs with raw innuendo and lyrical bravado. I became more daring, pushing the words as I had hoped Pamela would do in her renditions (the singer I could now hear with my words in her mouth). For my taste, the typical jazz lyric is too sugary. I desired a peppery, edgy sentiment (less sentimentality) in phrasing. I wanted the words to live alongside the music in my head—nothing like the jazz and poetry merging in the few pieces I'd written for AtmaSphere (with David Jones, Roger Frampton, and Steven Hunter) in Sydney.

Sometimes it seemed as if a different person or younger version of myself were writing *Thirteen Kinds of Desire*. I wondered if I had daydreamed myself back to the sonorous lyre, to where the simple rhymes ached to join musical instruments made of metal, catgut, and wood.

# New Blues

We are hurting
We are dying
For a new blues
One that doesn't rhyme
With worn-out shoes

We are hurting
We are dying
For a neo blues
Something to push against
To get to the evidence
Inside us

Forget the applause machine
Forget the corporate lotto
Forget the alchemist's gold scheme
And you can ditto
The sphinx's motto

We are hurting
We are dying
For a nouveau blues
To underline
What's left behind

Forget the Nazi doll
Designed in Detroit
And made in Beijing
Forget about this
Contagious computer virus
Traveling up the Tigris
Forget Batman
In this postmodern

Fantasia
Amnesia

A new shade of blue
One hundred hues
Down from the stratosphere
Up from the red sea
A hell of a journey
We are hurting
We are dying
For a brand-new blues

ah. Carving contests. Seeing
t are just second nature. Same
"Don't Go 'Way Nobody" like
get here? Did someone steal
Iuh? Did someone put a liz-
s? Tell me that. Did someone
? Why can't I stop touching
s and things. (*Shrugs.*) They
y? (*Pause.*) Women heard my
ew from a real strong muscle.
blew because I didn't know
vay. Not for me. (*Pause.*) Lord,
figure me out. I'd carve him
.ow-down. I'd put muscle be-
Sometimes I didn't know what
't been thought of. Not before
d to. It was like a pound of
Notes. And more notes. They
Getting fatter. Making more
nse. Notes no one ever blew
(*Pause.*) I'd make that cornet
wkers in the French Market—
and down Rampart, up and
ld rags, bottles, and bones. I
whore's moan. I could blow a
r Hattie. I blew what I knew
House Got Ready" four ways
all the way 'round. Anywhere.
*is head.*) Here. Lovers. Other
en who wanted a back-door
up nowhere. Anna Bartholo-
two-timers. On North Liberty
ocket change. Emma. Emma
re on her looks. She lived on
First, a few blocks 'round the
Last time I saw her she was
ith Remer's Vaudville. Some
know. All this helped to de-
can go and look up Alphonse
ost hold a note half the night.

# Shot Down

Have you ever been shot
Down by love
Blown out of the saddle
Cut down in the middle
Of paradise
With a throw of the dice
Taken out of action
By infatuation

Have you ever been shot
Down by love
Ever have to go
Inside your own metaphor
Open that door
Like Annie Oakley
Looking for Buffalo Bill
In a wild west show
In the Berkeley hills

Such a dangerous enterprise
I'll let the winter
Crocuses give advice
January, February
Is their only commentary
As they push up through the ice
What does it matter
Deep in the forest
Or in a walk-up
Cold water flat
Where there's a look-alike for Jack
Kerouac

Have you ever been shot
Down by love
Blown out of the saddle
Cut down in the middle
Of a city where you can't
Buy an ounce of pity
With a love chant

Have you ever been shot
Have you ever been shot down by love
Have you ever been shot
Have you ever been shot down
By real love

me some women back then.
who outdid who. Things like tl
way I blew my horn. I played
I made love. (*Pause.*) How did
the sweatband from my hat?
ard's tongue under my mattr
sprinkle salt on my doorstep
things? Love to handle drea
don't talk back. Can't, can th
silver cornet all over town. I l
The heart's almost as strong.
anything else. There's no othe
Robichaux. John could never
seven ways to the four winds.
hind everything I blew. (*Pause.*
I wanted to play because it had
I played it. I just played. I l
maggot-meat inside my head.
were always coming. Growing
and more sense. Making no
before. Like lice on a red ros
shout. Yessiree. Those street h
I talked their talk. Hawkers u
down Conti. Hawkers singing
blew those cries. I could blow
good woman's moan. I blew
and what I didn't. I'd blow "Tl
to the wind. Up and down, and
Nowhere. There. (*Pointing to
men's women. Back-door wo
man. (*Pause.*) We always ende
men and Ella. Two good-timin
and Conti, selling herself for
Thorton, trying to go somewh
Josephine. That's right. I was
corner. Yessiree. That's histor
performing in Lincoln Park
kinda shuck-and-jive fuss. Yo
throne The King. (*Pause.*) You
Picous and ask him. I could al

I'd squeeze it out till it was a drop of blood in my brain. Women would holler. They'd roll their hips like a Model-T Ford. Night wave. Blue and black. My sound reached the water and traveled Uptown. Everybody came to hear me. That's right. I played low-down blues. I blew what I lived and saw. What I hadn't seen or dreamt, I still blew it. (*Pause.*) Was that silver cornet my punishment? Was I doomed when I first raised it to my lips? Huh? Was I, doctor—Mister Sebe? (*Pause.*) Doctor, I had me some women. Good and bad. They fought to carry my horn, but I'd just hand them my coat and hat. Yeah, they did. Sure did. (*Falsetto.*) Let me have his horn. No, no, no. I wanta carry Buddy's cornet. No, I got his piece. (*Normal voice.*) Ha! I carried my own goddamn horn. Nobody touched my horn! (*Pause.*) I loved only three women. Only three in my whole life. Only three. Cora—my sister. Alice—my mama. And Hattie—my heart. (*Pause.*) I hate Buddy Bolden. I hate his no-good guts! (*He slaps himself across the face. He freezes.*) Okay. Okay, Mister Sebe, I won't do that anymore. I promise. (*Crossing his heart.*) I cross my heart and hope to die. I promise. But sometimes a man comes to hate himself. You know. Don't you, Mister Sebe, you know, right? (*Pause.*) My sister and my mama drove Hattie and me apart. Hattie's gone. Long gone. My son's gone also. They could be in hell for all I know. (*Pause.*) Now, Hattie, she was a sweet woman. Stole my heart and I never got it back. I was never all here (*pointing to his head.*) after we broke up. Nora, my second wife, my girl's mama, she was another story. She never could fit into Hattie's shoes. And she always knew, too. (*Pause.*) Berenedine, my girl, lost too. Loss? How can you measure loss, doctor? (*Pause.*) Come here. Come on, doctor. Look into my eyes. (*Buddy leans forward, and then pulls back.*) That's right. All I could do was blow my brains out—my silver horn. I polished it like a woman's leg. (*Pause.*) Devil's music? No sir. I know. The devil's music could never be so bittersweet. I played day and night. Night and day. Sunny and rainy. Uptown and downtown. But I never played no devil's music anywhere anytime. Not me. Horn shiny as a woman's leg. I blew wide open. Up-tempo. That scream lodged in the back of the throat, it had to get out somehow. But still sweet and easy. Honky-tonk my foot. I had an ear. Could read too. Go and ask Louis and Willie Cornish, if you don't believe me. Ask Red. Ask Cornelius Tillman. Ask

Zue. Ask Ray Lopez. And Brock. Ask Henry Zeno. Ask God knows who. Ask 'em all. And don't forget to ask 'em how sweet I blew on that cylinder we cut. (*Pause.*) Sometimes a man can be broken by what his mouth won't say, right? What the horn told me to blow. I've forgotten. Eyes behind these eyes you look into and see nothing. World inside my head. Someplace the women could never get to. Not but one. That Hattie. Lord, Lord. (*Points to his head.*) This door was even closed off to mama and Cora. It was no place at all. No room. Nora, I think, felt it. Somewhere. Somehow. Scared her to death. (*Pause.*) Hattie cried when we made love. She'd just cry. Make love and cry. Not moan, mind you. Really shed tears. I tried to play that cry. Over and Over, I tried. That sound. Sometimes after we made love I'd play for her. Just for Hattie—so soft I could hardly hear myself blowing. She'd be crying and I'd be playing. Notes. Terminals inside a lock. Doors to unlock. Doors inside the head. Doors. Flesh doors and wooden doors. (*Pause.*) I craved a new skin to crawl into. My color was wrong. I was wrong. All my friends were wrong. The music we played was wrong. The woman I loved was wrong. We were all wrong. Born wrong. (*Pause.*) Now I touch things. I walk in circles and touch things. In straight lines and touch things. Love to handle things. Things don't talk back. Can't. They just are. They can't talk back, can they, doctor, Mister Sebe? (*Pause.*) I got scared of the horn. It didn't have in it what my mind wanted to make it do. It betrayed me. It did. I just couldn't make the sound I had in my head. It hurt like hell. Awful. I felt the sound it couldn't make. Didn't make. Do you understand? Do you really? How can you understand, when I don't? (*Pause.*) Clem was in my place that night. Frankie Dusen said, "We don't need you no more, Buddy." I just fell into pieces. Frankie, of all people: he had listened to me like a mockingbird. But did I stand there and poor-mouth? Did I beg? Did I crawl? No, I didn't. I just walked out. Grabbed myself up into an empty bag and walked out. Yessiree, I did. Sometimes you have to holler. Nobody hollered King Bolden. Not a soul. Not a living goddamn soul. (*Pause.*) If someone had, I don't know what I would've done. (*Half-singing, half-talking.*) "Make me a pallet on the floor, make me a pallet on the floor, make it soft, make it low, so your sweet man will never know." Goofer dust? Never know. Whiskey? Never know.

Women? Maybe so. (*Bolden raises his horn to his lips, blowing a note or two.*) I don't care if you call Big Bradford in here, Mister Sebe. I just don't care. I don't care about the white jacket or Big Bradford. (*Bolden shakes his head. He reluctantly lets the cornet fall to the floor, turning on his heels and walking back toward the window. The attendant walks on stage and picks up the cornet and walks off stage. Bolden never notices Bradham; he continues talking.*) I was blowing. The sun was setting. Blowing. Setting. Setting and blowing. I was blowing and it had almost set. Now it's stopped. I was making the sun set, Doctor. Setting in the east. In the west. Nowhere to set. The sun was going home. I was blowing and the sun was taking me home. (*The curtain starts to close slowly. Bolden continues talking.*) Now it's gone. Home to Jesus. No sun. No sun in here. Gone. Long gone. I was blowing. Blowing. The sun was setting. I was going home. (*A very distant-sounding cornet plays "Get Out of Here and Go on Home" very softly and otherworldly for about thirty seconds. Then there's one loud blast on the cornet. Abrupt silence.*)

# Blind Stitches and Notes
# from First Takes

Here, sound
breaks into pieces
for gourd dancers

੨**

the nine wheels of my voice
roll through a haze of crickets

Fragments from some of my earlier poems are like half-glimpses behind a dark cloth.

Even when hearts crawl
out of excrement
embalmed with wine

੨**

Day grandmama died
Ma Rainey sang from grand-
papa's gramophone

I can see the edges of possibility. Hints. They tell me something about my earlier creative impulses.

thru eyes of flesh

੨**

i spoke an old man's eyes

These verbal shards are instructive: I can already see elements of what I wish to accomplish. And at times, the whole shape of the reflection eases through—into near focus.

> groans a golden room
> of C Minor Blues
> the rattle of dice
> pours out of brass

> 〜

> TCB, ostinato
> fingers on the pulse
> whistling in the darkroom
> waiting to see enemies
> go blind

These lines are like brushstrokes on an emotional canvas. "If I can do this once, I should be able to execute this again and again," I can hear an earlier Self whispering at some midnight hour.

> with your intricate bugging devices
> what you will hear, o lord,
> are all the hosannahs
> pent-up in the women of your family

> 〜

> copper flowers at dusk
> midnight men in love
> with waystation women

Am I searching for something I hope to reclaim? Why am I picking through these almost lost moments?

> Women dislike the dust
> I leave on them

> 〜

> wade into a murmur of sugarcane
> into the season of boiling suns

into the season of back-breaking work
into the season without laughter
that doubles you up

I can feel the heart's quiver and flash.

Hoodwinked shadows tiptoe
toward, intoxicated
on the power of shotguns
& cattle prods

જ

every time a gunshot
sounds in Africa
I taste blood

I can see where the leaps are about to happen. I can feel the
imagistic nerve endings and synapses.

Our heroes refuse to
give in to timeclocks

જ

Broonzy fell through six feet of darkness;
the meadowlark lost part of its voice
when lung cancer hunted him down

Challenges. Nudges. Glimpses at irony and satire.

Electric flowers
Spin their heads off

જ

only silent gods
suppose this
is death

Many of these instances show how I was able to continue
writing poems against the odds, and there are scary moments
where I still believe and trust these images.

# Shot Down

Have you ever been shot
Down by love
Blown out of the saddle
Cut down in the middle
Of paradise
With a throw of the dice
Taken out of action
By infatuation

Have you ever been shot
Down by love
Ever have to go
Inside your own metaphor
Open that door
Like Annie Oakley
Looking for Buffalo Bill
In a wild west show
In the Berkeley hills

Such a dangerous enterprise
I'll let the winter
Crocuses give advice
January, February
Is their only commentary
As they push up through the ice
What does it matter
Deep in the forest
Or in a walk-up
Cold water flat
Where there's a look-alike for Jack
Kerouac

Have you ever been shot
Down by love
Blown out of the saddle
Cut down in the middle
Of a city where you can't
Buy an ounce of pity
With a love chant

Have you ever been shot
Have you ever been shot down by love
Have you ever been shot
Have you ever been shot down
By real love

# Buddy's Monologue

*THE SCENE: Semi-dark corridor of the Insane Asylum of Louisiana.*

*THE TIME: Circa 1915. A late afternoon.*

*THE CHARACTERS: Charles Buddy Bolden, Mister Sebe Bradham, an attendant.*

*Charles Buddy Bolden, who played cornet, and apparently "went crazy," is a legendary figure in the early history of jazz in New Orleans.*

*Buddy Bolden plays "Funky Butt" for two or three minutes before the curtain opens. He continues to play, with his back to the audience. He stops blowing and turns around, obviously annoyed. Speaking to Sebe Bradham, an attendant, an imaginary character, whom he addresses throughout the piece, Bolden says:*

Mister Sebe, the horn was just sitting there. Sitting there like the cornet I found in the street back in New Orleans. Begging to be played. Believe me, Mister Sebe, I fought with myself before I took it. I walked three solid miles. Yeah, I walked three miles in a circle, before I unlatched the case. (*Pause.*) This is nothing like my horn. No siree. This thing's too light, and it ain't hardly broken in yet. Ain't kissed sorrow. (*He turns to the window again, playing the same tune. He stops, turns, and takes a few steps toward the imaginary Bradham, doubling over with a piercing laugh. The laughter grows slowly into a near-whimpering sound. He assumes a stern composure. He extends the horn, and he quickly pulls it back, holding it behind his back as he speaks.*) I had

---

"Buddy's Monologue" originally appeared in *Brilliant Corners: A Journal of Jazz & Literature* 3, no. 2 (1999).

me some women back then. Yeah. Carving contests. Seeing who outdid who. Things like that are just second nature. Same way I blew my horn. I played "Don't Go 'Way Nobody" like I made love. (*Pause.*) How did I get here? Did someone steal the sweatband from my hat? Huh? Did someone put a lizard's tongue under my mattress? Tell me that. Did someone sprinkle salt on my doorsteps? Why can't I stop touching things? Love to handle dreams and things. (*Shrugs.*) They don't talk back. Can't, can they? (*Pause.*) Women heard my silver cornet all over town. I blew from a real strong muscle. The heart's almost as strong. I blew because I didn't know anything else. There's no other way. Not for me. (*Pause.*) Lord, Robichaux. John could never figure me out. I'd carve him seven ways to the four winds. Low-down. I'd put muscle behind everything I blew. (*Pause.*) Sometimes I didn't know what I wanted to play because it hadn't been thought of. Not before I played it. I just played. I had to. It was like a pound of maggot-meat inside my head. Notes. And more notes. They were always coming. Growing. Getting fatter. Making more and more sense. Making no sense. Notes no one ever blew before. Like lice on a red rose. (*Pause.*) I'd make that cornet shout. Yessiree. Those street hawkers in the French Market— I talked their talk. Hawkers up and down Rampart, up and down Conti. Hawkers singing old rags, bottles, and bones. I blew those cries. I could blow a whore's moan. I could blow a good woman's moan. I blew for Hattie. I blew what I knew and what I didn't. I'd blow "The House Got Ready" four ways to the wind. Up and down, and all the way 'round. Anywhere. Nowhere. There. (*Pointing to his head.*) Here. Lovers. Other men's women. Back-door women who wanted a back-door man. (*Pause.*) We always ended up nowhere. Anna Bartholomen and Ella. Two good-timing two-timers. On North Liberty and Conti, selling herself for pocket change. Emma. Emma Thorton, trying to go somewhere on her looks. She lived on Josephine. That's right. I was on First, a few blocks 'round the corner. Yessiree. That's history. Last time I saw her she was performing in Lincoln Park with Remer's Vaudville. Some kinda shuck-and-jive fuss. You know. All this helped to dethrone The King. (*Pause.*) You can go and look up Alphonse Picous and ask him. I could almost hold a note half the night.

I'm afraid
you might take my hands
& place them on your belly

ک

Sweetheart,
what will we eat tonight,
dreams about peach pies?

Even when my mind has attempted to divorce itself from
these words and phrases, my body remembers across the
years.

woman blues
like the earth
turning inside

ک

Subtract "I"
& something unfixes

It is almost a hurting pleasure to know I still believe in these
words, and I am willing to let them keep teaching me something about my younger Self and Imagination.

**UNDER DISCUSSION**
**David Lehman, General Editor**
**Donald Hall, Founding Editor**

Volumes in the Under Discussion series collect reviews and essays about
individual poets. The series is concerned with contemporary American and
English poets about whom the consensus has not yet been formed and the
final vote has not been taken. Titles in the series include:

6285